WOMEN IN TEXAS MUSIC

Women in

BRAD AND MICHELE MOORE
ROOTS MUSIC SERIES

Texas Music

STORIES AND SONGS

Kathleen Hudson

UNIVERSITY OF TEXAS PRESS ⊽ AUSTIN

Requests for permission to reproduce
material from this work should be
sent to:
Permissions
University of Texas Press
P.O. Box 7819
Austin, TX 78713-7819
www.utexas.edu/utpress/about/bper-
mission.html

∞ The paper used in this book meets
the minimum requirements of ANSI/
NISO Z39.48-1992 (R1997) (Permanence
of Paper).

LIBRARY OF CONGRESS
CATALOGING-IN-PUBLICATION DATA

Hudson, Kathleen, 1945–
  Women in Texas music : stories and
songs / Kathleen Hudson. — 1st ed.
    p.   cm. — Brad and Michele Moore
roots music series
  Includes bibliographical references
(p.   ).
  ISBN 978-0-292-73467-8 (cloth : alk.
paper) — ISBN 978-0-292-71734-3
(pbk. : alk. paper)
  1. Women musicians—Texas—
Interviews.   2. Popular music—Texas—
History and criticism.   I. Title.
  ML82.H83 2007
  782.42164092'2764—dc22
  [B]

                      2006100418

To Alice Maude and Daddo, my deceased grandmothers,

To Annabel, my mother,

To Carolyn, my sister,

To Lisa, my daughter,

To Jessica, Angel, Erin, and Maya, my granddaughters,

To Donna, my daughter-in-law,

To Paula, Sunny, and Linda, my sisters-in-law,

To Ruth Jeanne and Barbara, my aunts,

To my girlfriends, too numerous to name,

To Jeanne Slobod, my own clan mother.

To them and to all the women writers who have encouraged me to find my own voice.

LET IT BE SAID

Let it be said
    when I am gone
        that I was an enabler
            of Ancient Wisdom

Let it be said
    that recognition
        came instantly
            through the eyes into the heart
  but understanding
        slowly permeated my being
            until at last it is almost whole
  True wholeness
      will not come
           until I am one with Ancient Wisdom
              for she is my Mother
Let it be known
  by those who love me
    that when this joining comes
      I will be home

        SO BE IT
        —JEANNE LAMAR SLOBOD, SEPTEMBER 22, 1990

CONTENTS

A Conversation with Lloyd Maines

Lloyd Maines—husband, father, musician, and producer—talks with me about his many and varied connections with Texas music. He started out in Lubbock, Texas, playing pedal steel guitar. The Maines Brothers are an important part of the history of Texas music. Lloyd started off on guitar, and then pedal steel became his main instrument. Then he met up with Joe Ely and Terry Allen, thus moving him into broader vistas and possibilities around music. Terry showed him that no boundaries exist when creating music. Joe informed him of the power of original music. Lloyd sees these two men as pivotal in his own musical history. One role he plays is father to Natalie Maines, a Dixie Chick. He has worked with many women. He began touring with Terri Hendrix in 1998 because he loved the music she was doing. And he produced her albums. He worked with the Texana Dames, Susan Gibson, Ruthie Foster and more. After producing the Dixie Chicks' award-winning Home, *he also toured with them and produced the Sony album* Live on Tour. *I wondered how he felt about their huge success in the world as well as their huge challenges, including the negative right-wing media frenzy following their remarks about President Bush and the*

Iraq War. I love the sense of life the Chicks' Live album conveys, and I love the writing. And every time I'm around Lloyd, I'm impressed by his sense of center and his sense of strength. His face lights up with a smile, and he seems to always connect with the person in front of him. I asked Lloyd how he manages to do all that he does. The following contains excerpts from a conversation in which I asked him about women and Texas music.

———

LET'S FACE IT. I have the strength of ten men. [laughter] I just enjoy it so much I never mind getting out of bed to go to work. I consider myself the luckiest musician in Texas because I get to work with all these cool people. For the most part, I've enjoyed everything I've done. I get to work with great artists, great people, great music, and make a living doing totally what I enjoy. I don't really relish traveling that much, but I enjoy Terri's music so much, and I know that traveling is part of what she has to do to move forward, so I accept that. We travel in a low-maintenance way; just the two of us usually go.

My family provides a center for me. As corny as that may be, I've always put family first. I had to leave Joe Ely's band in the early 1980s because of the amount of time he spent touring. I had been with him since 1972, but I had a wife and two little kids in mind. I've always tried to keep the family in the forefront of my brain. I have a very understanding wife who enjoys the fact that I enjoy what I'm doing. When I'm at these gigs, I have nothing to complain about. Maybe that is what comes through. At times, I've seen performers who just stare at their feet and act like they're mad at the world. I feel like I have so much to be thankful for. Luckily all my family's healthy, and I'm healthy. I have no complaints.

Before Natalie got with the Dixie Chicks, I knew the two sisters because I had played on a couple of their early albums in Dallas. I had played a few gigs with them and had done some TV shows. We really hit it off. I don't know if they looked at me as a father figure or just as a good steel guitar player. I respected their playing. Emily and Martie absolutely play as good as it gets. I think they respected my playing and respected me as a person. The folklore says that I pitched Natalie to them. That is not the case. Natalie wanted to go to Berklee up in Boston, so I did a little demo tape with her, just acoustic guitar and vocal, real simple. It turned out well, and I gave it to a few select people who I thought might enjoy hearing her. I gave Emily and Martie this burned cassette copy just for their listening.

It was a year before they were even thinking about changing singers. They kept the tape around on the bus and listened to it. Even before they needed a new singer, they told me that they might want to get Natalie if they ever decided to go with four girls up front. Natalie got the scholarship and went to Berklee for one semester. She liked the school but didn't like being that far from home. She came back and started at Texas Tech and literally, in the middle of the semester, Martie called, saying, "We're in a crisis now. We need a new singer right now." I reminded her that they hadn't heard her sing: all they had heard was the tape. I guess they just had a sense that she might just fit the bill. It was really blind faith. Martie and Emily went out on a long limb. They called Natalie on a Tuesday evening, asking her to be in Dallas by Sunday to practice for a gig they had that next Tuesday.

I was a little apprehensive from the point that she was young, only eighteen or nineteen years old. Just like any parent would be. Of course, I didn't realize she was stepping into a group that was going to become the number-one act in the country. The statistics are pretty mind-boggling. I knew what kind of people Martie and Emily were. That part was comforting. If she had to leave home, at least I knew she was with good people.

The record *Home* sold about seven million copies, and it continues to sell. They came back to Austin to do this with me down at Cedar Creek Studio. They sold almost as many of that one as they did of the first two. I know you've told me that you love the video of the live tour. When we did *Home*, the song that was the most emotional and the easiest to cut was "Godspeed." It's about being out on the road and thinking about your little kids back home. That one kind of stands out to me. Of course, "Wide Open Spaces" is special because it's the title of their first album. Susan Gibson wrote it. What really struck me when I first heard it is the way it captures that feeling of leaving home, having space to experiment and make mistakes. I pretty much enjoy all their songs. I also have toured with them from time to time. They asked me to do the longer tours, but I was in the middle of touring with Terri. Now their tours are as first class as it gets, but I've always been loyal to my word. I made a commitment to

Terri and to her career. We started working together in 1997, and I started traveling with her in 1998.

The women you are talking with, the women of Texas, do have something in common. Even though your list is eclectic, I do see a common thread. These women are all willing to work hard. Not one is afraid to get dirty doing the work it takes. You know, Marcia Ball, in the early 1970s, had Freda and the Firedogs. She's a good example of a woman who is not afraid of hard work. I remember when I was first working with the Chicks, they were driving their own motor home and hauling their own equipment. I remember when we first drove up to a gig, they would all grab some equipment and start hauling it in, just like everybody else. Even now Terri doesn't mind setting up her own stuff. She doesn't have to hire a keeper. The Texana Dames are the same way. They work their asses off and are not afraid to work. That sets them apart from the pre-fab Nashville "discoveries" who get signed and immediately have a keeper. And many, many of the women in Texas work hard, as you know.

The women you have listed are all about the music and the songs. They all go to extremes, as far as work, to be able to do their music. Didn't you get that sense when you were interviewing them? Even Emily, Martie, and Natalie still remember what it was like to haul their own stuff. Traveling with Terri, I see that the women not only have to deal with everything a guy deals with, but compound that with another forty percent of BS they have to go through.

In general, I think women are stronger than men. Baring one's heart and soul takes courage, and these Texas women artists have a lot of courage. They make me even prouder to be a Texan.

ACKNOWLEDGMENTS

Thanks

TO MY ENTIRE FAMILY, who provide ongoing support in my life; the women in my family who serve as examples: Annabel (mother), Carolyn (sister), Lisa (daughter), and Jessica (first granddaughter), who give me total love and total listening; my dad, who gifted me with my writing cabin, the House of David, and encouraged me to be true to my own voice; my brother David, who insisted that I participate in training with Landmark Education and continuously acknowledges me as I create my vision in the world.

To Schreiner University (the community that supports me; faculty development grants; Mary Ann Parker, the faculty secretary; a semester sabbatical; and a house for the Texas Heritage Music Foundation on campus).

To the John Anson Kittredge Foundation for a grant to support me during the last year of this work; Hal Robinson and his shamanic healing work; Jeanne Slobod, my dear friend and mentor who left us April 28,

2006, at age eighty-nine; Meredith Fund, named in honor of Jeanne's daughter; Past is Prologue for ongoing training; Landmark Education for training in commitment (Carol Redfield and Bruce Saxton); local music magazines (Hill Country Happenings, M.Y.T.H.) for providing outlets for my monthly column; Brad O'Quinn at the Family Sports Center, who supported my physical well-being; Kristen Jetton (a Schreiner student who served as a work-study in my office and a research assistant on this book); Stephanie Gaines, who became a research assistant in 2005 and helped organize my teaching office; and Tim Wilton and his family, who took added responsibility in the September Living History Weekend as well as the THMF office.

To Debbie Fowler, a Schreiner student who contributed to the office for a year; ALL the women who took time to talk with me; my friends (you know who you are) who listened and listened; club owners who supported the research by allowing me to attend the shows and interview the artists.

Mindy Reed, at The Authors' Assistant in Austin, Texas, has a brilliant editing eye and pulled together these interviews in a way that created a manuscript; Theresa May, senior editor at UT Press, had conversations with me that not only encouraged me but helped give me direction. I know she has a daughter who can sing like Janis Joplin! Roger Wood, author of *Blues in Houston* (UT Press), sent me a list of women to contact in the Houston area. Steve Davis, Dean of Social Sciences at Kingwood College in Houston, shared his extensive research on Janis Joplin with our Texas Heritage Blues Seminar in 2004.

Harold F. Eggers, Jr., provided a link between me and the women he has worked with: Barbara K, Susie Nelson, and Barb Donovan. He brought these women to my classroom and inspired me to continue with this oral history even as it goes beyond the boundaries of this book.

Brian Hawkins heard me talking about this in the hot tub at our sports center and requested the chance to create a television show for *Texas Country Reporter*. We went back to Houston and talked with Jewel Brown and Trudy Lynn again, camera running. I was blessed with more resources on the women of Texas: Adam Jeffries Schwartz, writer and world traveler, showed up at my house just in time to give this manuscript a close reading. Larry Gunn, a longtime love with an eye for detail, gave it a read. I'm proud to be part of the Texas music catalogue that UT Press in Austin is putting together for Texas and for the world.

The Author's Story

THE WOMEN in this collection have chosen to live life fully, to keep gen-
erating possibility, to celebrate and enjoy life. They tell stories of rich
and diverse lives where family and relationship matter, AND they are
committed to pursuing their dreams. This collection of life stories does
not reveal a group of women whining, complaining, or even ranting and
railing, but the subtle message of inequality is still present. This collection contains the stories of courageous women.

I've never labeled myself a feminist, but I may start doing so. I didn't
burn bras or participate in marches. My concerns were always with the
dispossessed, the downtrodden, the outsider. All of mankind. I did not
question the word *mankind*. Now I see, once again, that our language
reveals our cultural bias around women.

I began this project by talking to musicians and songwriters who
moved me with their music. I knew I wanted to give special attention to
the women. As I conducted these interviews in the field, I realized that
I did have similar experiences, unnoticed before, in my own life. I may
have started this project as a woman working alone in the world, but I
finished it with a deep awareness and understanding of my kinship with

all these women. I know intellectually that we are all part of the family of human beings, but I felt the connection in my body this time.

My work with Hal Robinson, shamanic healer and Gestalt therapist in Kerrville, helped with some important integration as I got in touch with voices I had abandoned in myself. During this project I spent a week with my daughter and three granddaughters in Wichita, Kansas. I watched these women interact, and I watched my daughter make life easy for her husband, as he worked and finished up school. She also taught fulltime. I was reminded, once again, of the many responsibilities women take on. I was also reminded of how we bend to the values of patriarchy without really looking at some of our choices. My mother, affectionately called Saint Annabel, was the force that kept our family strong while Dad was out living his dream of medicine and providing for his family. I have talked with my mother on a regular basis my entire life. Now that Dad is retired, I get to talk with him when he answers the phone. Balance.

I chose San Miguel de Allende as the place to put together this manuscript. The women in this community became friends. In December I spent ten days in San Miguel with Jeanne Slobod as my traveling companion. We not only shared a workshop by Life Path Retreats called "Awakening the Divine Feminine," but we spent mornings in my apartment talking and sharing stories. Her perspective from her eighty-eight years on the planet helped shape my own listening to the women in this book.

I had a dream in San Miguel de Allende that I was massaging a man's back, and then turned him over. There I found a little black kitten sleeping peacefully. I had read about Joseph Dispenza (Life Path Retreats) and his work with dream interpretations, so I joined the Tuesday afternoon group. At the end I saw the dream as a reminder of the work I am doing in the world, turning over the male perspective to discover and reveal the female perspective, the divine feminine energy that the planet so needs at this time. The workshop I later did with Joseph and Beverly Nelson worked on the distinctions between "domination and partnership." We used the structure of maiden, mother, and crone, the three phases of womanhood, to shape the workshop. I saw how difficult it is for a group of people, highly steeped in a dominant paradigm, to even talk about partnership models, like a group of fish trying to talk about water. What an amazing experience for me as I finished this manuscript. Joseph also reminded me, "Include more of yourself in this book."

I was shocked to find that over 800 women are listed in the Texas Music Industry Guide, yet most festivals around the state feature the boys' club. Even Willie's picnic lacks female performers. I know they are not all out there knocking on doors and being told no, but I also know festival producers are not looking them up and asking. The Billy Joe Shaver Birthday Concert at the Paramount in Austin, Texas, had one woman on the lineup: Pauline Reese. And I know Billy Joe appreciates the women. It seems the young guns of Texas music get a lot more play with a lot less work. I read through a magazine that runs my monthly column, and the lineups at many festivals advertised include men only. The covers are mostly photos of men. I am sure more men are out there on the road. What does that say? That more men are talented? I think not.

I do have a great appreciation for the men of Texas music. Just ask Charlie Robison. I went to his 2004 CD release in both Helotes and Kerrville, taking photos of Charlie and his son Gus onstage. I have a huge appreciation for Charlie and for the spirit of Guy, Townes, and Billy Joe that he evokes. I was thrilled that Emily Robison, mother and wife as well as Dixie Chick, decided to contact me and create some time for us to talk.

As I look back at my first book on songwriters, I am painfully aware that many women were left out. I wrote about the people around me, and it looks like most of them were men! This book became a deliberate search for the stories of women. It is not a definitive collection, but rather a sampling of a mine rich with treasures. Again, I am painfully aware that I cannot include all the stories I've heard, and that this collection is eclectic rather than definitive.

Lydia Mendoza's daughter took me to a rest home where I could sit with Lydia, a profound influence on the music of this state. Lana Nelson took time out from the Dylan/Willie/Hot Club of Cowtown tour to invite me to eat backstage with her as we talked. Stephanie Urbina Jones invited me to her home in Nashville, and we shared some time with her first baby, Zeta. Bobbie Nelson had me over for tea, and Susan Gibson came to my hotel for a visit during South by Southwest in Austin. Katherine Dawn, Darcey Deauville, Jean Prescott, Tish Hinojosa, Michelle Shocked, and more said yes to a possible future conversation. At times I wanted this project to last a lifetime, and maybe it will.

I could not include all the women I had chosen for the project. Some declared they were too busy to take time out to talk. Others said they were interested, and I never got back with them. Timing. Again, this is not a definitive collection, but rather a sampling of voices.

As I continued to talk with women, my own life went through changes. Each woman told me a story that inspired me. I began to live with more courage. I even got up onstage at the Mountain Home Opry (near my house) and sang "Mama, Don't Let Your Babies Grow Up to Be Cowboys." I sang "Richland Woman" at a faculty meeting after giving a report on my research for this project. And I had been a woman who did not have the courage to sing in front of others even though I wanted to. These interviews with brave women inspired me to be courageous.

This project caused me to stop and do some research. My work in Texas music has led me to many a wonderful festival, concert, and performance. I read Adrienne Rich with a new eye. When she said that it's time to "enter the text from a new direction," I saw the implications for an interpretation of the interviews I have collected. These women were doing just that.

With a focus on the contributions of women, I have discovered another layer in this rich mine. Watching Elana Fremerman (now Elana James) take the lead on her fiddle, with Bob Dylan on keyboard accompanying her, singing "Highway 61 Revisited" on the 2004 tour of baseball parks with Willie Nelson, was a highlight in my life. I am a longtime fan of the genius of Bob Dylan. His tribute album to Jimmie Rodgers in 1997 echoed the Texas tribute I created in 1997 with Willie Nelson. Both men inspire me to keep doing what I do, collecting the stories of Texas music. Bob Dylan called Carolyn Wonderland when he was in Houston one time, inviting her to join him in the studio. Our paths seem to cross without touching, and his life and work inspire me to do the work I do.

The material gathered in this oral history project provides material for my various classes at Schreiner University: composition, world literature, children's literature, mythology, and creative writing. Often I invite the men and women I interview to be guests in the classroom, at the coffeehouse, at the annual writing conference. I see my life as a tapestry rich with many threads of varied textures. My life as a teacher gives me the space to utilize all aspects of my life. I see patterns, I live them, I create them.

Read this collection with an eye for the patterns. You will see your own patterns, filtered through your own life's experience. Together we create this text.

Catherine Powers

Carolyn Wonderland on trumpet

Stephanie Urbina Jones at the Kerrville Folk Festival

Elana Fremerman (James) at the Continental Club in Austin, with Hot Club of Cowtown

Mandy Mercier one Sunday morning at Maria's Taco Xpress in Austin

Karen Abrahams rocks

Melissa Javors on dobro

Catherine Powers and Lee Duffy backstage at a Merle Haggard concert at the John T. Floore Country Store in Helotes

Lee Ann Womack and Willie Nelson at the Verizon Amphitheater in San Antonio

Neesie Beal at Casbeer's
one Sunday

Rosie Flores at South by Southwest

Ruthie Foster, Maggie Montgomery, and Cyd Cassone backstage
at the Austin Music Awards

Jewel Brown

Pauline Reese
at the Broken
Spoke in Austin

Terri Hendrix at Old No. 9, teaching a songwriting class

Sara Hickman at Flipnotics in Austin

Traci Lamar, a Texana Dame, at Güero's in Austin

Conni Hancock, one-third of the Texana Dames, at Güero's in Austin

Lavelle White at the Kerrville Folk
Festival

Rattlesnake Annie playing in San Marcos

Lloyd Maines and Terri Hendrix at Schreiner University

Wanda King at
Django's in Dallas

Eva Ybarra in her living room in San Antonio

Shemekia Copeland and the author in Monterey, California

Susan Gibson and her jeep, ready for the road

Ruthie Foster at Schreiner University

Marcia Ball on keyboard

Bobbie Nelson on piano

WOMEN IN TEXAS MUSIC

Reinvention, to me, equals longevity. You're not denying who you are; rather, you are getting to that next place that makes you feel like you're exploring new territory.

LIVING OUTLOUD

I knew that the Dixie Chicks were more than an overnight sensation. Even though I did not pay attention to these cowgirls in cowboy boots at the YO Ranch Social Club Party in Mountain Home, Texas, the first time they played there, by the time they invited Natalie Maines to join them and showed up on CMT, I was a new fan. Of course, I had to overcome my reverse snobbery that chooses not to notice mainstream country. I even attended the Country Music Awards at the invitation of Justin Harper. My appreciation for both the women and men of country music has grown. So much for stereotypes and snobbery. Maybe the mainstream does have something to offer!

The Dixie Chicks not only know their instruments, but they also write and deliver songs in a way that opens up a space in country music. I met Emily one evening at a concert by Charlie Robison, her husband and one of my favorite Texas songwriters. Emily, in ponytail and jeans, was being a great mom to Gus, their two-year-old, and a great wife and partner to Charlie, watching him and smiling as he performed. I introduced myself, gave them a copy of my first book, and made my request: "I would love to talk with you for this book project. Is that possible?" Several months later we did hook up and talk. I came away, once again, impressed with a woman who is willing to work hard for what she dreams. I came away inspired to keep following my own dreams. The Chicks have won awards and broken records touring, and each of these women has an important story to tell.

HUDSON: I totally respect the lifestyle you have chosen, and that often means time constraints. When I saw you with Charlie and that beautiful boy, I thought, "And she's a mother, too." When a young woman picks up this book fifty years from now, what do you want her to know about you?

ROBISON: Wow, that's a large question. People might say, "Who was that?" To me, longevity is important. I was sixteen when I joined the band. What is important to me is the change throughout my life. As far as the music is concerned, being relevant is important. Music is my passion, but my real passion is my family. That comes naturally when you get married and start having kids. I need to think on this. Let's start with something more specific!

HUDSON: Okay, what are you working on right now, in January 2005?

ROBISON: I leave in about ten days for the West Coast to be with a producer we're going to use on the next album. We're going out to L.A. for six to nine months. We're in the middle of writing. We've been writing since last spring with different people. Our goal is to write most, if not all, of the next album. Did you know I'm pregnant? I'm six months pregnant with twins. I can't fly after a certain time, so we'll have the babies out there. We'll do pre-production, write some more, and collaborate. We'll get a new vibe going for the next album. We don't really know what's going to be on there right now.

HUDSON: The articles I've read over the years address the ongoing changes you have all experienced. I think it's brilliant to keep reinventing yourself as an artist. Bob Dylan does that well!

ROBISON: Reinvention, to me, equals longevity. You're not denying who you are; rather, you are getting to that next place that makes you feel like you're exploring new territory. Just going back and playing the same songs over and over is not very gratifying. So, to us, it's about exploring that next step. Trying to decide on the radio format cannot be part of the equation. You end up chasing something that doesn't serve you well. For us, it's "what do we want to be playing onstage on the next tour? How do we want to round out our set?" We'll always be going back and doing songs from the last three albums. But what do we want the next sound to be to incorporate into our musical history? What is going to be fun to play for the next year? [laughter]

HUDSON: It's great that you are comfortable not knowing right now. I recently read an article by Pema Chodron, a Buddhist monk, and she describes this as "sitting in the fire." I like the place of being willing to not know and then create and invent from there.

ROBISON: That becomes a subconscious thing, but you have to get there by some conscious choices, like giving yourself an environment where that can happen. If we were all at home trying to get together and write, the everyday things would tend to distract us. We could be sidetracked easily by our life and homes here. For us to work, sometimes it takes getting away to a new place.

HUDSON: How do you balance the career with the family life? With Charlie such an amazing writer and performer, I imagine your situation is even tougher.

ROBISON: I feel so lucky. Sometimes there might be a three-week span where we don't see each other, and we have to be passing ships in the night. But at the same time, if we had a job that consumed us everyday, we probably wouldn't get to spend as much time with Gus and with each other. There's really a lot of quality concentrated time. It's feast or famine, and that comes with the territory. Charlie will call saying, "Oh my gosh, I haven't seen Gus in three weeks." Well, he's just had the last three weeks off, so he's been with us all the time. I think it takes getting used to, and I feel lucky at the same time.

HUDSON: You've figured out a way to really honor your family. I was so glad to see you pregnant in a commercial country video. What a statement that makes!

ROBISON: [laughter] I had no choice. I keep getting credit for that, but I had no choice.

HUDSON: I applaud the life you have chosen to create. You are sassy. You speak up and live fully from your heart. I love that. You all are examples of who we can be as human beings.

ROBISON: That's very generous of you.

HUDSON: I picked up a current *Rolling Stone*. There you were in the center of the cover, surrounded by male rock stars. How did that make you feel?

ROBISON: I have to say that was one of the highlights of my career at this time. If Natalie and Martie hadn't just had babies, I probably wouldn't have gotten that opportunity. It was one of those timing things. It was incredible. It's in my "to be framed" file.

HUDSON: What were some of the highlights of your "Vote for Change" tour?

ROBISON: The whole thing was a highlight. It was a really short tour, so it seemed like we were thrown into the middle of it, then we were gone. Being able to perform with James Taylor was incredible. We really made the show a collaboration rather than just taking turns doing songs. We worked out things on each other's songs. It's always fun to change things up like that. Everyone put their egos aside. It can be a little intimidating to be around all those rock stars, but at the finale in Washington, D.C., we were all just one family. Everyone was so nice and inviting. There was this sense that we were doing something bigger than any one person or one band. No one complained about the time for a set. Everyone seemed to say, "Whatever part you need me to play, I'm there."

HUDSON: That's powerful, listening to others and putting egos aside. Do you have a way that you honor and nourish yourself?

ROBISON: I go to the spa! [laughter] I'm not one to torture myself. It's very centering to me to go and have my own day, just let myself go back to being how I was when I was twenty-two. Go window-shopping and get my nails done. Just go do fun girly stuff like that. But really, my son and Charlie are the most centering thing for me. Take a breather. Being on the ranch and being around the animals is very spiritual to me. I think that's why we live out here. It's such an oasis, such a great change from the fast pace of the rest of the world. We are going out to L.A. to work for a few months, but our lives are back here in Texas. We all have so many projects going on in our individual lives that we are trying to step away from that. I don't want to be thinking about faucets for a remodel when I'm writing a song. Juggling those things gets difficult.

HUDSON: The Dixie Chicks have opened my eyes to the value of a lively performance. Your delivery gets described as rowdy, innovative, sparkling, exciting. How do you view the performance aspect?

ROBISON: We are having fun. Being on tour is the most fun for us. To make it fun every single night, you have to put the energy into the work, and it is a lot of work to pull together tours on the scale that we've done in the past. We know there's that payoff every night when we step onstage and the lights are just right. We've thought about the visual aspect of the performance as well. I think we knew early on that we wanted to be known as a touring group, the tour people want to return to every year.

HUDSON: What was your big break? I remember when you played for the YO Ranch Social Club. I remember the girls in the cowboy boots with the big hair.

ROBISON: It was a series of things. Being the local gals in the Dallas/Fort Worth area, everybody thought we were on the brink of something for about six years. That's a while to be on the brink. It just never panned out. Then Natalie was a catalyst. When she joined the group, things changed. We also put our foot down when we did the album, by declaring we were going to play our own instruments instead of doing the Nashville thing and use a studio band. It was important for us to continue to create what we thought our sound was. I think the single break came with "Wide Open Spaces." It kind of cracked it open.

HUDSON: Let's talk about a highlight from a tour, a shining moment for you.

ROBISON: It's hard to choose. I have career amnesia. It's hard to go back and remember.

HUDSON: I read that the Dixie Chicks are the only artists in history to be nominated for "Entertainer of the Year" at the CMA awards for a debut album.

ROBISON: Really? To me, that's record label promo stuff. That's not the stuff that gets me going. To me, especially what we've been through the last couple of years, the controversy is when you know why you're doing it. It's not the good times you remember; it's the fact that you didn't cave in during the bad times. There was a death threat on Natalie in Dallas on the last tour. I remember Martie and I going up to her and saying we could cancel the show. She said, "No, I'm not going to do that. That's not me. I don't want to let that kind of stuff rule my life." Even though we made the decision to go on and do the show, we were terrified. That five minutes before going onstage, when we said, "Okay, we're going to do this"—those moments are special.

HUDSON: Rather than, "We got album of the year."

ROBISON: Yeah, exactly.

HUDSON: I get the distinction; it's about the heart stuff. Those moments shine for you. Is there anything about that "controversy" you would like to say?

ROBISON: I'm very much a believer that things happen for a reason. Maybe it was a test. It gave me a special moment of knowing that when the chips are down, we are going to be there for each other. It's relevant, and yet it's not. Yes, it did happen. It's part of our history. I don't think about it much anymore. The only bummer is that we know that question will be asked forever and ever. And it's not so bad to be able to clear out about half your Rolodex. I say that laughing, but it's true. You learn who your real friends are. People don't have to agree to be friends. I don't know. It was a bitch. [thoughtful silence]

HUDSON: Is there anything special about the way you three work together?

ROBISON: We honor and respect each other, and our strengths are in different places. We just like each other. Even when we're not working, we end up at each other's houses, at Halloween parties together. Our lives do revolve around each other.

HUDSON: I read that some strong women have been strong influences on you: Emmylou Harris, Dolly Parton, who else?

ROBISON: Martie and Natalie, of course. Bonnie Raitt has been a wonderful friend to us. Getting to see from the inside what her life on the road is like has been inspiring. Seeing how she sustains her life and how she does it. She has incredible integrity. It's always nice when you meet your musical heroes and they live up to your expectations. I find that a lot more with women than with men. The women have had to work doubly hard to get where they are and to sustain where they are. The matriarchs are usually extraordinary.

HUDSON: Thank you so much for an inspiring story.

We are preservers, recorders, communicators, storytellers.
Being a woman makes you do all these things.

Susan Gibson

ON THE ROAD

I had a joyful conversation with a woman easy to know. My sister, Carolyn, joined me. This was the first time we had spent time together as sisters and as women. Sharing the conversation with Susan also created more glue for the relationship we were creating after years of going in different directions. I began to understand the concept of "sister" and all its significance. Carolyn and I became known as the Pillow Sisters soon after this, a name given us by Robert Brandes, a friend in Fredericksburg. Susan smiled broadly and laughed a lot as we talked. Open is the word for this woman traveling down the road with her dog. Now Susan has a place in our own family story as well. As the author of one of country music's biggest hit songs, "Wide Open Spaces," Susan has already left her mark on the world as a songwriter. Now she's ready to travel.

HUDSON: I first ran into you at a Mexican restaurant in Alpine. You and the Groobees were playing in Terlingua the next day. I told you back then that I wanted to interview you. Then Terri Hendrix mentioned you. After your name came up three times, I decided I'd better make that call. I'm glad to be here today, during the 2003 South by Southwest show in Austin. Let's talk about the influence of women in your life. I was about fifty before I really understood the importance of the women in my life. I'm thrilled to be sharing this conversation with Carolyn, my sister. We've connected after years of living separate lives, and this is our first trip together.

GIBSON: When I hear people talk about my work, I hear the comment that this is the woman's perspective. Because of our nature to communicate and our nature to preserve and our sentiment with each other, I see a historical, biological, genetic urge to do this. I just finished *The Red Tent*. Have you read it?

HUDSON: Just finished it. Loved it.

GIBSON: There are so many opposing views on what a strong woman is. This collection of stories from the women's perspective in the *Old Testament* of the Bible gave me another way to look at strength. Like this idea that if you are strong, you can't be feminine or delicate. You're either butch or Barbie. It's either this camp or that camp.

HUDSON: Men are strong, but women are strident.

GIBSON: I don't feel like I've ever suffered discrimination. Maybe I have, but I haven't perceived it in a personal way. There are things that disappear if you don't give them the energy. And, of course, there are some things that come and peck at you even when you aren't giving them any energy. I have a big lesbian audience, and that's an unusual thing to reconcile with my boyfriend. I don't know what it is. Maybe it's because I'm so cute. [laughter] I think that's explained by the woman's need to communicate. I'm a feeling person. I will distort the facts, but I'll nail the feeling. I get in trouble with that sometimes. I won't hear what you said. I'll hear what I felt you said. I'll remember how I felt when you said something. The distinction between facts and feeling can be the male/female distinction as well. Being in a band with four guys was a real learning experience. One would ask, "What time is it?" And I'd answer, looking at my watch, "I think it's about five till eleven." I can see the time there, but maybe I don't trust myself that I set it at the right time. Always ambiguous. I want to give myself a little room for error. If you ask the guys the time, they will give you the facts, whether or not they are wearing a watch. I don't think that's arrogance, just a masculine trait. Emphasis on the facts. I don't think a masculine trait is a negative thing, just like a man shouldn't think a feminine trait is a negative thing.

HUDSON: Many strong women get tagged with masculine traits. When you create something that lives in the world, your energy is masculine, according to Carl Jung. Penetrating, hard, aggressive energy that goes out. The kind of energy that is passive and receptive is called feminine, and we need both. All you have to do is look at a plug and a socket.

GIBSON: I think the songwriting is the feminine part, and the delivery is masculine, which is weird if you think of it in human terms. The conception is the only part that includes the masculine. And the delivery is the female. Interesting.

HUDSON: I've always been comfortable with the juxtaposition of opposites.

GIBSON: For me, the good and the bad are almost the same thing. It's a coin. Both sides are included.

HUDSON: You wrote a huge hit, "Wide Open Spaces."

GIBSON: That enables and disables at the same time.

HUDSON: Yeah, I can see that. Do you liken that to parallel universes? Do you think that way?

GIBSON: This is more metaphysical than I had thought, but perhaps that is why we can have seemingly random things happen that are not really coincidences, based on other decisions we have made.

HUDSON: I find the chaos theory in physics fascinating.

GIBSON: Have you read *The Dancing Wu Li Masters* by Gary Zukav? Our bass player in the Groobees, Bobby, was telling me about this book. He talked about the particle versus the wave theory in measuring light, how the act of observation changes what is being observed. He was giving me all these examples of trying to measure things that are not measurable. I've just been turned on to *The Four Agreements*. Have you read that?

HUDSON: Yes. My favorite is the one that says, "Do not take anything personally."

GIBSON: And that's tough. I cannot take myself out of my situation. In one way, everything is personal. And yet I know that everything is personal for you, and for you, and for you. Then it's not personal.

HUDSON: Your upbeat spirit and energetic approach to life feel like the same energy I hear when I talk with Terri and Ruthie, as different as you three are.

GIBSON: I love being in that group!

HUDSON: It's up, it's together, it's woven, it's moving, it's experimental, it's curious, it's leaping. It's all those things . . . and more. What do you attribute that to?

GIBSON: I would attribute it to the acceptance that we don't know things. I'm really confident when having exploratory discussions. I feel passionately about everything, but I'll ride the fence on everything. I can see so many sides. I think that's an openness to explore, and that takes a willingness to admit that you don't know. I feel like I talk a good game, but when I look at the fiber of my life, I'm the biggest mess I know.

HUDSON: I feel the same way.

GIBSON: I feel like I've learned a lot, and I write about some of that. Then that's misleading because I don't really know. I realize at times that I'm at the beginning. Sometimes I learn more about myself after singing a song and having someone come up and tell me what they heard in that song, what their impression was. I'm speaking about a song called "Gatesville," which I wrote just driving through the town when I had no idea there was a woman's prison there. The whole song is about making bad choices and being trapped. I wrote about a gate looking like a fence. Two different things. One person in my audience asked me if I knew someone in Gatesville, telling me her sister was in prison there. That was the first I'd heard about that prison.

HUDSON: So, when an audience hears a song, they are listening to it through their own life and identity, and the song that you wrote changes. Stanley Kunitz wrote a book on literary criticism, saying that the reader creates the text. I say that the listening creates the song! The song is on your CD the way you wrote it. Every single listening creates a new text that then disappears.

GIBSON: And, subscribing to Zukav, everything breaks down to light and energy. Now that is an interesting way to look at songs and performing. I even think that we're all vibrating at our own frequencies. My performance will be different depending on the combination of frequencies in the room. Not just the individual perception in the audience's brains, but also in the energy in that room.

HUDSON: Rooms do have a vibration.

GIBSON: Yes, at the Cactus Café you can look every single person in the eye. That is a direct communication. There is something so satisfying about sitting around a campfire, sharing that moment of exchange. You don't get that when your song is number one on all the radio stations. You get the mailbox money, but not that rich moment of exchange. Everybody is putting the song in her or his own context. A song then becomes this transparent thing you just lay over something else—a lens to look through at some event, say, that the lyricist knows nothing about. So a song can offer either a moment of rich exchange or a poor lens through which to peer at something otherwise fuzzy.

HUDSON: And it sounds like you're a reader.

GIBSON: I love to read. Tom Robbins is one of my favorites. He's such a goonybird.

HUDSON: Don't tell me! Another coincidence that isn't a coincidence. I'm a Tom Robbins freak and love knowing that I've read every book he's written.

GIBSON: He's the only one I'll go look for. Ani DiFranco is that for me in music. I like her so much I'll buy anything of hers. I'm a little too white-bread middle class, Ward and June Cleaver background, to share in her experiences, so there are some things I hear that seem to be for shock value. Then I imagine that perhaps she did have a shocking life. I have had a really good solid life. I've had love and support that make it easy to take risks. Sometimes it makes it easy to see that you don't know how high you can go until you hit rock bottom.

HUDSON: And I'm not sure I've ever hit rock bottom! What's wrong with me?

GIBSON: We used to pretend we had retainers by putting paper clips on our teeth. It seemed like we just wanted to have this hardship to deal with. [laughter] I feel like there are circles and stages we go through. And as we go back, we learn step one of another phase. Then we go on to the next phase.

HUDSON: There's a word for all these ideas we seem to share: not *coincidence*, but *synchronicity*. Carl Jung came up with this to describe events that happen together in time and create meaning—meaningful patterns.

GIBSON: I could talk to you forever. Check out *Just Plain Folks* on the Internet. They have 22,000 members, and I'm one of them. I'm their newest success story because of "Wide Open Spaces," which became a monster hit with the Dixie Chicks singing it. The award ceremony was eclectic. I was no longer just a female singer/songwriter who works the Texas market. I was part of a world group that is creating something temporary and forever. It is as temporary as it is infinite. It is as frivolous as it is an absolute necessity. It seems like buying a CD can be frivolous, but it can also be a way to feed the soul. In order to live, I think people will feed their soul first.

HUDSON: I feel like a lot of people have given up on that, not realizing how important it is to feed your soul. At many schools, when the funding gets short, the arts are the first to go. I have a proposal to create a songwriter's chair at Schreiner University. Once that is funded, I see the songwriter staying on campus for a week, sharing classrooms and workshops and ending with a community concert. I think that makes a statement that we value our songwriters.

GIBSON: I see what you mean. I believe that God is everywhere, and He has blessed me so much. And in advance He's blessed me. So, I feel the need to give it back. That's the only way I'll hang on to it. That's where that transfer of energy happens. I think your proposal is a fantastic idea. It would take so little, and it would do so much. That would be my drop in the bucket. And it would encourage others to drop in the bucket. [We discuss getting various Austin songwriting groups on board. We brainstorm ways to get these groups on campus. Songwriters who have already visited the school include Billy Joe Shaver, Guy Clark, Tish Hinojosa, Terri Hendrix, Ruthie Foster, James McMurtry, Bett Butler, Steve Young, and Kinky Friedman, and that's just the beginning.]

I got to open for Guy Clark in Dallas last year. I knew the name, but I didn't know why I knew his name until I heard him play. What an awesome discovery! I certainly knew those songs. It was like hearing the writer of "Happy Birthday" sing it. His songs were that familiar to me.

HUDSON: My favorite Guy Clark line also happens to be his favorite: "She Ain't Going Nowhere, She's Just Leaving."

GIBSON: I so identify with that. I move around and don't get anywhere.

HUDSON: What are the things we need to talk about in the future?

GIBSON: To bring it back around, I was thinking about *The Red Tent*. The women of this time [Hebrew, tribes of Jacob] would go into the tent and menstruate together. It is this honoring of your connection with the moon, your part in nature, your connection with other women. Sure, the men had a certain legacy to carry on, the accumulation of land, hunting. The women's responsibility to each other included the daughters' keeping the stories for their mothers. If you didn't have a daughter, you didn't have anyone to give your stories to. The women were the storytellers in this way. They would have this intimacy of combing their hair together and for each other, not in a sexual way, but in a physical way of bonding. It was nurturing and comforting. I get a picture of this mother whispering these stories to her daughter, saying, "Be sure you remember this story I'm about to tell you. It's about how we live."

HUDSON: And you think that the women in Texas music are like that?

GIBSON: I do. I feel that is the clay of what we are. Whether we are writing, singing, teaching, sewing, or whatever, this is the clay, the raw material. I mean our womanness. We are preservers, recorders, communicators, storytellers. Being a woman makes you do all these things. It's our nature, our clay. Texas music seemed like cowboys around a campfire for a while. That makes sense too. But now I'm really seeing the contribution of women. We've had so many good images. I'm trying to incorporate this idea of a Greek goddess in a cowboy hat. There are so many archetypal roles that women play . . . the telephone operator, the woman behind the counter, the hairdresser, the first-grade teacher.

HUDSON: We could also talk about your favorite food.

GIBSON: I love so many kinds of food. I love Chinese food . . . but that doesn't seem like my mama's cooking. I love my mama's cooking because I have a recipe box that has grease stains on the recipes where Aunt Berle picked up the card. And all the recipes are in my mama's handwriting.

HUDSON: Did the wide open spaces of Amarillo also affect your world?

GIBSON: There was an Austin punk band that had a great line in a song: "There's nothing to break up your view of nothing out there." You get this idea that if you were able to see forever, you'd be able to see something. And you can't.

HUDSON: How do you explain every song being different?

GIBSON: You know Michael O'Connor. He plays guitar with me. That puts this pearl of wisdom in a context. At times we struggle for creativity, get writer's block. But really creativity is unlimited. If three of us wrote songs about the same object, we'd have three different songs. I write a lot of driving and traveling songs, so I end up writing about this "vehicle," pardon the pun, for writing. Your pathway. Your road. The turns you make and whether you signal or not. You can apply all these principles to living.

CAROLYN PILLOW: How can there be so many different tunes as well?

GIBSON: In the western scale there are eight notes. Research also covers the effect on the brain of two notes in harmony. Now that's interesting science. Rhythm does certain things to your body. I think the sound and rhythm appeal to something in us that is so much older than we are. I feel like that explains why there can be a trillion love songs with many variations. None are exactly the same, because the human brain and creativity are limitless.

HUDSON: Let's talk about collecting stories and songs.

GIBSON: I think that archiving contemporary stories is getting history while it is happening. That is more accurate than waiting for the dust to settle, then going to dig it out.

HUDSON: I spent an hour with Rosie Flores last night.

GIBSON: She's awesome. You know, the Groobees opened a couple of shows for her several years ago. I felt like it was happening in black and white, and you could hear the scratch of the record or the radio station behind her voice. That took me back to another era. I think that about every other style of music, other than what I do. That seems like really here and now. If I go see a jazz or blues band, something different, I feel a thread connecting me to all the music.

I've had the conversation on the genre of Texas music a lot. People ask what it is. It's like having the last name Smith. You know you all come from the same line, but there are so many different Smiths. It's a broad name that speaks of a common lineage. That has been one of the coolest aspects of being put under the Texas music umbrella. You're in a category that puts so many varied musical styles together. Carolyn Wonderland and I are both pretty strong women. We both like the ballads, even though she's blues and rock, while I'm folk-oriented. I think of the musical landscape. Is Texas the great plains, the piney woods, the mountains, or the sea?

HUDSON: Do you think that Texas can mean "eclectic" with many threads woven together in one song?

GIBSON: I do. I think there are certain patterns that repeat again and again. In the political history, well, we've been under six flags. There's the German influence in New Braunfels and the Louisiana sound in East Texas. Same with the food. Do you want chicken-fried steak or tamales or black-eyed peas? I do think there is something distinct and unique about Texas.

HUDSON: I know some people who do not want to be grouped in a Texas music frame. And I've talked with artists who claim no interest in Nashville as being commercial, but in some way most artists do want to be commercial.

GIBSON: Not wanting to be grouped under the Texas umbrella was strictly a business decision. And notice I say *business*. The key thing is to act with integrity. I was reminded of this recently when I attended the Folk Alliance. I went to see Janis Ian. She put out that song "Society's Child," about interracial dating in the 1960s. She was so young when she wrote that song. A manager told her that only one line said it was about black and white relationships. He suggested she take that line out. She said that it was a watershed in her career, at the age of fifteen. She had to decide about that line. As it turns out, everyone picked up the song and played it because of that controversy. It had not been dealt with on radio before. She felt this choice really set the tone of her career. The Dixie Chicks cut "Wide Open Spaces," and they cut out a stanza of the song, wanting it to be timely. I really had a hard time with that. The verse was about a U-Haul. I think it was to make it the right length for radio play. It was not quite as universal as the rest of the verses. But I don't think it changed the integrity of the song.

HUDSON: This was not something you had to make a stand about. Perhaps you might have with other verses?

GIBSON: Absolutely.

HUDSON: How did they end up with that song?

GIBSON: The Groobees were putting out an album. We had made a demo to send to Lloyd Maines. Scott, one of the Groobees, had an album out where I sang vocals. That was how I got in cahoots with those guys. We weren't really a band that was playing together at that time. It grew and evolved into a band. I had been writing solo stuff and doing some solo gigs since about 1991, in Amarillo. I moved up to Montana. That's where I started running open mikes. That's where I wrote "Wide Open Spaces." We had given Lloyd a demo tape, and right at that time Natalie started singing with the Dixie Chicks. A little later, they were signed to Sony and to a developmental thing. They were looking for songs for a record. Lloyd agreed to produce our album, and he mentioned that he had a daughter singing with a group called the Dixie Chicks that had done really well regionally. They were getting away from their bluegrass and cowgirl thing, wanting to get more mainstream. They had been playing my song live for a while, and they got a good response. He asked me if they could record it. I had no idea what that meant, really. I was doing my own songwriting, and I was very naïve about it all. I thought Reba McEntire wrote all her own songs. I thought maybe she started out by calling and getting her own gigs. I don't know her history, but I was naïve about the business.

My favorite part about writing "Wide Open Spaces" is that I wrote the song at my mom's kitchen table the first Christmas I went home after moving to Montana. When I left, I left my notebook on the table. She found the notebook—so much for doing it all by myself.

HUDSON: I can now value the interpretation and expression, but I was surprised when I found out that George Strait did not write many of his own songs.

GIBSON: I've heard, in the shady corners of the business, that some performers demand a cut of the publishing with the songwriter. I know that I made more off "Wide Open Spaces" than Natalie did. And she's out there singing her guts out with her picture on the billboard. I don't know that I'd write if I didn't also perform. I like putting a breath of air in the songs. That's like the full circle. Getting the applause every three minutes when you play a show. That's a paycheck. When you have to perform and deliver songs, it's like being accountable for what you write.

HUDSON: I am going back to a conversation I had with Terri Hendrix. She spoke so highly of you.

GIBSON: As little time as we spend together, I feel that we really have tight threads with each other. She steps out in front of me to open doors for me. But in the same sense, we're in the same place all the time. I think about her a lot. I wonder what she would do in some of the situations I'm in. There's just this kind of energy exchange going on. When we got together to write, we ended up writing songs about each other. We went and had lunch together and decided to "bang our heads" together. I have a song on my album called "Shape I'm In," and Michael and Eleanor [two band members] helped me with it. We've had conversations about jumping off from a comfortable place. We get comfortable, and jumping off is scary.

HUDSON: I have this friend, Paula D'Arcy, who was a successful counselor. Then she decided to see what was next, in the face of being comfortable and successful. She's written five books and is performing a play about her life right now. That's a leap.

GIBSON: It seems to get harder to create because of the risk of doing something that someone's already done.

HUDSON: I'm on this edge doing a lot of different projects that I created. And I'm looking at what it would really look like if I took a leap.

GIBSON: Yeah, yeah.

HUDSON: You just have to decide to leap.

GIBSON: Yes, yes.

HUDSON: Guy Clark says, "Always trust your cape." Have you written about that jumping-off place?

GIBSON: I have. "Even water jumps from a comfortable cloud, for crying out loud. For just a moment of individuality before it hits the ground and washes out to sea." Details matter. Whether you jump or fall or get pushed. You react to it differently. You look at it differently. Your rewards are different. In fact, a fan once said she loved the song about water falling from a cloud. I said, "Oh no, baby, it's not FALLS. The word is JUMPS. You're not pushed, you don't fall, you do it." It's like a detail that's so minor, but it makes all the difference in the world. Each word brings a different reaction.

HUDSON: A lot of people have a goal of getting comfortable.

GIBSON: One of the most depressing things I heard after the Dixie Chicks' success with my song was "Wow, Susan, you'll never have to work again." How depressing when you love what you do. That was the kiss of death. Now it's easy to get lethargic. I have a nametag I can wear until I do something that outshines that. And that might mean just writing another song, not a better song. I mean getting up and doing something not quite as good as what you just did takes more guts at times.

HUDSON: Do you have a sense of a new direction for yourself? I know you're on your own now.

GIBSON: Yes, it is a new direction. Because of the way our band, the Groobies, terminated, there were some hurt feelings. Some things to get over. I feel like that's what I've been doing the last year. And now I'm not feeling like I'm over it. These things take time.

HUDSON: Trust the process.

GIBSON: It was a process to get there, and it's not going to be one decision to get over it. Pain is an easy thing to write about, and if I keep looking back there for my inspiration, I might just be stuck. Hurt, vulnerability, and loss are easy to write about. Sometimes it's more uncomfortable to write about good. You tend to get sappy.

HUDSON: Terri Hendrix can do that . . . write about the good.

GIBSON: Yes, where it's lighthearted but not taken lightly. She walks that line really well and gets way off that line really well. I love that about her music. She defines a sound. That's another girl I look to. She can do something traditional and still sound like Terri Hendrix. She can do this far-out pop, eclectic "teeth of the lion"-sounding stuff and still sound like Terri Hendrix. She's made it all Terri Hendrix. She's got that whole wide margin.

HUDSON: I've never heard it put that way. I like that description of a distinct sound.

GIBSON: I'd like to walk that line, find out where the Susan Gibson line is. I really feel like humor is such good medicine. It's a drug: when you're feeling good, it makes you feel better, and when you're feeling bad, it makes you feel good.

HUDSON: And scientists are measuring the effects of laughter, finding that it's more healing than many drugs. I also read that the chemicals in your tears when you are laughing are not the same as the chemicals present when you are crying in sorrow.

GIBSON: [long, thoughtful pause] Yeah . . . I think my lyrics get pretty conversational. I have a song called "Anything to Keep from Crying." I wrote it from conversations I had with my sister, Jane. We are really sentimental. If my mom is behind a car with your birthday date in the numbers, she will probably follow it for a while! Or your initials. If she sees SLG, she just might say, "That's Susan Laura Gibson. That's my girl," and she might miss her exit. She notices everything. Many times Jane and I start out laughing and end up crying, or vice versa.

HUDSON: We could talk about family for a while, couldn't we?

I caught up with Susan again at the 2004 Kerrville Wine and Music Festival. She and Michael O'Connor delivered an opening set that created the tone for the evening. I asked her to add an update to this conversation. Here's what she said:

GIBSON: What a year since March 2003! I've been trying to put down some roots in the Hill Country without getting too stagnant. I've played and driven, and driven and played, collecting new songs and new people to sing them to! I think it is so cool that I have run into your sister since the interview—thanks for the new friend. I don't know much more than the last time we talked except this—we are blessed as we are, thankfully. I'm trying to keep that as a balance in my life.

I gave myself a time frame. If my idea didn't work, I was going back to school. . . . There's a common perception about doing anything creative, that you're going to starve. . . . Not true.

Terri Hendrix

A FORCE OF NATURE

Terri has been part of my life for a long time. I first heard her with a trio playing at John T. Floore Country Store in Helotes. I was there to interview Marcia Ball, but I was intrigued with this opening band. That was just the beginning. Terri graciously visited my English classrooms at Schreiner University each time she played a coffeehouse on campus. Then she started doing weekend songwriting workshops in Waring at the Old #9 educational facility. Her career just kept growing as new opportunities opened up for her. Not accidentally, I might add. She had a vision, a purpose, and the tools to keep moving along a road that she created. In September 2002, she and Lloyd Maines played the annual Literacy and Learning Concert that is part of the Texas Heritage Living History Weekend. I saw her band transform into a rocking folk group at Floore's one evening. Her style of dress had changed. My last interview with her occurred at a place we both love, the Kerrville Folk Festival, in June 2004. Of course, I saw her again in January 2005 at the birthday celebration for Rod Kennedy, founder of the Kerrville Folk Festival. Terri is a woman who has a following in the world of folk/pop music, and she loves what she does. Lloyd Maines, who has accompanied her since March 1997, is an integral part of both her sound and her success. What follows are selections from my years of talking with and knowing Terri Hendrix.

HUDSON: Great overalls! Let's hear a story from your life.

HENDRIX: I started wearing overalls in 1997. I wore overalls because they were a low-maintenance outfit to wear. As the waistlines on jeans were creeping lower and lower, and the skirt lengths were creeping higher and higher, I safely performed in overalls. I was unaware of how it became the way folks identified me. Soon, it caught on with my fans. At one time, I had over seventy-five pairs of overalls I had collected. One problem, they are too hot to wear in the Texas heat, so I don't wear them anymore.

STUDENT: Do you have a central theme to the songs you write?

HENDRIX: I do have a theme to what I write. It has to be true to my life. It is my wish to inspire. Sometimes I just write the music. Sometimes I just write lyrics. And sometimes the two come together and end up being a song. As I grow older, I feel I have more experience to bring to the table and a deeper pool from which to write. But I think it's important to not take myself too seriously. If I get too abstract, I tend to lose my audience, and it is the connection I aspire to achieve when I perform the songs I've written. I don't have just one way I write. I got this great thing from Guy Clark: "The method is really not having a method." If you don't limit yourself, you'll come up with anything true to life. [She talks to the class as she's tuning. Then she sits on the desk to perform a song.] Any other questions? There's got to be something.

STUDENT: Do you have any regrets?

HENDRIX: Yeah, I do. Letting fear and doubt limit me. Playing for as long as I did on the River Walk in San Antonio and not embarking on my career path. I was making good money playing for tourists on the River Walk for about five years. When I left the River Walk gigs, I was able to really focus on being a "performer." There's a huge difference between playing while people are eating dinner and playing while people are really listening to you. I closed a door so that other doors would open. After a few years, the listening rooms that I wanted to play began to hire me. I gave myself a time frame. If my idea didn't work, I was going back to school. My fourth CD is coming out May 2. One of the things I did in 1998 was start my own record label. Anybody can do that. You take $100 or so, start a bank account, go to the courthouse, and start a DBA. It gives me the rights to all my songs and gives me control over my music and my destiny. It's been very rewarding.

HUDSON: So you're still Tycoon Cowgirl Records?

HENDRIX: No, I changed the name to Wilory Records. Tycoon Cowgirl Records was limiting. It sounded "country." I do country music; I'm just not sure what country it comes from. [smile] Because I do so many different styles of music, I didn't want a name that put me in one genre of music. Ani DiFranco is a real pioneer in doing it your own way. Another is Jerry Jeff Walker. He had a lot of success with "Mr. Bojangles" and started his own label a long time ago.

STUDENT: Did you ever consider signing with Righteous Babe, Ani's label?

HENDRIX: No, I didn't try. But I did set up my company the same way. For instance, in Europe, I lease my music to someone in Europe. I rent it to them, then get paid royalties. They provide me with a quarterly financial statement. When you're on a record label, for example Sony, and your CD sells for $15, you might make about $3. As an independent artist, you make the entire amount. I like selling 1,000 CDs and making $15,000. I think it's important to control your masters and add up what you would make on a label versus what you would make going independent. The cost of making the CD is not that high. Are you ready for a song? I hope I haven't been rattling on too much. On the way here, I got behind this huge truck going about twenty miles per hour, and I couldn't pass them. So I feel like now I'm rattling at you at 100 miles per hour. A friend of mine, Susan Gibson, wrote "Wide Open Spaces." Lloyd pitched the song to the Dixie Chicks. They ended up not only cutting the song, but naming their debut record on a major release after Susan's song! To celebrate, Susan came to San Marcos on a fluke. We went to a local gift shop. Susan started buying gifts for everyone she knew, I think, even her first-grade teacher! I thought about how generous she was. We kicked back, laughed, and had a real nice time. Being around such a special person inspired me to write "Good Time Van." You see, most of the women I know settle for less than they deserve because they are unaware of their gifts. They wake up, and then one day they wake up some more. They look back and say, "Now why the hell did I stay so long in that situation?" and hopefully make a change. I have done this when I was too scared to quit, and it's been hard to stay.

I'm thirty-two now. I think music is like wine. The older I get, the more wisdom I hope that I have. I can say a prayer now with much deeper meaning because I understand where my faith comes from. My appreciation for family has deepened. Singing this song the last time I was here was different. Raised Baptist, it's been a long haul to be comfortable with the type of free religion I embrace. It has changed how I pray. Let's get back on the topic of the woman thing. I enjoy being a woman. A song can take on a different meaning when a woman sings it. I think the gender issues do relate to content of songs. I am aware that I'm a woman. I think it's always been important to portray myself as a strong, independent, and free-thinking spirit. I attempt to do this in the songs I write. I don't want to be the victim.

[The same day, Terri visits a literature class.]

HENDRIX: I'm going to start with a song I've been working on. It's been hard for me to finish songs these days. I've been touring nonstop for the last five months. Bouncing like a ball from state to state makes it difficult to complete a sentence, much less a song. I came home a month ago to work on my new record. On a day off, I visited my folks. They are getting older, and it's important for me to spend quality time with them. My mother's been going through her things. She's always been, like me, something of a pack rat. One of the items she found was a quilt that my grandmother's mother made. I was given this quilt. It was symbolic of the relationship I have with my mother. We are very different. We come from different pieces of cloth, but we are sewn together, and we become one, as a family unit, in spite of our differences.

HUDSON: One of the ways I started this class was to remind students that our stories matter. My family is mixed racially, and my parents have had to shift their perspectives to accept all that we kids have done and all those we have brought to the dinner table.

HENDRIX: Blood is thick in families, but principles are also important. We can't sacrifice all we are just to please parents. It's a fine balance, for sure.

HUDSON: I'm glad you brought up that distinction for this class.

HENDRIX: We have to have morals. Sometimes kids have them and their parents don't. That's tough. I think as individuals we must all find our way and be willing to take a stand. If you have kids, this is really important. They learn from our actions.

HUDSON: What's been the biggest challenge for you?

HENDRIX: [long pause] On several different levels I see keeping integrity as a challenge. That means a lot of hard work. Perseverance. When I was younger, I had a hard time just eating one piece of pie. If I liked it, I wanted more. At one time in my life I've pushed 200 pounds. Discipline with my time is what I find most difficult. In order to create new songs, I have to better myself as a musician. The two have always been connected for me. The larger palette I have, the more I can dip into and write. I'm connected to the music. But it takes the discipline to practice. Writing takes discipline too. My purpose is to write songs and then share those songs with others. It brings me great joy to communicate this way. At times I feel writing is the last thing on my list. I get so very busy with "life." Fixing the leaky faucet, changing the burned-out lightbulbs, doing laundry . . . then next thing I know, I'm packing and heading to the airport for a tour. I have come to the conclusion that I'm going to have to have more discipline as a writer to go where my heart wants to go with my songs. Another challenge is health. It takes discipline to eat right. I have epilepsy. It's challenging to maintain my health on the road. This disease requires that I get a certain amount of sleep and eat a balanced diet. It's been hard to travel and get the sleep and food I need.

HUDSON: Now that's hard to believe, looking at you now.

STUDENT: Have you ever felt like you didn't know what you were going to do?

HENDRIX: I always knew that I really didn't have a choice. Whatever is burning in my heart. If we all look deep inside, we will know what that is. It may be as simple as working on trucks, but it is burning inside. We must follow that burning. Honor that. I always knew I wanted to do something with music. I was paying for it, too. I was going to college and failing, waiting tables all the time. I received no help whatsoever with the cost of my education. I had this coach suggest I drop out and get my act together. I stopped going to school, and I started doing music. And I've never looked back. There's something I want to say. There's a common perception about doing anything creative, that you're going to starve. Part of the story. Not true. If you keep your overhead low, you can live within your means and afford to do what you love. I make choices that keep me on my path. I could be writing and singing commercials, but that doesn't support the path I want.

HUDSON: How would you describe your calling to music?

HENDRIX: It's like something inside of me that I can't stop. I even love the smell of 7-11s. Call me a nut. I love it when we are on the road and stop at a convenience store. It's almost like a road ritual. I love the way a place smells before we play a festival. Waffles and powdered sugar. I love the way it was in Europe. People, not knowing what we were saying, bouncing along, wearing Willie Nelson T-shirts and loving the music. Now that is fun. It's the funniest thing. The desire to experience new things, meet people around the world and travel all call out to me. I'm called to communicate to others through music. I enjoy the feeling I get when I know I have made a difference in someone's life through my music.

HUDSON: For you, it's the performance component and interaction with the crowd that calls to you, right?

HENDRIX: Yes! More important than anything else. It's also when I'm driving down the road and hear something I love, I write it down and go buy it. It was like that when I heard "The Cape" by Guy Clark. It was like that when I heard Patty Griffin, Ani DiFranco, Eliza Gilkyson! It's like that when I put my pen to a piece of paper and come up with a song. Like someone higher than me is involved.

We have so much to be thankful for, no matter our background or experiences. It's a blessing to be able to hear, right? Every day is a gift. What I'm trying to bring out here is that we're all creative beings. Human beings create. I don't believe in talent . . . alone. . . . I believe that people are born with the "I can" or the "I can't." Perseverance. We can all sing and dance. We can all write poetry. We can all dance.

HUDSON: That's my ongoing mantra: "You can do this."

HENDRIX: I think I'll do a song for you about that. This is a mandolin, and this song's called "The Wallet." I keep this journal of what people say, and once a goofy man came up to me at a show and said, loudly, "Live with passion." I watched him walk away, and I wrote it down. My lyrics come from situations like that.

[Terri strums that mandolin and plays a song, one that encourages everyone to live full-out: "Own Your Own Universe."]

HENDRIX: When I wrote that line, it's about owning the world that you live in, as if you created that world. What you create is what you own. No matter who we love or who we date, they can never take our universe. The two can be side by side, but no one can take your universe. That's what that whole song is about, needing to just be who we are. Any questions? It's such an honor to be doing this, and I love it.

[On June 12, 2004, I took my first granddaughter, Jessica, to the Kerrville Folk Festival to hear Terri perform. Jessica, age eleven, joined me on this interview, both of us absorbed in Terri's genuine way of being. On the way home, Jessica played the new CD, The Art of Removing Wallpaper, over and over. By the time our trip was over, Jessica was singing all the words to her favorite Terri songs. Below is an excerpt from our conversation.]

HUDSON: I love the songs on this new CD, and I can see the organic unfolding of your career as a writer. How do you perceive the changes going on in your work?

HENDRIX: That's wonderful. As a woman, I get older, and my goal is to move forward with what I'm doing. I want to get stronger at what I do so I can communicate effectively. Communication.

HUDSON: You said the magic words there: "Getting older." Age and appearance seem to play a distinct role in the careers of women.

HENDRIX: Oh, it does. For years and years I wore overalls because they were comfortable. But as a woman I found it started to be more about my overalls than about my songs. I had a problem with that. I'm thirty-six now, and I decided to just wear blue jeans for a while, hoping people would think about my songs more and not ask so many questions about my overalls. I have guy friends who wear overalls in a band, and they don't get asked about them. Interesting. I'm finally realizing things are different for women.

HUDSON: I remember seeing you the first time and hearing that funk / jazz rhythm that is so hard to categorize. I wonder what you hear about your music.

HENDRIX: I don't think about what others say too much. I can tell when I'm off, though. I care about making it worth people's time to come see me. I very much appreciate positive feedback.

HUDSON: You have a beautiful brochure with this new CD.

HENDRIX: I have a talented team working with me, and Melissa Webb is really talented. I've learned to control less by finding people who are good at what they do and letting them go. Melissa works her best when she creates on her own. I'm proud she works with me. I have this same philosophy with my band. Rather than tell them what to play, I just have this unspoken rule: "Just play what you feel." Time is short, and we can only do so much. I have to give certain things away, and at times, I fall on my face doing so. People who will do what they say are hard to find.

HUDSON: Who are some of your favorites right now?

HENDRIX: I really adore Ruthie Foster and Cyd Cassone. I love their music, and I love the female camaraderie that we have, calling each other and leaving phone messages of encouragement. We tour across the country and talk about each other across the country. I've always admired Joe Ely. I've learned so much by watching Joe and Jerry Jeff Walker. They both command the stage. I also like a lot of techno stuff, like Kinky and A3. I'll get on a jazz kick, and then I'm off. I love the Pointer Sisters. Working with Lloyd over the years has introduced me to other elements of music. I love the mix of acoustic with other things . . . horns, for example. I've never been a huge fan of strong electric guitar, but I love it when the acoustic gets tough, like Suzanne Vega and early Rickie Lee Jones. I love the harmonies of Supertramp. I am a huge music fan.

HUDSON: Let's talk about your band tonight.

HENDRIX: Glenn [Fukunaga] and Paul [Pearcy] and Lloyd [Maines] really get the most out of their instruments. We cross capo at times to get a jangling twelve-string sound. The textures are important onstage.

HUDSON: I suppose the audience makes a difference, and this is a great listening audience. How do you plan the song list?

HENDRIX: In a forty-minute set, we do need a list. But at Floore's, with the entire evening ahead, we can be more creative without a set list. Play in tune, play in time!

HUDSON: Let's talk about a favorite small venue.

HENDRIX: I like it informal and comfortable, anywhere there's no pretension. I like "down home." That goes for anything. I get a lot from the audience, and I like them close.

HUDSON: You are still running your business, with seven CDs to your credit. What is the biggest challenge right now?

HENDRIX: We had over 3,000 pre-orders on this new CD. In my garage there were 6,000 envelopes. My whole house was nothing but people, and the A/C had gone out that week. I got a blister on my hand from autographing, and it was a sweatshop that week. I'm really fortunate to have the fans I do. The music has to come first.

HUDSON: Let's end with some weird questions I use in boundary-breaking exercises in my class. What item of clothing are you?

HENDRIX: I am a soft, fuzzy, warm quilt or a down comforter.

HUDSON: What room in your house are you?

HENDRIX: The kitchen with lots of windows where I can watch the birds.

HUDSON: What color are you?

HENDRIX: I am this purple color . . . almost neon.

HUDSON: What direction?

HENDRIX: South. I'm always going south, looking in other directions, saying, "That's where I'm supposed to be!" [laughter]

HUDSON: Earth, wind, fire, or water?

HENDRIX: I wish I moved like water, but I don't. I would love to be earth, but at times I'm more fire. I worry too much at times. I'm the wind.

HUDSON: Favorite book and movie?

HENDRIX: *Da Vinci Code* and *Shrek*. I'm a horrible Shrek-head right now. I loved the first one. I loved *Finding Nemo* and *Barbershop*. I love comedy.

[We wrapped up our talk, and Terri took the stage with her band. The audience loved her, and she loved them. What a show.]

When I listen to a woman telling a story in a song, She's not hiding anything. It's all out for anybody to see, and it's usually something that came from a process of healing and there's a story to be told and there's other people that can relate to it and that's what they want to reach out to.   [CASSONE]

Ruthie Foster *and* Cyd Cassone

THE HEART OF TEXAS

I first heard Ruthie Foster at a Willie Nelson picnic at Luckenbach. She then showed up at the Kerrville Folk Festival, performing with Cyd Cassone on percussion. Ruthie's voice and purity of soul moved me, and I invited both of them to visit my classes and play at our Texas Music Coffeehouse. Each time, each album, they just get better. One performance that stands out in my mind is the Literacy and Learning Concert they played at Schreiner University in September 2003. My sister, Carolyn, and I got up in the aisles, dancing, as we sang along to these words: "Walk on" and "Got to get my travelin' shoes" and "Got a hole in my pocket where it all slips away." Carolyn was leaving a long marriage, and I am always called by the road. What a moment for the Pillow Sisters, a name given to us by Robert Brandes, a man who always encourages us to get up and dance!

HUDSON: I want to hear you tell that story about the beat again. I was raised in a Southern Baptist Church, and my whole experience of life, worship, joy, and celebration was with the music and ultimately the beat and the rhythm. I love that story you were telling.

FOSTER: Well, growing up in the Southern Baptist Church, sometimes you would have a piano player and sometimes you wouldn't. And a lot of times you wouldn't. And what my grandmother and her sisters would do is sit in their amen corner with these heels on, and they always had these heels that would make noise on a wood floor when they're singing. [Ruthie hums.] And then they'd start clapping with that. Well, sometimes they'd clap and sometimes they'd just hit on their purse. And that's how we'd start. And that's how you start fellowship. Sometimes you would even have what they call brother superintendent up front. And let the amen corner start the fellowship. They always knew what song to start with. Whether it had words or not, you knew they were singing a song. They just had to hum it.

HUDSON: Now, was this an official amen corner?

FOSTER: Well, no. See, at our church we had one side where the sisters would sit, the older sisters. And then there was a side where the brothers and the superintendent would sit. And then the rest of the congregation sat out in front. So it was usually the older men over in the brothers section, the brothers of the superintendent section, and then the sisters. The sisters, usually the older women, would sit on the other side of the church. I don't know if there is any other church that does that. This was our church and the way it was.

HUDSON: Right.

FOSTER: It was usually just overflow seats, the seats in our congregation. When the benches were full, that was just overflow. But these sisters had their own spots, you know, set out.

HUDSON: So many of the songwriters and musicians I talk to, especially in Texas, have a story that happened in a church: Billy Joe Shaver, Willie Nelson, or Willie's sister Bobbie.

CASSONE: Me too. I grew up in a Protestant environment. We'd go to camp meeting, and the older kids had their own tent. I always got an older cousin to take me to that tent. It was more fun. They would go to celebrate, and it's almost all music. We sang for hours in this tent. The particular camp meeting that I used to go to seemed to be really steeped in the old spirituals. I wouldn't go to the one that was for my age group; I would go with my older cousins because it was much more interesting. I loved it. I grew up going to camp meeting every summer singing those songs, black spirituals. My aunt Esther loved those songs, and she would sing them. I lived with her for a lot of my childhood. She was a big influence on me. My mother loves that music, as you know, Ruthie.

FOSTER: I was surprised your mother knew "Precious Lord," because I always looked at that as a black spiritual.

CASSONE: She knows all of them.

FOSTER: Here's this white woman in Seattle, and we're in the kitchen washing dishes and she goes, "Ruthie, do you know 'Precious Lord'?" Yeah . . . and I'm thinking to myself it must be another "Precious Lord" that she's going to sing. She breaks into the same old thing that we would sing down in Teals Prairie, Texas, and New Hope Missionary Baptist Church.

HUDSON: I haven't heard of that.

FOSTER: You probably wouldn't. It's small. It's just a little community. It's just a little farming community near Caldwell in Burleson County.

HUDSON: When you were in College Station, did you become part of that music scene?

FOSTER: Not really, I don't think so. Because I had just come from New York, and my sound wasn't country.

CASSONE: Yeah, they thought we were going to break out into "Copenhagen" or something like that.

FOSTER: Yeah. I've just started to learn the Guy Clark song "Home Grown Tomatoes." I love the song. I mean, I grew up picking tomatoes every summer. And I just thought that would be fun.

HUDSON: So you can sing it with authenticity.

FOSTER: Yeah, I could throw in my little story right before it and then go right into "Home Grown Tomatoes."

CASSONE: I'm always so surprised at so many of the parallels that we have growing up in completely different countries, as far as I'm concerned. Growing up in the Seattle area, in the Pacific Northwest, and she grew up in Central Texas, born in East Texas. And, you know, we did the same things in a lot of ways. We were both from families that were relatively poor.

FOSTER: Yeah, we were talking about that earlier.

CASSONE: We did, I did a lot of picking in the summer. Did a lot of having to get up at five o'clock in the morning and go out there and work in the fields and pick flats of berries, or pick whatever needed to be picked that time of year.

FOSTER: At least y'all had fruit.

CASSONE: Yeah, I didn't have to do the tomatoes. Didn't have to do that. We grew them at home. I had to pick my own, but I didn't have to go work in the fields for that. But I did a lot of that fieldwork. My mom was basically a migrant worker when she was young. She only went through the eighth grade, and my grandfather pulled her out of school, and they worked with migrant workers on the West Coast.

FOSTER: That was common where I'm from. My mother and her brothers talked about when they would go west, go to West Texas into the Lubbock area and all that and pick cotton during certain times of the year, usually the summer. And sometimes they would pull them out of school when it was time to go pick.

HUDSON: I feel that we can choose to see how different we all are, or we can take a look at how similar we all are. What do you think is distinct about the woman's perspective?

CASSONE: I believe that, from my experience with things I write myself and listening to the writing of other women, there's a wanting to make a connection with the people you are relating your music to that I think is stronger in women's music in a lot of ways. It's hard to put into words. It really is more visceral. When I listen to a woman telling a story in a song, she's not hiding anything. It's all out for anybody to see, and it's usually something that came from a process of healing and there's a story to be told and there's other people that can relate to it and that's what they want to reach out to.

Or there's a message: it's a lot more globally oriented, more open to other people, open to humankind, open to the universe. I feel more in women's music than in men's music. That's not saying that men can't write that way, because I've heard it there too. But we have a friend, Rachel Bissex, who wrote a song called "Dancing with My Mother" that no matter how many times I hear it has the same effect on me. And it's a simple song—very simple. I always cry.

FOSTER: And we heard it a lot on tour.

CASSONE: And we heard it a lot because we toured together for a long time. She's from Vermont. She comes to Texas a lot. But that song, in its simplicity, tells a story about how important the mother/daughter relationship is and makes everyone in the room, especially women, think about their relationship with their mother. And that kind of a song is talking about relationship. It's talking about the importance of that relationship to everybody in that room, whether your mother is with you or not. And, so, something simple like that. And I see that women get a lot more involved in issues when they write, too. Taking a stand on something that's maybe hard to take a stand on. They're willing to stand up there and put it into words and put it in front of all these people. And maybe you like what I said or maybe you don't, but this is important.

HUDSON: My research uncovered this quotation by Tanya Tucker: "It's a lonely business being ballsy."

FOSTER: I love that!

CASSONE: The women that really make me stand up and take notice and really listen to what they are saying have "cojones." They aren't afraid to say it.

HUDSON: Is there a time, Ruthie, when you felt like maybe the door was not open? Has being a woman played any particular role in your life?

FOSTER: Not really, no. I've never really run into any barriers as a woman.

CASSONE: I think the only time I ever noticed hurdles, I wasn't expecting it. I didn't know there was a problem with a woman doing what I was doing, but when I decided I wanted to do sound engineering, I was all over the place. I started out in sound engineering in Oregon and helped build a recording studio there. And I was the only woman in the group who wanted to be a sound engineer. There were other women involved, but they were kind of groupie personalities, and they wanted to be a part of the thing, but they didn't really want to know what was going on with the equipment. And I wanted to jump in with both feet and get in it up to my neck and learn it. And when I met Ruthie, that is what I was doing. I had gone back to working as a sound engineer. Kind of going back to my intention of being involved in music from as many angles as possible.

FOSTER: That was interesting to see in College Station.

CASSONE: I was the only woman sound engineer in College Station at the time, as far as I know.

FOSTER: I don't know if it's a Texas thing or just that area. Bryan – College Station area. After moving from New York, and then bringing my band into this particular venue, and then seeing her walk in and say "Hi, I'm Cyd Cassone. I'll be running sound for you." Well, now, in Texas?

CASSONE: I did butt heads with some road managers. Road managers would walk in and say, "Where's the sound guy?" And I would say, "I'm the sound guy." And they would go, "No, really, where's the sound guy?" "I am the sound guy." "No one else is going to run sound?" "Nope, nobody else knows how, except me."

HUDSON: Let's just go to the end of your life. How would you like to be remembered?

FOSTER: You first.

HUDSON: She went first before.

CASSONE: Yeah, chicken.

FOSTER: I pass the buck quite a bit.

CASSONE: Yes, you do that.

HUDSON: We're not going to let you this time. How would you like to be remembered?

FOSTER: I would like to be remembered as this beautiful black woman, and I would have to say black because that has been the one thing that does stick out with me sometimes with the music thing, because I feel I am bringing my experience to folk music. Now that I'm in folk, I guess you could call it. And my experience is, growing up with all music, that's country and R&B and soul and gospel and spirituals and everything else that was running through the house.

HUDSON: And what else was that?

FOSTER: Folk music. But I grew up listening to spirituals along with sermons. My mother had albums with sermons. She would put on Reverend C. L. Franklin and drop the needle, and we would just sit and listen to a whole sermon. And then you'd hear singing. Aretha Franklin was on that. And how I would like to be remembered is as this person who brought all this to music, this circle of music, that they call folk music. I'd like to bring a little more power to that, push the forefront. Does that make any sense?

HUDSON: Yes. And that is a broad base of experience. And I would have loved hearing those sermons. I bought a Martin Luther King CD, a whole CD of all his speeches. I just want to hear the music of those sermons.

FOSTER: There's a rhythm to the way preachers speak. And that's what I would like to carry myself when I'm singing, too. I get people coming up to me going, "You're going to preach one day. I know you're going to preach. You're a preacher." I grew up with that.

HUDSON: You say that Ruthie Foster brought more soul to it. Whatever it is.

FOSTER: To me, it's just about the music. Yeah. Putting my family in there too.

HUDSON: And Cyd, how would you like to be remembered at the end of all this?

CASSONE: I've been one of those people who are always trying to make a difference or bring attention to something that needs changing. And I guess, to me, music is the strongest tool for anything like that in the universe. It's at the core of a lot of the change that takes place. And it's one of the strongest communicators, the strongest way to send your message. I would like to be remembered as someone who has made a difference in a positive way through music. Because, you know, music is in everything. When armies go to battle, they have their music they take with them. Advertising uses music. Political campaigns use music. Everything—

HUDSON: Bob Dylan used music!

CASSONE: You know, it's not just the people that get up onstage and do a show, but it's actually in everything, if you really think about how music is woven into everything that is used to influence people.

FOSTER: See why I hang out with her? She's so well spoken. You know, I'm just a little country gal. I can teach you how to pick a tomato without pulling a plant up. But this girl can talk. From eight to ten is when I realized that I was going to be in music. And, you know, it starts in the church. I was watching my uncle. I have a group of uncles that sing in a quartet. And watching them just set the church on fire, all these women in the amen corner in a frenzy because he's singing. This is in church!

My uncle would start on this piano riff. And then my uncle Sonny would just open his mouth. You see all of us kids sitting in the back 'cause we ended up sneaking into the back row, and we'd end up going to the front row when we knew my uncle Sonny was going to sing and get the church going. So, it was anywhere from eight to ten years old, I knew that's what I wanted to do. I wanted to sing. But I didn't really open my mouth to sing until a little bit later than that. I figured I'd just learn to play an instrument.

CASSONE: Well, it's hard to compete with all those.

FOSTER: There are so many singers in my family. Oh my gosh.

CASSONE: Had to be intimidating.

FOSTER: But it was so cool to watch. You know, watching TV, I was into the 1970s variety shows. You know, I loved Glen Campbell and Olivia Newton-John. *The Mac Davis Show*. All these variety shows that had these songwriters. You know, I looked past the little stupid comedy stuff they do, and I'd wait for them to sing. And that was it. That was it. I know it sounds simple, but that was it. What about you?

CASSONE: I think it's just been a constant awareness that music was the thing that gave me breath. When I wasn't in music, I felt myself fading; I felt myself dying inside. And I knew that if I didn't go back to submerging myself in music, which is where I knew I had to be, if I didn't go back to it, I would die inside completely. I sang in choirs and I did a little bit of recording and sang at people's weddings. You know, did stuff that was safe for the relationship that I was in at the time. I did some of that, but I came to a crossroads where I said I have to go back to this. This is who I am. It's what I need to be. And I'm going to go back to it full-time. And I took a huge, huge risk. My marriage did end because of my choice to go back to music full-time.

HUDSON: Do you have kids?

CASSONE: I have two children. I have a twenty-one-year-old daughter and a fourteen-year-old son. I am still mom, still do mom stuff. Even the twenty-one-year-old calls me from Austin, saying, "My car got towed!" I say, "Well, you're going to have to go get it, aren't you?" Being a mom is just the most incredible thing. I had 100-percent support from my children when I made my decision, made my choice. And I still do have support from them. Yeah, I think it's always been awareness that music is who I am and that I really can't live without it.

When I was a little girl, one of the aunts I lived with for a while had me watching Shirley Temple movies, item for item. And I was in love with Shirley Temple because I identified with her character a lot because she was always in these situations where she wasn't with her parents. But she was this singer. And she could get up in the middle of everything and sing a song. And, I don't have really strong recollections of this, but apparently my kindergarten bus driver loved me because I would get up and kind of trip down the aisle in the bus singing Shirley Temple songs, entertaining. I was on the early bus, with the high school kids, and there weren't very many little kids going to early kindergarten. I would get up and entertain the high school kids with Shirley Temple songs. So, I guess it's always been there.

[Tuesday, May 28, 2002]

HUDSON: Let's talk about your projects now. What plans do you have for the future?

FOSTER: We have a new CD coming out next month. Lloyd Maines helped us with that, and of course, Terri Hendrix put her two cents in. We let her! We're hoping that this is going to be the CD that says what I want to say. I dug deep. I went into the gospel, the spiritual side of my music, my influences. I also went into the blues.

CASSONE: This is the first one that is not 100-percent original songs. One-half is digging deep into the roots of American music, finding some spirituals and old blues. Some of the songs come from the 1930s, a Maybelle Smith song. And some songs from the Carolina Sea Islands off Georgia. Some field holler songs.

HUDSON: I think a creative personal interpretation of someone else's song can be just as creative as performing one you have written yourself.

FOSTER: We did some of our own arrangements with "Woke Up This Morning" and "Death Came a Knockin'" on this CD. The first one was a spiritual I grew up with as a piano player in church. I've also heard a version by Sweet Honey in the Rock that was "Stayed on Freedom." I was using that song as a practice song in the studio with Lloyd. We had to be there about ten in the morning, after playing late! I needed the practice song. I used "Stayed on Freedom," and Lloyd suggested adding that one. I think we started playing it in the nursing homes. I would also love to do a completely spiritual and gospel CD. That will happen pretty soon. This one was a mix.

HUDSON: How does this recording make a difference in the possibilities that you create? Will this open a new door for you?

FOSTER: [thoughtful pause] I think so.

CASSONE: I think it's going to broaden the spectrum of where we get booked, more blues and jazz festivals. Before, we didn't have a product that said that this is what we were going to do. It was easy to do the singer/songwriter thing with our first two CDs. This one will move us into new arenas.

HUDSON: I think you are defying all classifications.

CASSONE: We have a back-burner concept that is so cool we both want to do it. We want to go to the Sea Islands off the coast of Georgia and do some research for more songs. Not just go in and take the songs and go record them, but rather, live there for two or three months, learning the people and the songs. Texas State University is interested in helping us with that.

FOSTER: Those people don't come off those islands. You have to go in there, live with them, go to church with them to get them to open up to you.

CASSONE: I think a lot of research projects, collecting songs, do not capture the essence of the people. You have to live it first. Doing that one song on our CD gave me a hunger for that.

HUDSON: I knew and loved Glen Alyn, who is no longer with us. He set up a teepee near the house of Mance Lipscomb and recorded him for over 200 hours over several years, getting to know the family and the area. His book, *I Say Me for A Parable*, is a record of those conversations.

CASSONE: We started a project with Glen and Tary Owens [a blues musicologist from Austin, now deceased] at the Navasota Blues Festival. This is our seventh year to be involved in that festival and help raise money for a scholarship fund. It's on June 29 this year. We try not to run into Juneteenth. The sponsors just aren't coming in to us the way we would like, so we cut it to one day. Tary Owens will be there this year. We're on the board and put the music together. It's in honor of Mance Lipscomb.

FOSTER: Mance chose that name after he got to a certain age. Emancipation was the name he wanted to try and use, but he ended up shortening it to Mance.

HUDSON: Let's talk a little about your other interests.

FOSTER: We get involved in our community. We do a nursing home tour in the Bryan–College Station area once a year. We work with the police department there, D.A.R.E. We put on a big concert for screaming fifth and sixth graders each year.

CASSONE: When we are on the road, we do play for colleges and universities. And we take part in Gary Hartman's Texas Music Unplugged concert each March at Texas State University in San Marcos. We also do other levels of schools. When we did Folk Alliance this year, we did a performance for a wonderful elementary school. We did a variety of styles of music, blues and reggae. The kids loved the live music. We explained differences in music and talked about the black writers who created the music. It was February, Black History Month.

FOSTER: I had been in a blues band in college. Then I joined a big band while in the Navy, as the singer. Then I was in a funk band where we would go and play all the high schools in the Southeast area. We would walk into a rough situation, and the Top Forty music we played really worked. They were cool to that. After the Navy, I went into the folk realm with the hope of bringing more black songwriters to light. Nobody was doing Sam Cooke at the time.

HUDSON: I was listening to Lavelle White at the Kerrville Folk Festival this year, noticing that not many blacks attended this kind of event. I did see you on the front row at the Threadgill Theater. What is that about? Do you have many mixed audiences?

CASSONE: The Pacific Northwest seems to have more integrated audiences. Segregation still exists in this part of the country. It really struck me, coming from an integrated way of growing up, how less progressive some parts of this country are. Ruthie and I are six years apart in age, but it's like we grew up in different times completely. It's like you grew up in a different time completely than I did. Ruthie was born in 1964. By the time she was old enough to recognize discrimination, it had disappeared in some parts of the country. She still had to deal with it in this part of the country. Small towns out in the country.

FOSTER: I remember having to put on my little patent leather shoes and nice dress to go into Bryan and go to Woolworth Dime Store. I remember my mother saying we had to be "dressed" to go into town. I'd have to go to the back doors when running errands for my mother in Gause, where I grew up. A town of 500 people. A different church on every corner. My mother was a housekeeper, and she kept house for a lot of the white women in town. I remember helping her clean house. I grew up on the cusp of being accepted into the homes. Some black people weren't. We lived in an area of Gauze called "Nigger town" by the white people. Just a little black community in Gause.

CASSONE: There was also discrimination where I grew up, but we were also a melting pot. You grew up knowing there were different races and cultures. The Northwest was filled with Native Americans, blacks, Orientals, and many other mixtures. Seattle is a port city, so the diversity seems to make the area more progressive. The biggest discrimination there had to do with Oriental people because of what happened when Pearl Harbor was bombed. Putting them in concentration camps.

HUDSON: Let's talk about the distinction "woman." Is there anything particular that comes up for you in this business?

FOSTER: [long pause] To me, it's about being a black woman from a farming community. I grew up in a town that was segregated, and music opened the back doors and the front doors in my community. I had a chance to play a lot of white churches there, with piano and guitar.

HUDSON: Do you think music has opened the doors for lots of women?

CASSONE: As a representation of women and a representation of diversity, a lot happens when we walk into a place. Being women, we don't experience aggression directly toward us. I don't know if it would be the same with two men coming into an East Texas juke joint. We just played Nacogdoches, and the music brought down any walls that might have been there. It goes the other way too. When we go into situations where a lot of blacks are playing, I feel a little trepidation, wondering if I'll be accepted. What the hell does a white woman know about the blues? I can feel that question in the air. Once we get up there, it's all okay. I'm family now. Ruthie's family has accepted me with open arms. I feel so at home. I forget I'm not black. We're talking a lot about race here, but that gets pointed out a lot with us.

HUDSON: I think you both, as a duo, get to do a lot of educating.

FOSTER: And some of our booking comes from seeing the picture of us. We get booked for our diversity at times.

CASSONE: Sometimes when people help us unload, they put the drum in front of Ruthie and the guitar in front of me. Now that's an interesting stereotype.

FOSTER: I just think it's funny.

CASSONE: One thing about women is the traditional role we seem to have of being healers. And I know many men who are also healers, but I feel like that is what we do in many places when we go and play. We're in that role. Women write music that is spiritually healing to people. I can see the response in the audience when people just let go. And they come up and talk to us about it afterward. A healing has occurred because they let go.

FOSTER: I have a gospel song I wrote that's on the new CD called "Joy," and we get everybody in the audience rejoicing. It's not so much about religion, but it's about being spiritual.

CASSONE: We try not to address any denomination directly. We just believe in what we do, and we address the spirituality. We don't even have the distinction between Christian and Buddhist. It's all about being spiritual.

FOSTER: We get churches that label me because I grew up in a Missionary Baptist background.

HUDSON: One bit of research says that women communicate horizontally for relatedness and men communicate vertically for power.

FOSTER: That's interesting that you said that. When my ex-husband and I decided to part ways, I wanted to move back to Texas, back home to be a part of a community. I wanted to get back into my family. James wanted the total opposite. He wanted to move back to California, get this great-paying job, and work his way to the top. That's where we clashed.

CASSONE: He's a really cool person. I went on this mission to get these two talking to each other again. I had a great conversation with him. You all were friends before you married.

FOSTER: Yeah, he's my buddy. I am glad we're back in communication.

HUDSON: How about a final story when you experienced a lot of that "joy" you write about?

FOSTER: Every time we play. Especially when we play to a new audience, one that knows nothing about us and can't figure out why we're onstage together. I love seeing that reaction. It's cool to watch their faces change.

CASSONE: Last year at the Winnipeg Folk Festival, we were scheduled to only do workshops. That's a standard role the first year. Somebody called and canceled a "tweener," when you get up and do two or three songs between other acts. We happened to walk into the office at the time they were looking for us to do this. We quickly accepted, of course. We got up and did two songs, "Full Circle" and "Death Came a Knockin.'" Thirty-eight thousand people gave us a standing ovation for two songs. I didn't want to do any more. Just get off the stage.

FOSTER: Looking out at the audience made me weep. You don't see faces, just colors and shapes. I had my eyes closed for that long note at the end. I opened them to a sea of people responding in a huge way. That was pretty cool.

CASSONE: It's not about the rock star persona; it's not about being famous. It is about touching somebody emotionally. We're not doing any songs I've written; we're doing Ruthie's music. I feel what she's feeling when the words to something she has written have that effect on somebody. Since I'm personally close to her, I feel for her. My ex often says, "Now you get to be a rock star." I keep telling him that is NOT it. It is about connecting emotionally.

HUDSON: I want to read you a piece that was inspired by "Home." This is one way I use your music in the classroom.

CASSONE: You understand.

HUDSON: Talk about "Runaway Soul" and the "business" of being a musician.

FOSTER: We put two CDs out before this one. They were mainly about my music, and Cyd accompanied me. We wanted to present this one, wanting people to know that we are a duo. Ruthie Foster and Cyd Cassone. So we decided to use photos of both of us. How we got into the graveyard was not my idea at all. Cyd liked it, and our great photographer, Laurie Drum, from Navasota, liked it, so they relaxed me about it. We were in Calvert, Texas, and took a lot of pictures of the people there.

CASSONE: The original concept was to call the CD *Small Town Blues*. We wanted to get all these small-town photos. We put on an impromptu concert on a street corner and invaded a domino game. This album has the blues and the gospel feeling, showing both sides of this concept. We wanted pictures of these guys playing dominoes across from a church they will go to the next day, showing how integrated life is in a small town. A diversity of activity to draw from.

FOSTER: The poster shot is of us sitting in front of an old store. We're "small-town girls." That poster is getting around quickly.

HUDSON: On the back of the CD, I see a chalkboard with the word "hymns." Tell me about that.

CASSONE: That was shot at one of the churches, and I thought that was a great way to line up the title for the CD. Ruthie thought of it to list the songs.

FOSTER: That has confused a few people who thought it was all gospel. I tell them it's also about breaking up and all kinds of other topics as well. I thought it would be cool. I'm very proud of how the CD looks; I had something to say about the graphics!

HUDSON: A lot of musicians don't have that much say when they are with another record label.

CASSONE: Usually I've done the layout for the CDs. I got Ruthie more involved in this one. I think we're both artistic visually as well as with the music. We don't just throw an idea at a graphic artist and say, "Make it pretty." We have design ideas in mind. Ruthie picked the cover photo. She ended up really liking the graveyard concept.

FOSTER: We didn't think too much about it. We just did a lot of songs that we like doing. We did some blues songs that I've written, some gospel, and a song by Terri Hendrix that I love. It's more folk-oriented. I just made up my mind that I wanted it on there.

HUDSON: What about the "business" of creating CDs, traveling, and performing? You have signed with a record label now, right?

CASSONE: Communication is the biggest part of it. We're used to having all the irons in our fire. We had to let go of some of that, and communication was the most challenging part. We're learning a lot about that skill. It's actually harder work to have this team, because you become the coach.

FOSTER: We meet once a week to get everybody on the same page. Then we have a meeting with promotional people, booking, management, record label. We try to meet with them every couple of weeks. Twice a year we have a big meeting, to plan the year.

CASSONE: Getting the promotional people to send the right material to the right people at the right time is important. We've been in situations where we play a festival and the CDs haven't arrived yet.

FOSTER: Like we're playing a coffeehouse tonight. First, we know you, and we want to do it again. Then you have to call our booking agent to see that we are clear. Most people start with the booking agent. Except for the many people we do know personally in this business. Then there are the contracts that fly back and forth. It's important to get the times right, the length of the concert, the time to load in equipment. Lots of details.

HUDSON: And Nancy Fly, your booking agent, certainly takes care of business. I appreciate the way she does business.

FOSTER: Then there's the promotional material that gets sent out ahead of time. That's important! I stopped by the music store in town, and it was great to see our poster on the front door.

HUDSON: You have created this business for yourself from the inside out. Not all performers have as much say as you.

CASSONE: We won't give that up.

FOSTER: I have actually done that. I was signed with Atlantic Records for four years. And one of the first things you give up is your right to do anything except show up and be where they want you to be. It was one of those things that just started happening. I was told to go write. I had a publishing deal with them and a recording contract. I was going to write ten to fifteen songs per year, which was nothing for me. I was a prolific writer at the time. They would call me and let me know someone who wanted to write with me. We write, we demo the songs, then take them back to Atlantic. They either take the songs or not. Then we would go into the Atlantic studio to rerecord the songs. In my case, I was not allowed to record. It was just one of the parts of the contracts that I did not understand. I was not there to record; I was there to write. I just didn't have a lot of say about where I wanted to record even. The only thing I had freedom with was where I wanted to gig. I did use the time to play and work on my craft. New York kicked my ass, but I kicked it back. I learned all these different ways of writing in those four years. Like starting with a title. . . . I had this long process. I needed lots of paper and lots of light. It was cool learning how to write other ways. Atlantic was a major label. I learned a lot from them. Lots of horror stories, but I learned a lot. I'll probably run into some of these people at South by Southwest. And I might get a free meal! Now that's a good thing.

CASSONE: It's obviously what you do with it. You have lots of positive energy and always use things for the best. She brought all that to the table when we started working together. She had already been off the porch.

FOSTER: She started playing with me on the acoustic gigs.

CASSONE: Now I have eight drums and two suitcases full of percussion toys.

HUDSON: What inspired you to write songs?

FOSTER: I was filling time. I got out of the Navy. I was in Charleston, and there was this boat club opening up. I was doing a lot of covers, Sam Cooke and Aretha Franklin. I guess I needed more songs to fill up that two hours. Then I went to New York and learned how to write. I was also a vocalist in the Navy. I also went to college for music. I had a lot of fun in the Navy, singing, and the only reason I got out was because I wanted to go to Italy, and they wouldn't send me. They weren't sending women there. Just the guys. We played a lot of urban high schools. We were known as the Top Forty funk band.

HUDSON: What defines Texas music? When you claim yourself as a Texas songwriter, are you claiming a state or a style?

FOSTER: Now that's a good question. Lots of people are trying to answer that.

CASSONE: Texas music represents a huge spectrum of music. If you look into the folk encyclopedias, you will see many of the Texas musicians referred to as folk artists [Mance Lipscomb, Lightnin' Hopkins] back then. Some of the crossing over from Louisiana created a distinct Gulf Coast blues sound. Then there is country-western, and there are a huge number of songwriters in and from this state. It's as hard to pigeonhole as we are! People try to put us in a category, and it doesn't work. We are representing the full spectrum of music that comes from Texas.

FOSTER: When I was with Atlantic, they didn't know what to do with me. My sound was everything. They signed me hoping to get another Tracy Chapman because Columbia had Tracy Chapman. The way major labels react is that if one artist on another label becomes popular, then all labels want "one" of those. That changed while I was with these guys. I did a photo shoot and couldn't even see myself in the photo. I sent one to my dad, and he said that he had received a photo of "a white woman with my baby's nose." I had a lot of makeup on.

[Ruthie and Cyd tour extensively, sharing the spirit of Texas music with the world.]

I got my work ethic from all the women in my family. . . .
I'm constantly setting new goals and moving forward.
I like challenges, and I like work.

Lee Ann Womack

A TEXAN IN NASHVILLE

I first heard Lee Ann live at a Willie Nelson picnic and concert held at Verizon Amphitheater in San Antonio. I did not have a chance to interview her, but I stood in line with fans and introduced myself, saying I wanted to talk with her. Several years later the timing worked out, and we had a talk by phone. I was glad that I had seen her perform with Willie live. Of course, the video of these two riding horses up the street to the Texas Capitol building in Austin is a classic. I knew of her East Texas roots, and I often read stories about her prefaced with "Texan, Lee Ann Womack." I figured that she was okay with that Texas connection. I also read about the fuss over image when she made some changes. I'm not sure we've had that much fuss over men and their images. I remember one comment she made about the cost of a photo shoot and what that means. What I heard in her voice as we talked on the phone was a sincere commitment to her family, a love of the music, and a pride in being from Texas. I hope to see more of her with our own Texas Buddha, Willie Nelson. They work together well. The entire world knows about her awards and her chart successes. I read the words to "I Hope You Dance," by Tia Sillers, to my parents on their sixtieth wedding anniversary.

Lee Ann wrote the foreword to a book of the same title, written by Mark D.
Sanders and Tia Sillers. Lee Ann took that song out into the world, where
it became a hit. Lee Ann and I spoke by phone in October 2004.

HUDSON: I met you first when you were singing with Willie at the Verizon
Amphitheater. I have some photos of you with Willie in the background
and of Willie with you in the background. You were quite lively that day.
Let's look at the role of women in your own life. Friendships and family
members.

WOMACK: I've always said that I got my work ethic from all the women
in my family. My mom has a master's degree in education. She did that
with two kids, going to school at night. I watched her make it work. I
learned how to do that. Now I have to do my career, take care of my kids,
and figure out how to make it all work. My mom's mother had her master's
in education, as well as my great-grandmother. That's a lot of hard work!
My sister went on to become a lawyer. I watched all the women in my
family work really hard and balance their family life with their careers.
My mom's sister, my aunt, has also taught me a lot. My mom always told
me I could do anything I wanted to do and be anyone I wanted to be. She
made me believe it. She never pushed me. I never had a stage mom; I
had a mom who gave me the tools then encouraged me to go work hard
for what I wanted.

HUDSON: As I read some of the interviews with you, your deep roots
in a work ethic come across.

WOMACK: I hope I'm able to pass this along to my girls. I told my oldest
daughter, who is looking around now at what she wants to do, that it is
not always the most talented person who becomes successful. It is always
the people who work hard.

HUDSON: I started interviewing musicians in 1985, and I know the
value of persistence and hard work. I think when my first book came out
in 2001, some people were surprised. "You're still here doing this?"

WOMACK: You figured out how to make it work rather than just saying,
"The cards are stacked against me." That's what my mom taught me.
Figure it out.

HUDSON: You're in the middle of a tough business, the music business,
and based in the city of that business, Nashville. What are your challenges
right now, after success?

WOMACK: You never stop. I used to think I would get to a point where things would be automatic, and I wouldn't have to work as hard. I have lots of role models around me, like Reba and Loretta. The public has a short memory. I am constantly setting new goals and moving forward. Loretta has a new album out with lots of new publicity. Trying to reach higher and higher. I enjoy what I'm doing. I like challenges, and I like work. It's been a little difficult for me because I've done everything I've wanted to do, and I have these two beautiful and wonderful girls that I enjoy spending time with. I do have to make myself get up and work at times. At times I just want to go hang out with my kids. And I do enjoy my work and the people I work with. It's a constant balancing act.

HUDSON: What do you do to nurture yourself?

WOMACK: I joined a church last year. I was raised in church, and that's one thing I want to take time for. I work out with a trainer. I'm bad about not spending time on myself, so I have to create some goals around that as well. I get on my treadmill every night, but I'm also listening to music or catching up on the news. I'm always multitasking.

HUDSON: I think most women do. We are good at that.

WOMACK: I choose the treadmill because I can do that and something else!

HUDSON: I really love your choice of songs, "I Hope You Dance" and "Orphan Train," both by other women. Julie Miller, writer of that last song, is also from Texas, right?

WOMACK: Right. I choose songs that touch me.

HUDSON: Let's talk about the writing process for you.

WOMACK: I wish I were better at it. I wish I did it more often. It's hard to jump from the businessperson or the mom into the writer. That's a real leap for me. It's hard to have two hours one day and all of a sudden be a writer. I love it, though. I wrote one on my new record called "Twenty Years and Two Husbands Ago." The best way for me to write is to really bring my own life into the song. I think people enjoy that. Audiences seem to enjoy hearing something that is real.

HUDSON: Let's talk about some of your favorite performance opportunities. I see that you performed at the awarding of the Nobel Peace Prize.

WOMACK: When I was first offered this opportunity, I didn't want to go do it. I hadn't traveled that much, and it sounded kind of far away and improbable. Who's going to understand a country girl from East Texas?

It turned out to be a great experience in Norway. And I did connect with the audience. There were a lot of artists from different genres in music there that night. I didn't enjoy it as much as I'd enjoy playing Gruene Hall or something!

HUDSON: Do you still perform at some of the smaller venues?

WOMACK: Yes. For instance, this week I was at two shows put on by radio stations. They let listeners in, and the first show had about one hundred people. The next day there were a few hundred. It was in a House of Blues. Nashville also has the opportunity for songwriting circles. I like the intimacy. That's my favorite. It's more about the song and what it's saying. Since I'm not primarily a songwriter, I don't get to do it often. But I love it.

HUDSON: Articles about you often state the Texas connection. You obviously still have your roots here.

WOMACK: I'm a Texan. I'm squatting in Tennessee right now. Thank goodness I married a Texan. In fact, I married two of them. [laughter] Frank's from Houston. I'm sitting here right now drinking my coffee out of a cup with "Texas" on it and "Crawford" written on it as well. Everything around here has a little something about Texas on it. My girls just got something in the mail making them honorary Texans. They are thirteen and five. Aubrie and Anna Lise. I just bought a house back in Texas. It's weird. I feel like I'm still in college or something. I came up here to go to Belmont, and I just haven't gone back yet.

HUDSON: We want to claim you here. I can hear that Texas woman in your voice. I loved the way you responded to questions about image. Women have to respond to that a lot. Do you think men have to?

WOMACK: [more laughter] Oh, no. I've always said that country is not something you put on and take off. It's inside you. I know when the Dixie Chicks came out, they had to face those comments: "They're not country. They're wearing Marc Jacobs or something." I just remember thinking how ludicrous that comment was. You can't get any more country than they are. It doesn't matter what kind of shoes are on their feet.

HUDSON: Are you a reader?

WOMACK: Yes, I am. I read many different kinds of books. Lately all I've read have been things about politics. I've read all the books that have come out. I'm in the middle of about five different ones right now. I went through a period of time where I read a lot of Larry McMurtry books. I love that. I love Cormac McCarthy.

HUDSON: Those are two of my favorites as well.

WOMACK: I go through times where I want to read novels and just get away. And at times I want to educate myself. We are all big readers around here.

HUDSON: Imagine someone is reading these stories in about fifty years. What is the most important thing they can read about you?

WOMACK: [pause] I love my career, and I love country music. But I hope people look back and say, "She was a good mother." That's my primary job.

Manuel, my grandfather, crossed over from Mexico by walking. He did not know how he would even live the next day. That inspires me.

Stephanie Urbina Jones

SAN ANTONIO MATTERS

I first heard Stephanie at a venue in Comfort, Texas, called Armadillo on the River, which was a renovated old bowling alley. The lanes stretched out behind her as we sat at a table in front. The life in her eyes caught my attention first, and her enduring energy. She was obviously passionate about her music and about each performance. Since that first time, I've seen her play at the opening of the Hill Country Opry in Kerrville; at the Comfort, Texas Music Festival; at the Kerrville Folk Festival; and at the 2003 Willie Nelson picnic. Her T-shirt that day said "Espiritu," and she meant it. Her spirit reigns on the stage as she reaches out and touches our spirits. Singing "Crazy" while looking into the face of Willie Nelson was a highlight for her. Knowing that he wrote the song, knowing that Patsy Cline made it a hit only enhanced Stephanie's joy at singing this duet at a picnic. Her dark beauty blends in with the passion she portrays. Her business is family run, with Uncle Rudy taking care of many loose ends. She spends her time traveling between Nashville, her home with her husband, and Texas, her spiritual home and home to her largest fan base.

Stephanie has never been one to sit back and let things happen. Proac-

tive in all areas of life, she got herself to San Miguel de Allende, Mexico, just when she needed the time to reflect and heal. She has toured behind her CDs, visiting radio stations and playing in small towns as well as big cities. She has been a queen on a float during San Antonio's fiesta, and she works hard in the studio. There aren't many aspects of the music business that Stephanie has not experienced. I appreciate the fact that she noticed I secretly wanted to be a percussion player. She invited me on stage several times, with my castanets or bones or even a tambourine from time to time. I experienced her song about her grandmother, "La Reina de los Angeles," as a sidewoman playing percussion. I enjoyed her music in one more way by actually playing along.

HUDSON: Tell me what you are most excited about right now.

JONES: I'm most excited about two things: How I'm being received in Texas with "God Loves It When You Dance." That message is getting out there. It's been a long two years getting prepared for this point. The second thing is how I've been led spiritually these last two weeks to make this Christmas album. Within three days I wrote five new Christmas songs. We went into the studio for four days, and it was a magical experience, covering the entire landscape of my musical terrain from blues to country gospel, to soul, to rockabilly.

HUDSON: You have an amazing voice, as well as delivery and songwriting . . . You used the phrase "led spiritually." Some of your songs move me to tears. Yeah, "Mariachi music always makes me cry" too. I have spent a lot of time in San Miguel de Allende.

JONES: I have spent time there. I don't talk to a lot of people about this, but I've worked with a lot of healers down in San Miguel. I've had some very powerful experiences. Something happened in me, and I realized that when the voice of the Great Spirit beyond talked to me, I would follow that voice. It was a connection, something like a train getting on a track. The evolution from that moment of commitment has been amazing, one miracle after another. I kind of call my tour the Spirit of Texas Tour. I just got married about two years ago. I thought I was going to start having babies and write songs on the side. I got a call from San Antonio to play for Henry B. Gonzalez. I came to San Antonio, and my father had heard a mariachi band, and we got them to play with us. I played two songs I had written. That acceptance in San Antonio inspired me, and I decided

I wanted to do this. We started playing in some hotels in San Antonio, and the performance aspect just took off. For me, the synchronicity leads the way. When I speak of something and then it shows up, I know I'm on the right path.

HUDSON: That's how it works in my life.

JONES: I have an instinct. I follow that instinct. I ask for guidance, and I know I'm going in the right direction when things show up that keep me moving in that direction. When I have a setback, I know that I need to get some distance and perhaps change my thinking. It's been an incredible learning experience because I'm a very willful, strong woman, and I have a sense of where I think I should be going. It would not have been my choice to come play little honky-tonks in Texas for two years. And yet I am so grateful because of the experience that I've had. I've learned something. Now I can come to any experience and just let go. If there's one person in the audience or 500, I choose to connect.

HUDSON: A writer named Paula D'Arcy has written a book called *Gift of the Red Bird*. She talks about balancing the creative energy with the acceptance. How did you figure this out at your young age?

JONES: Well, "willful" can get a lot done. Ten years of therapy, six years of sobriety, being surrounded by some very wise souls who have guided me.

HUDSON: I want to talk more about the Mexico connection. I resonate with the rocks when I go there.

JONES: It is so powerful. There are so many things that are beyond what I can understand.

HUDSON: Your faith, whatever it is that allows you to listen, really shows up onstage.

JONES: It is my dream to have a publishing company, to publish books and to mentor young writers. I don't always want to be on the road. [When I saw Stephanie a year later, she had designed a set of cards illustrating the Spirit of Texas theme.] I've been through a big publishing system; it's hard to pull me away from my soul just to get a song published. I do have a home and a husband in Nashville now. I tour Texas about three months each year. He knew when we married that I was following this calling. I would hate to be sitting on a back porch rocking a baby right now. It's not the time. I married him because I believe it will work, and it will be for a lifetime.

HUDSON: In some of my conversations with women, we end up talking about the balancing between the creative process and our love of family and home.

JONES: My husband and I have bet everything to do this album. We put our house up for mortgage. It was so scary to step out that far to produce an album. In the past year, it is amazing what has shown up for me. A couple in Austin opened up their home for me, then one in Dallas and one in Houston. They all made sure I had a place to stay when I came to Texas. These people have invested in my career. I am trying to further define what the spirit of Texas is. I want to write a weekly piece on my website on where I find it. Recently I found it in a bathroom at a Texaco station in the middle of Northeast Texas. I was worn out and tired. I got a Subway sandwich and went to the restroom to cry. Then I thought of Manuel, my grandfather, who crossed over from Mexico by walking. He did not know how he would even live the next day. That inspires me. Somehow that is all connected with what I'm doing.

[As she performed that evening, Stephanie told the stories of each song. Once, in Nashville, she was pulled into a publishing house and told that she could make a lot of money if she would just change a few things. She was just a little left of center. "I did what every good Texas woman would do," Jones said. "I ran home and wrote a song called 'Left of Center.'" We talked again at her baby shower on June 10, 2004.]

HUDSON: We've chatted about babies, family, relationships, Libras and Virgos, and more. This is such a great gathering of friends honoring you. And you look gorgeous! I want to capture what you are saying about your husband, Jason, right now.

JONES: We've always had this dream together, both of us. He agreed to work and support me until I could support us. He's worked and allowed me to be on the road these last five years. We bring more into the relationship together. We've grown and bloomed in our separate lives, and then we bring these lives together and create a rich relationship. We have a lot to share. Now we're about to share having a child together. Her name is Zeta Anaya West. Anaya was my great-grandfather Manuel, and I took his name as my middle name, Urbina. It's very symbolic and meaningful. Our hope is that in the next few years we can travel as a family together. Jason is a writer and a computer programmer. Uses both sides of his brain! He's pretty amazing. He's very nurturing, and this is encouraging to me because my career takes a lot of nurturing too.

HUDSON: I do well with a nurturing man. And here I am talking with you at your baby shower.

JONES: I wrote a song inspired by you, actually. It's called "The Hell on Wheels Roadshow." It's about fiery women. Not just women being crazy, but women being on fire with intention. I think it would be great to have a Texas-based road show featuring these women: Ruthie Foster, Terri Hendrix, and more. I've been dreaming of that concept.

HUDSON: You mentioned that you had been very emotional this morning, close to tears. Want to talk about what brought that on?

JONES: Honestly, it's so powerful, this gathering of women to help usher a new life into this world. These women have encouraged me to do what I do in the world. I'm overwhelmed with gratitude and love.

HUDSON: I want to thank you for having this party at this great Mexican restaurant.

JONES: We still office here; my record label is based here. My great-grandfather, Manuel Anaya Urbina, celebrated his 100th birthday here. He inspired me to do what I'm doing as an artist. Can you feel the Mexican angels dancing here? We have men at this baby shower because we are not going to do things like other people! Men are nurturing too. My *tio*, Rudy, is nurturing, and I wanted him here. Along with my dad.

RUDY: It's a Hispanic thing.

HUDSON: Now for a chat with Dad. You were telling me something very interesting about the history of women in Nashville.

CHARLIE JONES: I'm Charlie Urbina Jones, Stephanie's dad. I call myself the minority person here. What I have to say has parallels in both the country and the Hispanic communities. In the 1950s and 1960s you had a brand of music coming together, country and conjunto. Both went through some changes and fell on hard times. You saw Willie leave Nashville because they did not recognize his genius. I think the conjunto music here in San Antonio began to die off for a while. Willie came back to Texas to play his own music. You saw the rise of the Tammy Wynette types in Nashville. They were the people who served as the bridge and savior for that music. They played straight into people's hearts, both men and women. Nobody talked about the maladies women had gone through.

I remember driving through Alpine, Texas, in my pickup truck, in 1967, hearing Tammy sing "Stand By Your Man," and "D-I-V-O-R-C-E." That resonated with me as a young man. This woman was a heroine of sorts. She made a lot of sense. Conversely, in the Hispanic community you had Selena speaking out. She was the beginning of a crossover. Her early death made her mythic. I was running for Congress at this time. I talked to many people in South Texas, and to them she was a heroine. She represented who they were! If they went to HEB, Selena went to HEB. There was no differentiation between her and regular people. It's good to look at the place women have held in music history. We, the men, tend to beat our chests, saying it's all about us. That's unfortunate, for here is this other side that really moves societies. My father would tell my mother, "I wear the pants in the family." My mother would respond, "Yeah, but I buy those pants for you." There is that unwritten thing in all families; every woman is a heroine in her household, and as a group, they were the heroines in communities. The music was a reflection of this, I think.

HUDSON: What do you think of the differences between women in Caucasian households and women in Hispanic households?

CHARLIE JONES: In the Hispanic community we are very matriarchal. Dad is very macho, but in the background Mama carries a big stick. Everyone knows that. Look at COPS here in San Antonio (Communities Organized for Public Service). Ernie Cortez was the organizer, but the women went house to house in organizing this group. Then this group ruled San Antonio politics. Within the Anglo community, I think it's the same. Just a different face. Our cultures are similar but different.

HUDSON: I have met some interesting political figures here in this group.

CHARLIE JONES: Melody Cortez is twenty-three years old, and she ran Kerry's campaign here in South Texas. She's a St. Mary's graduate and was one of Henry Gonzalez's aides. Her grandmothers are on the west side of town. She understands the plight of poor people, and she has the ability to put these issues in front of people. It's unusual for young women to have access to this power so early. She's part of a powerful group coming out of St. Mary's University. St. Mary's in the early 1960s had a mission statement that included community empowerment. I think Melody is a reflection of this mission. You, as a university teacher, can understand how these mission statements sometimes get pushed aside by other concerns. I came through this school in the 1960s, then went to war as a young army officer.

HUDSON: And you had political leanings as well?

CHARLIE JONES: My political awakening occurred in Vietnam. We were heading into a hot area, and I saw a newspaper lying on the ground. It mentioned that all troops were in a defensive posture. Well, we were not just defending, and I realized I was being the tip of a spear. And what was being told to the people was not the truth. As a young officer, I did what I was supposed to do. Many years later, when I went off to law school in Houston, I got involved in city council races and had a political awakening. I ran for the state legislature and lost, then eventually ran some successful campaigns for other people. Politics have always been a part of this family tradition. My grandfather participated in the electoral process and worked at getting people elected. When I was running for Congress, Stephanie went to many towns and sang her heart out for me.

HUDSON: Do you support the direction her path has taken?

CHARLIE JONES: Yes. Her music is her politics. Music from the heart. You can support political parties as well as true political issues. Her issues, because of her heart, are about helping people. Her music is about "chiseling out my soul." You can be of one persuasion or another, but the truth is, the truth is the truth. That is her political banner. I always tell her to use her gift to help those who are less fortunate.

HUDSON: I sense that in talking to her, and I had a suspicion there was strong family backing for this. I can sense the principles here.

CHARLIE JONES: She would be a sixth-generation Texan. Her great-grandfather, on my mother's side, Manuel, was an old Baptist minister, an alumnus from Baylor. We referred to him as Old Jerusalem on the Brazos, for lack of a better term. And he inculcated all of us with the importance of education and participation in community building. Even though I'm divorced from Stephanie's mother, Stephanie comes up to me with the philosophical questions. I always encourage her, as a young female, to make up her own mind and follow her heart.

HUDSON: You seem to know everyone here.

CHARLIE JONES: Grace Padron, the mayor's assistant, is here, as well as the mayor's wife, Mary Alice Cisneros. Our families grew up on the same block. When Henry Cisneros married her, we were very happy. Henry took a real liking to Stephanie when she did the kickoff at a tribute to him. And this woman, Yolanda Arellano, is the head of the Mexican Unity Council. Quite a gathering of powerful women. And my wife is the best "behind the scenes" worker there is. Cindy Reed Quinlan is here, married to John Quinlan, former chief of special crimes for the county of Bexar. He wrote the Texas penal code that we follow today.

HUDSON: Thanks for adding your perspective to this conversation!

I am committed to writing in my future. I'm at a point where I can't go on until I claim my own authenticity.

Jill Jones

RIDE 'EM COWGIRL

I first met Jill Jones after Buck Ramsey told me to call her. I was producing a tribute to Jimmie Rodgers in Kerrville and had added a yodeling contest. "Call the Hays County Gals," Buck said. Buck was the real thing in the world of western music. He is no longer with us, but his legacy lives on in the songs and performances of many. Jill Jones, one of the "Gals," entered and won the yodeling contest. I have kept up with her career ever since, watching her take awards (2002 best band, given by the Academy of Western Music) and take her music to new places. I attended the Cowboy Gathering in Lubbock in 2001 with my friend Jim Wilson, and I heard Jill perform one of her original songs, "Buck's Song." My heart was moved as I thought back through the memories created by knowing Buck. Jill Jones is one of those treasured people who gives her heart to her music. She is willing to let her own voice speak, and she is willing to dance with the mystery of not knowing what will happen.

HUDSON: I'm so glad we decided to do this at your house. What a peaceful spot hidden away here in Driftwood. Glad to see you still have a horse! Mine still lives with me on my little place west of Kerrville.

JONES: You know, if you're going to talk with women, you need to find Cindy Walker. I heard a story she told when she was being inducted into the Hall of Fame. She pointed to her dress, saying, "My mother gave me this dress when I first started writing, and she told me that I needed to wear it when I was inducted into the Hall of Fame. I just laughed it off. Now I'm wearing that dress!"

HUDSON: I know she lived with her mother, who played a big role in her life, even providing the music for some of her songs. Women helping women. I can't help but notice the way you support your daughter and her literary endeavors.

JONES: I think we met about ten years ago. It's been eight, at least, since the Hays Country Gals were together.

HUDSON: Let's talk about the genre of western music. How did you get into it? What was the appeal?

JONES: My interest naturally unfolded. I grew up as a musician. I started playing as a kid. It was a lonesome, therapeutic experience where I started just playing by myself, old Joan Baez songs.

HUDSON: I started out playing that way myself, at summer camp. I didn't end up being a performer, though.

JONES: Maybe you didn't have as much heartache as I did. It was just something I did without thinking. A feeling thing. I started playing in little R&B bands in the early 1970s. I was the backup singer. I could snap my fingers and sing a chorus. [laughter] I was a chick singer. We just had a ball. We were all UT (University of Texas) students, hanging out on campus and playing in the dives. Remember the One Knite? We kind of became successful, and the serious members formed a core group, playing progressive country music in Austin. We became successful with the Doc Jones Band. I was playing guitar then and singing mostly harmony. That was my ex; we married over that deal. We played for around eight years in Austin. We were the house band at the Split Rail. We played every Friday night. We got married and started having children. My son was born, and I remember calling up Marcia Ball, saying, "Marcia, I have this baby, and I don't intend to quit playing. Give me some advice." We were playing a lot. She told me just to pack him along. I played the night before he was born with the guitar on my belly. In fact, I love the videos of the Dixie Chicks, with Emily just pregnant and performing. I knew

Marcia had a baby and kept playing. So, I did. He slept under the bench in the bar. He had grown up right under that guitar, so music was not a disturbance to him. He did okay with it; I got worn out.

HUDSON: I used to drag all mine to the barrel races, taking a playpen and a sack of peanut butter sandwiches.

JONES: I didn't do as well as Marcia did. I wasn't able to maintain coming home at 3:00 in the morning. A baby waking up sick with colic. I just became too grumpy. That's the nice way to put it. I didn't know I could be that much of a bitch. And then my daughter came along two years later. I realized that I'd rather be at home cutting out valentines. I had a ball doing that. We moved out here to Driftwood, and I quit. I became a housewife and mother. I missed the performing, the music.

HUDSON: You know Sara Hickman just made that choice to be with children.

JONES: What happened, fortunately, for me, is that my next-door neighbor was creative and production-minded. We discovered that we both liked to sing, and we decided to do some shows for the kids up at Wimberley School. We started with all the kids' songs, and we'd dress up. By Easter we had a big production with bunnies and eggs and things in each egg. At Christmas we had a twelve-member cast. We would get all the homeschooled children to be the elves and reindeer, then we would put on these giant productions. We enjoyed putting together all of the sets and all of the songs. We got another mother to join us. We each had two small children, and we had this rabble around us at all times. It was fun and therapeutic. There were times during rehearsal that we would just cry on each other's shoulders. Otherwise our lives were often tedious. This gave all three of us an outlet that included our children. We definitely put our own kids in the productions. And they remember it, lo, these many years later. Then the school asked us to create a sesquicentennial program in 1986. So we got our little boots, our little bandannas, and our little cowboy hats and put together a show. It was so dorky, these three housewives playing cowgirls. That was our beginning of western music. We learned all the Texas stuff, patriotic stuff. We did learn "Whoopi ti yi yo, get along little dogie," and I kind of liked that song. The harmony worked out. From there sprang all of the research, and everything else fell by the wayside. We went on as three women singing classic cowboy songs. We were also going to the Kerrville Folk Festival and making a little splash around the area. We had done our homework. A dobro player showed up around a campfire one night, and he just kind of fell into the act, coming out to rehearse with us now, and we loved the camaraderie of it. We found Ginger Evans, a bass bluegrass player in Hays County. Joanne Roxell was my neighbor who played a timid fiddle. That was the core of the Hays County Gals. As groups started asking us to perform, we started building an audience and a certain professional pressure entered the mix. One of our members wasn't ready for that. So Ginger and Greg Lowrey and I became the Hays County Gals and Pals and started traveling. That's when we started going to the cowboy gatherings. An unwieldy name, but we kept it a long time.

HUDSON: What did you know about the genre of western music then?

JONES: We just fell into it blind. The first thing we did was go to the Western Music Association. We had never heard anyone else singing "Riding Down the Canyon." We went there, and everybody was singing "Riding Down the Canyon." It was then that we realized what we were really doing.

HUDSON: You found your tribe.

JONES: From that WMA meeting we had arrived. We got gigs from there. Immediately, we were hired to go to Branson. We were a new, exciting group. I was yodeling, and we had a good instrumentalist. We were probably above standard for the industry, and we had no idea what we were doing. Then we started going to these festivals and found a new slice of life where our music fit.

HUDSON: Did that lead you back to more research?

JONES: Oh, yes. Then, in earnest, I started looking for obscure songs to perform. People started handing them to me. Scholars would send me information about things never published. I was just really blessed.

HUDSON: Then the trio transformed, right?

JONES: I started growing, noticing the contemporary songwriters [like Andy Wilkinson], and I took it on to find some of these songs and put them out there. Of course, Andy does a great job with his own songs. I started moving into contemporary music more. We loved the old songs, but I'm not a cowpuncher.

HUDSON: Did you discover some songwriters that you wanted to promote?

JONES: Oh, yes. Do you know Bob Campbell? Nancy Thorwardson? She's a hoot. So I changed and started doing that. Ginger and Greg stayed with that transformation. I'm making a new CD right now, and it doesn't sound like your old guitar around a campfire.

HUDSON: What about awards?

JONES: In fact, in 2002, the Academy of Western Artists voted Jill Jones and the Lone Star Chorale Group the western group of the year. This group includes Doug Floyd (lead and harmony vocals, mandolin, and guitar), Lynn Daniel (harmony vocals, bull fiddle), and Greg Lowery (accordion, banjo, gut string guitar, pennywhistle, harmonica). Ginger moved to Arizona to pursue other interests. Patty Clayton, in Denver, joins us when we play out of state. We have played with Keith Carper. We trade around with bass players sometimes. We've been doing this for about four years. I just peck away at it, waiting for the phone to ring. I don't devote all my time and energy to it. I haven't marketed the group, but when we go to one festival, we'll get several offers for others.

HUDSON: It sounds like you've kept some sort of balance for yourself.

JONES: This life has worked being a single mom. I had the time to be home with them during the week when they needed me. I was the only mom who could carpool at 3:00 p.m. during the week. I was gone over the weekends and missed a few soccer games. [Jill's daughter, Amanda, is sitting on the couch studying and laughing from time to time during this interview. The kids of working moms might have other stories to tell.] I love to perform. The travel and three-day festivals get a little weird from time to time. I'm fifty-one now, and I pace myself more. I used to feel like I couldn't miss anything!

HUDSON: I know we were both so close to Buck [Ramsey]. That was such a loss. Who are the people you are close to now?

JONES: Jeanne Prescott is very successful and a dear friend. A great singer. Of course, Andy Wilkinson is great. And Bob Campbell. Liz Masterson and Shawn Blackburn are wonderful people, living up in the Denver area. I could go on naming names for a long time.

HUDSON: I've found so many wonderful, big-hearted people in the music business, people who are following their hearts.

JONES: I don't do the business either. I don't want to sit at that desk. Time for me to find an agent. So, that's something new I'm going to look at. I did send my CD to one agent who handles western artists several years ago. He said it was the best CD he'd gotten, with the worst cover. I guess I need to look at that. I agree with him.

HUDSON: What about songwriting? I know in this genre a lot of traditional songs are performed.

JONES: Yes, you have your original cowboy songs, songs of the range. Then western music moved into the Silver Screen era of the 1930s to 1950s. Wonderful stuff was written, but it was written by someone named Ira in New York. It had nothing to do with the real experience. It was a very romanticized scenario with fabulous chords and music progressions. Here came the blend of these Broadway songwriters writing for western scripts. The Sons of the Pioneers took off with this smooth harmony. I kind of moved into that. People our age and older remember that. They knew Gene Autry and Tom Mix. That's our audience now. That's where their memories are.

HUDSON: You run the risk in western music of finding people who are "trying" to be authentic.

JONES: Sometimes I don't feel very authentic when I listen to the poets. They really have something to say. In fact, that's the direction I'm heading next. Finding my own voice.

HUDSON: I love Andy Hedges. Of course, I felt Buck when Andy was performing.

JONES: Andy's the real thing. He's not a poser. Joel Nelson, I highly recommend that you listen to him. He lives in Alpine. The attention to detail and subtlety from being out on the land, which is the cowboy's job, to pay attention, is phenomenal. When somebody gets tuned in to what's going on around them, and they're out there in the wilds, it is so inspiring what can come out of them.

HUDSON: That's true of all writers, I think. Careful observation and attention to detail.

JONES: Pat Richardson said this about cowboys: "Nothing fans the inspiration in the eager minds of youth, like the cowboy dancing lightly round the edges of the truth."

HUDSON: What role does your own writing play?

JONES: I am committed to writing in my future. I'm at a point where I can't go on until I claim my own authenticity.

HUDSON: Your own voice.

JONES: I wrote that song to Buck. I'm beginning to write a little more now. I have about six I started that I have not made myself finish.

HUDSON: What are some festivals or events in your dreams? Have you performed at Elko?

JONES: Yes, two times. I'd like go back as a writer. California lately has discovered me. I love it. There's a listening audience out there, and they're into it as a recreational activity.

HUDSON: Let's talk about some favorites. Songs? Places? Moments?

JONES: There have been a bunch of them. We did a tour this last October, and we did our own show. We had a hall, and we created the show. It was in Salado, Colorado. I had this sense of being part of a bigger thing. I also had this sense of making a connection with an audience. I'm not a naturally entertaining person, like some people are. I'm good at going out and laying out my best song with my heart in it. I get nervous about the stuff in between. The jokes and stories. I've struggled with this. I think that was a point where I realized that my struggle was paying off. It worked. We just connected.

HUDSON: Where did that idea come from?

JONES: Dennis Fisher, a wonderful poet and friend, told us about this hall. We created the show, and I really enjoyed that.

HUDSON: You're interested in ongoing growth, evolution, and transformation.

JONES: I think the only thing I'll be happy with is to write my own material. I don't know if it will be cowboy music. What I have in me to say is not about punching cows. I may be able to put the story in a western setting, but what I have to say may be better suited to a gospel setting. However, there's a huge movement as a subtext in the western music genre, of gospel music. I don't know if it's everywhere, but we played in Prescott, Arizona, and it was big there. We played in Ruidoso, and it was big there. The general overall feel seems to be value-oriented. These events are put on in communities by the community, often as a fund-raiser for a bigger cause. There is a spirit about it. There's a bigger purpose for it, so I want to serve that. I always volunteer for the Sunday gospel hour. I don't know how much that can bleed over into the Saturday night show without running some people off. The audience is early retirees with their RVs. A sea of gray hair faces me when I sing, happy as punch to sit there and listen to every word. I appreciate that. I don't feel like I have to have a young audience to be legitimate.

HUDSON: The concept of listening is important to the songwriter. No one writing wants to be background music, unless they are writing for a dance band.

JONES: We are playing in state-of-the-art theaters, also. I'm no better than any other professional musician, but I have had some wonderful opportunities to perform because of this genre.

HUDSON: Have you played West Fest?

JONES: No.

HUDSON: I've attended a couple of these shows, and I can see you really fitting in. I bought a piece of art from Buck Taylor at my first West Fest.

JONES: I have a piece of his art, as well. You know, I feel so incredibly blessed to have these stages and this audience.

HUDSON: I do what I do because of the people.

JONES: I've been meaning to ask John Aielli on KUT if I can go down there and do a couple of hours of cowboy poetry. I bet he would let me do that. You know, there are some women right up there at the top of the list.

HUDSON: There's so much bad poetry in the genre, that the good stuff really grabs me. You should hear me defending cowboy poetry as I mention Buck Ramsey, Andy Wilkinson, Red Steagall, and others.

JONES: You know, I wrote a song for my son. That's easier for me to do, take a specific subject. I have received a big response from the poem to Buck. In fact, I wrote that for a lot more than just Buck, and I didn't know it at the time. There's a lady up in Colorado whom I just love, Peggy Godfrey. I could just sit at her feet. Listen. It's called "In Forty-Five Years." "I've come to see the mountains as more than stone and mud/I've come to know my neighbors as more than flesh and blood. I've come to see the work I do as more than passing time/Poetry means more to me than getting words to rhyme. I'm now aware each day is more than getting on with life. I see myself as more than just my role as mom or wife. Life offers me a framework, like bones stripped bare and white. What I can do is flesh them in with muscle, love, and light."

She's been run out on a rail before because it's so heavily spiritual. She ranches out in barren country in the San Luis Valley. She has sheep and cattle. She's a midwife for first-year heifers for neighboring ranches. This woman is so tuned in, that life is a tapestry for her, and every event has a metaphysical element.

HUDSON: That's how I see my life.

JONES: That's what it is! For her, everything has this significance. There's much more to it. [Jill gives me a copy of this poem.] Her name is Elizabeth Ebert, a favorite at Elko, too.

HUDSON: How would you like to be remembered?

JONES: In many ways, I feel like my life is beginning at this late date. I see myself more in service to those around me than to myself. It's a dead-end street to just serve yourself. Whether it's what is right in front of me or on a larger scale in the world, I don't think it matters one hoot, but I do want to be able to take what is meaningful in this human experience and put it into words and put it to music. And it seems overwhelming to me that I could aspire to do that, but I'm drawing closer.

HUDSON: You are an expert on what's meaningful to you.

JONES: And so much is shared. It is the everyday stuff that we share. I've been reading the parables in the *New Testament*. Now there's a storyteller. He taught with stories.

HUDSON: At Schreiner University I talk about the power of stories in education. We can't just strip away the information and deliver it.

JONES: No, you can put yourself into it. The story gives a place to enter the learning. People can identify.

HUDSON: Whatever I do comes out of the commitment that stories and songs make a difference in the world.

JONES: We got to do *Prairie Home Companion*. We were one of six national finalists for the Towns Under 2,000 Talent Contest. What a joy to be onstage with him in 2,000. Driftwood had 1,900 at that point. We did one song and lost. We were the only one doing western music, and one of two adult groups. Several child-prodigy groups.

HUDSON: Let's bring this to an end with a story.

JONES: I know after all these years of performing, if I will enter the story, I don't forget chords, I don't get distracted. I've transcended myself, and that's what it's about. That's why people go to be entertained. They want to be transported out of themselves. It's an elusive thing to be that present to the story, but it's not that hard to do. The rest just takes care of itself if you can do that.

HUDSON: When has that happened?

JONES: It's what I've worked for all these years. It's like stepping through a curtain into the present. You're not trying, you're not thinking about it. You just lose yourself. You just step through this time barrier; of course, music is so temporal. It's here, and then it's gone. You have to stay with it, or you get off the track. I can't say that I do that all the time, but more and more I do. I'm going for the story; I'm going for the song. It's not about me. It's like being a surfer and riding a big wave of energy. All you have to do to ride it is stay balanced. Especially when you're with others, and you're all on this wave. You kind of need to have a good sound system. Then you have an audience really listening and you're present, and you're leaning into it. It's just energy. That's when your heart just breaks open and pours out. That's what it's about. That's what people want to experience. That's one of the songs I'm writing: "It's Not Me." That has given me more liberty to realize that. It's freedom.

I'm sure I'll be known as someone who just stuck it out! I haven't had an easy road, but I do hang in there because I get joy out of what I'm doing. I've figured out a way not to get jaded. I do it for the creative satisfaction out of the process of writing.

Rosie Flores

A ROCKABILLY WOMAN

Rosie Flores takes the stage by storm, entertaining in a way reminiscent of Wanda Jackson at times, a real rockabilly woman. I first met her at the Frutigen Songwriters Festival in Switzerland, watching a crowd of about 7,000 go wild as she strummed that guitar, singing her own version of country and swing. She works hard, like all the women on the road. She is generous with her fans and dedicated to her life as a performer. Others speak highly of her as well. Her photo appeared in a 2005 autobiography of Billy Joe Shaver, published by University of Texas Press, revealing a friendship tried and true. When that's your reputation in the music business, you have a loyal following wherever you show up. Rosie writes and entertains from coast to coast and throughout Europe, taking that Texas story with her. We talked about this on March 12, 2003, at South by Southwest in Austin, Texas.

HUDSON: I was listening to your album, thinking how much I love roots music, Americana music. And I love the song "Speed of Sound" on your album.

FLORES: "Speed of Sound" is my favorite song on the record. That's the one that moves me. I sometimes put in my own CD and enjoy listening to it! I enjoy listening to Tammy Rogers play the fiddle in the style of Stéphane Grappelli. My songs, as they were recorded there, sound different than when I'm playing with my band. It's a whole different sound. My live band is really coming into its own, and this studio band also creates a beautiful piece of music.

HUDSON: I love the minor chords.

FLORES: I do too. That song was one of the three songs I wrote on that record. When that song comes on, nobody gets to talk. I go on a cinematic journey with this song. It's the perfect song for driving alone at night with the windshield wipers going, beating along with the rhythm of the road and the rain.

HUDSON: I listened to that song driving here today through the fog with windshield wipers going. And I thought, "This woman has lived this song."

FLORES: It's a very true song. You're one of the few people that have pointed that song out to me. That's why I'm gushing right now. It's one of my favorite songs to deliver. It's one of those moody songs you can get inside of. It's not my first broken heart, but I can still hear the sound of a voice saying good-bye as I'm driving away. You're going over the scene in your head. And you keep thinking, maybe there's still a chance because I'm feeling so much. And maybe he's feeling it too. That's why I call it "The Speed of Sound." Eventually it does go away, as the sound becomes fainter as you realize it's time to move on. This song is written about that moment of good-bye. We've all had this experience when a relationship ends.

HUDSON: I was remembering seeing you play at Frutigen in those cowboy boots.

FLORES: You were there! They thought I was Bruce Springsteen. It was so crazy with 7,000 people under that tent. That was probably the biggest moment in my whole career. Never again have I ever been so darn popular. They thought I was it. I was the Beatles. I heard them calling "Rosie, Rosie." I never had a chance to return with my band, Rosie Flores and the Bad Boys. Greg Leisz, Duane Jarvis, and Dusty Wakeman. Now they all have major careers on their own.

HUDSON: What is your take on the wholeness of your life as a woman, on the road and traveling a lot?

FLORES: It seems to fit together for me. I've never opted to be a mom. From early on, I said that I wanted to change guitar strings, not diapers. I knew this instrument was going to be my baby. My friends and fans became my family. I've been to the UK and many countries in Europe and across the USA. I look at this as a richness, even though I did give up a chance to raise a child. And that does tug at my heartstrings. Last year in three different places, eleven-year-olds were brought to my gigs because they were huge fans. Then I did a song for a Bloodshot Records Compilation called "Tonight the Bottle Let Me Down," and I did "Red, Red Robin," and it went up to number four on the kids' chart on XM radio. It touches my heart that kids really like me. Music was so important to me when I was a kid. I remember those records that made me jump up and down. I really loved the music. If I can sing one of those songs that makes a kid say, "I love music, and I want to sing," or "I can play the guitar," then I'm thrilled. I love it when the little girls say they are going to play guitar because they wanna play like Rosie!

HUDSON: You are part of a small group of women who do play lead guitar.

FLORES: There are some really doggone good ones out there. Most that I know are more into the blues, playing slide. I'm more into rockabilly, western swing, and honky-tonk. I grew up playing in the bars in L.A. and San Diego. My training shoes came from there. I like that country-picking stuff. Later on I tried some blues, but I've never indulged myself wholeheartedly like Sue Foley.

HUDSON: What about your San Antonio connection?

FLORES: That little girl I was talking about, who loved the music so, was me living in San Antonio, Texas, until I was about twelve. My first falling in love with music was through the Dick Clark Show and Hit Parade. We never missed a musical television show. My father took me to every live play that had music in it. I wanted to be in musical theater when I grew up. I wanted to play those parts. Out of that grew a love for melody. I took up tap dancing and developed a love for rhythm. By the time I was fourteen, I had learned how to count measures, and I could put measures of rhythm together. I was about fourteen or fifteen when I learned guitar from my brother over one Christmas vacation. I was already singing by age seven. I asked him for three chords, and I went into my bedroom and practiced. Then I came out, knocked on his door, and asked for three more.

HUDSON: What do you call your roots now?

FLORES: I think of myself as a Texas-influenced, West Coast performer. I was in this Austin scene when South by Southwest was starting out, playing in a band with Katy Moffatt, Butch Hancock, and Jimmie Dale Gilmore. We started this little Americana group. I completed a new CD with Katy Moffatt, produced by Wendy Waldman. It is very cool. Katy is so incredibly talented, as is Wendy.

HUDSON: Time for a Wanda Jackson story.

FLORES: I have spent a lot of time with Wanda. I met her in L.A., and I was hired to sing background vocals for her first live performance in years. In fact, I said I would do it for free! She knew who I was because I had just recorded "I Gotta Know" [one of her early records] on Warner Brothers Records. We bonded right off. The next time I got to see her was in 1995 when I had just recovered from a broken wrist. Pam Tillis had hired an all-girl band that included Cindy Cashdollar, and the featured guests were Pam, Wanda Jackson, Tammy Rogers, Iris Dement, and me. Those are like four main singers. The show was called "Live at the Ryman." That night I asked Wanda Jackson to sing a couple of duets with me on a rockabilly CD. I flew myself to Oklahoma City, and they put me up in their extra bedroom. We hung out for three days, working on the songs. I put her vocals down on the existing tracks. When *Rockabilly Filly* came out, she agreed to do a six-week tour with me. We toured the US, her first time in many years. That was great fun and a dream come true for me.

HUDSON: What has been an obstacle for you? A place of struggle?

FLORES: Well, right now. It's not very easy, I feel like I've been struggling every minute of the way. It's never been a piece of cake. Right now, I'm putting everything I have into starting my own label, Durango Rose. I'm putting out my first solo, live and acoustic CD, and it's called *Single Rose*. I could be giving you a copy right now, except we have to do some remixing on it. Eminent went bankrupt, so I have to buy back the masters and put them out myself. They were my favorite label to work with.

HUDSON: Let's hear a story about something upcoming.

FLORES: I'm writing a book called *Wacky Truck Stop Candy and Road Stories*. I've written two chapters of it. You have no idea what I've been collecting. When you're on the road with a band, you get to see lots of candy in truck stops. I can find candy that looks just like a tape recorder, and the tape that comes out is bubble gum! So, in my story, if I were talking about doing an interview with you, I'd have a picture of that tape-recorder candy. Match the candy to the story. I have dirty-laundry candy. I do need to go to a place where I'm so undistracted, I can finish this book. Maybe your place in San Miguel de Allende. Of course, I need to wait until my record sells in order to do this.

HUDSON: One last comment from you on women and Texas music. How do you want to be remembered?

FLORES: I'm sure I'll be known as someone who just stuck it out! I haven't had an easy road, but I do hang in there because I get joy out of what I'm doing. I've figured out a way not to get jaded. I do it for the creative satisfaction out of the process of writing. And I don't give up the dream that something good can really happen right around the corner. I don't think you should just set goals that include an ending date. You might miss out on something. I still have highs, and I have lows. Those highs are worth it. I'm working with a guy from Berlin, Gandulf [Hennig], who has his own record label. I played lead guitar all over his CD and toured with him for a month. He later directed a documentary called *Fallen Angels* on Gram Parsons. People in Switzerland and Germany love American music. I'm going to be in Switzerland. Aschi Maurer's son, Robert, has put together a two-week tour for me. Aschi did the Frutigen Festival, you remember. Then I'm flying to Dublin and doing a festival there. I'll have two weeks in Ireland on my own, solo and acoustic. I perform with Billy Joe Shaver tomorrow night at nine. Hope you can make it.

[In 2006 Rosie added the following: My career has never been a piece of cake. However, I find myself in a great place at this time. A place of change, a chance to reinvent myself. I spent seven years in Nashville and never quite fit in. There I was trying to fit my hand into a four-fingered glove. So the move back to Austin feels comfy and exciting. Here in the next year, I'm going to finish writing my book, Wacky Truck Stop Candy. I'll be in a good place to write dozens of new songs. The struggles will seem less, hopefully, as I continue to run my record label and put several bands together while I try out different styles of American roots music, including a project where I'll be singing songs in Spanish.]

When I've had a vision, I've simply tried to follow it, learning what I need to learn to fulfill it.

Betty Buckley

BROADWAY TO TEXAS

I first met Betty Buckley in a dance class with Ed Holleman and Larry Howard in Fort Worth. I was attending TCU and taking jazz classes. She was also attending TCU, but I chose to drop the dance class, buy a horse, and start barrel racing. It was the late 1960s. When we talked in Fort Worth on July 20, 2003, she was buying a ranch and coming home to live in Texas once again. She had been riding cutting horses and loving it. We talked about how it feels to be a woman our age and still enjoying life even as we made changes. By the end of the conversation I was fully inspired to keep following my dreams just as Betty follows hers. I still have a horse, but I ride only for pleasure. Twilight is my favorite time of day, that liminal space when light is becoming dark. That is when I love to ride Brownie, my granddaughter's horse that lives at my place west of Kerrville. I've always loved music, as has Betty. We shared memories of the Casa Mañana Theater in Fort Worth, of our dance teachers, of our challenges as women. When I first heard Betty Buckley singing in the original Broadway production of Cats, I had chills running up and down my body. Her voice, singing those words of the power of memory and the challenge of the impossible, became a

beacon on my own pathway. When you go to her website (www.bettybuckley.
com), you will find a newsletter called "Heart to Heart." This is where Betty
Lynn shares herself in another way with fans. Her list of favorites includes
one of mine as well: her old high school buddy, singer/songwriter/guitarist
Stephen Bruton. He has performed with Betty Lynn and most recently worked
on a new collection of songs with her. Again, a Fort Worth connection. I
remember Record Town, the great record store across from TCU owned by
the Bruton family. I remember the family playing music around town. It
seems we are all connected in some way. My sister, Carolyn, accompanied
me on this interview in November 2004 at Joe T. Garcia's in Fort Worth.
She also received inspiration from the conversation with Betty.

HUDSON: Let's talk about your progress through this amazing life you have created. Was there a point where you recognized your own success?

BUCKLEY: Well, there was a moment. This story goes back to when I was thirteen. I was listening to the radio in my room in our house in Western Hills. I had this view of an old windmill on the plain behind our house. I had this flash, call it a vision, of what my voice would sound like someday and how it would affect people. I knew at that moment I would be a Broadway leading lady. It was a deep inner knowing.

When I was eleven, my mom took me to see *Pajama Game* at Casa Mañana, the original Bob Fosse production, and I had this awareness of higher consciousness rising up through the tip of my head saying, "That's it. That's what you're going to be doing the rest of your life." I've always had a strong inner guidance, except for those periods in my life when I didn't listen. I knew as a child that I had a unique talent.

People's response to my voice started when I was very young. I was not a socially adept child, at all. I could communicate with animals and adults, but not my own peers. And I went to schools that were cliquish: Morning Junior High and Arlington Heights. But my singing made me kind of notorious.

Most people wanted me to make it as a singer, except my father. And that's a bit odd since he was the one who introduced me to music. As a young child I used to sing old South Dakota folk songs with him while he played the guitar. I was also in the youth choir in church, and I loved it. And I was in the all-city chorus. My chorus teacher was a woman with platinum hair and long red nails. She used to put me in the back row and say, "Blend in, Betty, blend in." Thank God for musical theater. I realized there was a purpose for my loud voice. I had a big voice and I was very tiny for many years—a late bloomer. When I was a kid being rejected by the other kids, I remember thinking, "Just wait until you hear me sing." I knew that I would not only get people's approval when I sang, but that I could overwhelm them.

When I was on Broadway in *Cats*, I was thirty-five and they brought a recording of "Memory" into my dressing room. I wanted it to be perfect when we recorded the song, and I kept asking to do it over and over. The producer said to leave it alone. It was good. So, when I was listening to the final mix, it was nice. And I had this flash of the moment when I was thirteen and looking out over the plain, knowing what I was going to do.

By that time I had studied for many years. I found my teacher in New York when I was twenty-two. I was thirty-five listening to my recording of this wonderful song. I had been studying with this beautiful white-haired man who always wore fine Italian suits. His name was Paul Gavert. His vision for me was finer than my own. He was the first positive father figure I had who encouraged my talent. I think that is what a great teacher does, inspire in you a bigger vision and help you to hold it in space so that you can grow into it. After applying what I had learned from Paul to the singing of "Memory" in *Cats*, I knew then that I knew how to work. I finally knew what I was doing. It wasn't just luck anymore based on talent, but technique of concentration. It was a learned expertise and, of course, God's grace that allowed me to communicate in song. I then knew how to evoke in an audience the connection that one hopes for people to experience. It was a gift, but combined with knowledge and expertise.

That moment, when they played the recording for me, I got it. It took from age thirteen to thirty-five. I learned a lot about achieving potential at that point. I tell this to my students, as well. You know what you want to do. You might not achieve it in the timeframe that you want, but if there's a genuine inner vision and you commit yourself to that, the opportunities to succeed will come to you.

In our world, everything is so youth-oriented. "Do it all in your twenties or don't try." Well, I knew from a young age that it would take whatever time it took, and that my best work would come later in life. I feel I am one of God's singers. It was a path that called me rather than a random choice.

HUDSON: I knew when I was four that I was going to teach. I understand what you are saying. Do you have a particular way that you nourish that inner knowing?

BUCKLEY: Meditation and prayer. That's a way of life for me. I made a commitment to this path in my mid-twenties. My life works best when I stay true to my spiritual practice.

HUDSON: One of my dreams was to run barrels at the Fort Worth Stock Show and Rodeo. I ended up competing for about seven years during the 1970s.

BUCKLEY: Very cool! I had my own barrel horse from the time I was twelve. He was a champion, and his name was Black Bucket. I always wanted to barrel race there and never did. I was a rodeo reporter for the *Fort Worth Press* when I was in college. I was at the Fort Worth Coliseum every year covering the rodeo. I had a dream to have a cutting horse. I fell in love with Señor George, a legendary cutting horse, when I was a teenager. Sonny Perry was his trainer. They used to show at the Fort Worth Rodeo before the NCHA (National Cutting Horse Association) grew so big and became its own thing. Now it's this huge sport. I wanted badly to have a relationship with a cutting horse one day and experience that oneness I witnessed between horse and rider. It's like watching a great dance team. I have never seen anything so beautiful as when these teams of horse and rider were cutting cattle.

In the months after September 11, I kind of woke up one day with a loss of focus. I was very weary. I had spent all these years focused only on work and career. I was tired of the projections that are an inevitable part of life as an actress. People have a tendency in our culture to project onto any woman of authority. It's a difficult mantle to carry. I've been in analysis with a brilliant psychologist for over ten years. She's a terrific woman my own age. She has taught me that there seems to be a big need in this society to find "the perfect mother." She's helped me to understand that many women of authority in this culture become the object of other persons' projections. People add their own inner longing to what we create or do in this world. Then, when they find out that we are not going to be this perfect mother figure for them, that we're just ordinary persons with our own issues, all of this rage stemming from unmet needs from the family of origin comes up. Most women in positions of authority go through this. It's very complicated, but that's the short version of a complex topic.

In the months after September 11, I woke up more weary than usual, like a lot of people, I think. I called my friend Stephen Bruton and just burst into tears, telling him that I didn't know what to do anymore or what to sing anymore—that I had lost my vision. He was very kind. He happened to be free at the end of January, and I asked him to come to New York and help me develop a new repertoire of music. So he did. We debuted the collection at the Bottom Line, a renowned music club that used to be downtown in New York. I called the show "Deep in the Heart," because it was about going back to the kind of music I loved best growing up in Texas. I did four nights with the Fort Worth Symphony after orchestrating the show for symphony orchestra. Then I did another version at Feinstein's in New York. I was well received. It hasn't been recorded yet. And after that show was finished, out of the blue, I became obsessed with finding my cutting horse. I was turning fifty-five, and I realized I'd forgotten to pursue my cutting horse dream.

HUDSON: I'm fifty-seven now, and I'm discovering all kinds of problems with my body. My horse fell on my knee several years ago, and now I have no cartilage in it. And I'm riddled with arthritis. And I thought I was superwoman!

BUCKLEY: Yeah, they don't tell ya, but when you hit that fifty wall . . . everything just seems to happen. Anyway, I had been a member of the National Cutting Horse Association for about twenty years. About two years before 9/11, I had gone on a spa vacation where I had spent some time with horses. All these longings for my horse came up. And all this guilt about leaving Black Bucket in Texas. I got him when I was twelve and he was five. I thought I could just leave, go off to find my life in show business, and come back someday and take him to the ranch I would have. I told him to wait for me. I paid for his upkeep all these years by loaning him to little girls learning to ride. When he was thirty-three, my uncle said, "You'd better come back and say good-bye to Black Bucket." So I came back to Fort Worth to see him, and told him that I was sorry I had gotten preoccupied with my career and had not purchased my ranch yet. I told him if he needed to go, then he could go. I left, and three days later he lay down and died. All this guilt came up about Bucket at the spa. I told the riding teacher there that I had a dream of having a cutting horse. She replied that it was past the point and that I was too old. "People who ride cutting horses have been doing it all their lives." I didn't have a chance at that point in my life, she told me. I went home, threw out all my "Cutting Horse Chatters," and canceled my NCHA membership, thinking this was something I could never do. But after September 11, I became obsessed. My assistant, Cathy, couldn't figure it out. I started making cold calls to trainers and answering ads. I was determined to find my horse. That was in about March. And then I started wondering what kind of ranch I could get if I sold my co-op in New York. I started making fact-finding trips. I met Lindy Burch, the only woman to be president of NCHA. She hooked me up on the East Coast with some people who helped me get my riding skills back. Trainer Bill Freeman returned my call. He's a man who has won more money than anyone in the cutting horse business, and he took all the fear out of it for me. He's a tremendous teacher. I started riding with him. He found my horse for me in October 2002. I won my first belt buckle and my first big check at the Summer Spectacular this past spring. And I bought my ranch. That's where I'm at. Living my cutting horse dream.

HUDSON: Everything you've said connects with my life, down to the experience and connection with horses.

BUCKLEY: My new horse is a dapple gray named Purple Badger. He's a champion, and he's so funny.

HUDSON: What are some images that come up when I say "Texas"?

BUCKLEY: Sky. Space. A sense of being at one with the world. What I love about being on my horse is that I don't think about anything else when I'm with him. Just sky, grass, trees, and butterflies. I really thought I would live in New York City the rest of my life. I never anticipated coming home. I am really happy here.

HUDSON: I spent a wonderful time in my life living in Annetta, teaching in Aledo, and riding near there. This is beautiful country.

BUCKLEY: I'm a little perplexed about all this change in my life. I didn't plan it. It just seems to be the thing to do, so I'm doing it. I need space. Maybe it's from living in apartments all this time. I want to see land and wide open spaces.

HUDSON: I know that when I was training my horse, I was so completely present in the moment. It was as good as yoga for me.

BUCKLEY: Exactly. They require that. And they give back so much.

HUDSON: I can see you, Stephen Bruton, "Deep in the Heart" at the Willie Nelson picnic.

BUCKLEY: That would be nice.

HUDSON: I have this thing about the West. I live west of Kerrville with a wolf dog, and I'm happy there. I spent a lot of my life valuing men and not valuing women. I went through this transition, and it was about mothering. Women offer something that men cannot offer. I also work with Hal Robinson, a Gestalt therapist and shaman, who has helped me see more about my own life. I actually got around to mothering myself instead of looking for others to do this. Whew, I thought I had issues with men, then found out I also had some damaging stories about women. We call my mother Saint Annabel, because she is the ultimate mother. Maybe I always felt like a failure next to her. I never had a relationship with my sister until now. I'm glad she's here with me. I've resolved all that now and enjoy the different ways we relate to men and to women. Out of our own stories, for sure. What would you say to other women?

BUCKLEY: I think being an independent woman in this culture can sometimes be tough. Egos are so fragile in my business. It took me years to understand this. When I was young, I thought since theater was all about collaboration, people would be interested in what we have to say to each other. But as a Texas woman, I am bold and outspoken. I've had to learn to tone it down through the years. But I've always known that as an older woman I'd be eccentric and outspoken again. On a certain level I don't care anymore. I don't like "sissyness." I just want to live life from my heart. I don't want to have to pussyfoot around because I'm strong and have a point of view.

HUDSON: I think this awareness comes with age. I do not want to spend much time worrying about what other people think. I'd rather live life out of my commitments.

BUCKLEY: There are certain scenarios that I can smell coming, and, for the most part, I've learned to remove myself.

HUDSON: I think this awareness comes with age. I do not want to spend much time worrying about what other people think. I'd rather live life out of my commitments.

BUCKLEY: Carolyn Myss, author of *Anatomy of the Spirit*, has an image of the plug in a socket. This is how people drain us. She says, "Unplug."

And I've done that with people and situations in my life. I am at a point in my life where I can honor and love all that has happened to me. I mean ALL. It took an entire journey to get me right here now. And I love where I am.

HUDSON: I've spent a lot of my life living in my head. Since I've started working with Hal Robinson, I have started paying attention to what my body says to me, what my heart says. It gives me a more holistic communication with myself. I do believe we know what we need to do in all situations. We just need to listen to more than just our head.

BUCKLEY: None of us know when our time will be up in this life. I want to do what really matters to me. I want to go on the road with my truck and trailer and learn to be one of the top non-pro riders in cutting. But it costs a lot of money, so I gotta keep working. God willing.

HUDSON: And I want to take my horse over to the state park near Bandera and spend the night with horse and dog! I'd love for you to come visit Kerrville sometime. Have you met Leon Harrell?

BUCKLEY: Yes, he's an elegant guy. I've read his book, too. Cutting is an amazing sport. Everyone is so supportive. My wonderful assistant has been with me for three years. She wanted to be the assistant of an actress/singer. Now that I've become a cowgirl again, she's trying to adapt. She told me she would move to Texas and try it for a year. She's learning to ride.

HUDSON: I rode my first and only cutting horse at Leon Harrell's. He invited me to ride at a media event and to produce the music and entertainment. I also took a batch of photos for him. What fun! Thank you for the time you have given me today.

BUCKLEY: Thanks for including me. All the best with your book.

Nobody's ever asked a man if he had trouble combining his relationship and a career.

$\mathcal{M}arcia$ $\mathcal{B}all$

FREDA LIVES ON

Marcia was part of my first book; I first met her at the Kerrville Folk Festival years ago. She is a woman of the Southwest. We started this conversation on the Saltillo tile floor of a room that served as music studio and gallery for the art of her husband, Gordon Fowler. He entered the conversation as we moved to the kitchen later, fixing a squeaky cabinet door as we sat and talked. He was heading out to paint "en plein aire." Before heading to Austin that weekend, Sandy Wolfmueller, owner of Wolfmueller's Books and Records in Kerrville, took me on a short drive to the new ambulatory care center. There on the wall hung several paintings of the Texas Hill Country by Gordon Fowler. He told me later that he once did a lot of painting in the Hill Country. Watching Marcia check the bulbs in her Christmas tree lights as we talked at her house in December 2002 reminded me how women often do several things at one time. This natural woman, dressed in jeans and a T-shirt, is still willowy, articulate, comfortable with herself, and gracious. She is also responsible for the Center for Texas Music History, based in San Marcos. She still tours and writes, while staying connected with her commitment to family. Her history is part of the history of Texas music.

She represents a strong place at the center of the Austin music scene, and she has toured the world, carrying her keyboard, her strong sense of self, her joy, and her talent.

HUDSON: Marcia is sitting cross-legged on her new Saltillo tile floor. [I spread out an array of her CDs in front of her.] We met years ago, so let's begin by talking about change. I do see a thread that is constant throughout this music. Do you?

BALL: [looking at the CDs] This one, *Gatorhythms*, was a turning point for me. I wrote a lot for that one. It was named after the publishing company I had created for my own material. It was a harbinger for the future, in a way. From then on I would include more of my own material on my records. 1980 was a big turning point for me. I played more variety then, hanging on to the country music. I was influenced by the people playing in my band. In 1980 I went back to R&B, playing more of my own roots music from Louisiana. The most profound change was when I began to write more. *Gatorhythms* was pretty successful, so then you're scared to put out something else. Meanwhile we had created the "Dreams Come True" idea. We had been recording and working on it for about five years.

HUDSON: So you and Lou Ann Barton and Angela Strehli had been talking about this?

BALL: Angela and I had been talking, after all these years of playing side by side, that maybe we should try singing together. We cast about for something to do. The first song we did was "It Hurts to Be in Love." We had also done, live, "Little By Little," a standard blues song. That was when Antone's Record Label was beginning. Clifford [Antone] loved the idea, loved seeing us work together. He pretty much gave us carte blanche to do what we wanted.

HUDSON: That's a great recording. I love it. Do you like it now?

BALL: Yes, I do. There's something that happens when you get to record with friends that way. You share the responsibility; you share the spark. [She proudly holds up a string of bright lights, saying "Ta-dum!"]

HUDSON: You do not appear to have fallen into many of the traps that catch many performers [treatment centers, abuse], people who have really struggled with their art. I see you as someone creating out of a positive place.

BALL: I've been very lucky, for one thing. I'm not genetically inclined to habitual use. I'll admit I can dabble, and I have. Second of all, in many, many ways I have very fortunate timing. The good old days of pot smoking, beer drinking, and playing music were so innocent. Even then we could have gotten in a lot of trouble, but we weren't killing ourselves or anybody else in the process. Ray Charles said we didn't have a drug problem, we had a police problem. We managed to get through all that. By the time it got weirder, by the time cocaine and all that awful crap started coming into our lives, I had already decided I wanted to have a long life and have a long career. I just didn't want to burn out. The flip side of that is that a lot of the people who have struggled the hardest are also the most creative artists that we know. Townes Van Zandt is the perfect example of someone who created a masterwork out of a mess. In spite of his habits.

HUDSON: I think you've done something even more rare. You have created a great body of work out of this commitment to a centered, healthy, clear focus.

BALL: When Austin got weird, I got pregnant and moved out to the country. All of a sudden it wasn't about me. It wasn't about the party anymore. I took myself out of that scene, so I never was really surrounded by that scene. I was just lucky, too. I had Luke and a supportive family around me with Luke's dad and grandparents. Then when I remarried, I married Gordon, the same thing. A lot of help exactly where I needed it and when I needed it, to do what I wanted to do.

HUDSON: Let's talk about where you are going. I keep seeing this solid road of good music and strong performances.

BALL: I feel like the progress in my career is so incremental that you would have to line me up with something to be sure I was moving at all. I feel like it has been forward and upward moving, positive growth. It's not calculated, except that I do try not to make false steps, anything destructive. Way back at the beginning, I must have struck on the one part of the formula that works for me. It's entertainment; it's not surgery. Art melded to entertainment. I don't get all self-involved. There's a lot of personal expression in it, and there's often a message in some of what I write. I've met people along the way that inspire love songs. [looks over at Gordon, who has entered the kitchen] Also message songs.

GORDON: Sappy songs.

BALL: Like "Saint Gabriel," a song about a woman who went to prison over defending herself in a domestic violence situation. There's been a message as well as entertainment.

HUDSON: Sounds like you have such a great balance. I have to say this is a wonderful moment with Gordon fixing the cabinets behind us. I also wonder if conversations are different with a significant other around.

BALL: So far not. I did kind of lower my voice when I talked about love songs. He's at a point where he can't hear that well anyway. [laughter]

HUDSON: It seems that relationships do make a difference with women in a way that leads to different conversations with a woman than with a man.

GORDON: We don't have relationships; we have old ladies.

BALL: There's this comment circulating the web: Nobody's ever asked a man if he had trouble combining his relationship and a career. That may be less accurate now than it used to be. More men are trying now to be part of the family.

HUDSON: As I was listening to this CD coming in, and laughing at "Play with Your Poodle," I realized that I really like the song "The Right Tool for the Job."

GORDON: You know how that happened? I had my license plates sitting around on the counter. She asked me why I hadn't put them on. "It takes a special tool," I answered.

She replied, "Yeah, a screwdriver." Then she started that song.

HUDSON: I love the song as it applies to struggle.

BALL: You know, this record did not do as well for the record company as *Gatorhythms* or *Blue House*. As I look at this song for song, it contains some of my favorite writing. I like that song too. I love "American Dream," a short story in four stanzas. "The Story of My Life" is a good one for me.

HUDSON: What inspired that?

BALL: That song is not lyrically all that deep, but it does have some cool images. I was inspired by Dan Penn on that one. It's another little short story. It holds together. Being an English major, there are things I do that I'm proud of. Nobody else would even notice. On *Presumed Innocent* I have a song called "She's So Innocent." First of all, it's inspired by the poems of Edna St. Vincent Millay. You won't hear that in a lot of rock-and-roll conversations. I wanted to grasp the sweetness of her. There's a point in the bridge where I've included internal rhyme along with end rhyme.

I've reached a point in my songwriting where I don't think I knew I was doing that until I looked at it later. "She holds the world in the palm of her hand; she's just a girl in the arms of a man/And when she's hurt she folds like a fan."

HUDSON: You were and are a reader?

BALL: [leading me to another room lined with shelves of books] As Sarah Bird said, "This is my friends' shelf." She's reading tonight at BookPeople.

HUDSON: I guess it would be hard to talk about favorites. What about influences?

BALL: I like Shelby Hearon a lot. I met her last year, and I like her a lot. I've read all of Bud Shrake's fiction. I really loved Willie Morris's *North Toward Home*.

HUDSON: I was listening to the wide variety of sounds in your music. The only thing not present now is country. I hear lots of boogie-woogie, soul, blues, rock, and Cajun.

BALL: I haven't gone back to early country songs. We just put out the Freda record after thirty years. I was on the radio last night with Bobby Earl talking about it.

HUDSON: How has the Internet affected things for you?

BALL: Personally, I hear from people who wouldn't write me, couldn't find a stamp for the letter, but can find me on the Internet. I'll end up being in communication with the sister of someone I went to high school with who wants me to say hello to someone else when I play Juneau, Alaska! What a web of communication. You get many connections. Musically you're spreading information around. I can also see that becoming a problem. Too much. I'm happy where I am right now, working on a new album with Alligator that will be out in April 2003. Stephen Bruton produced it, bringing in lots of friend musicians as well as my own band.

HUDSON: Who are your regular musicians?

BALL: Don Bennett is my bass player and has been for twenty-one years. My guitar player is Pat Boyack from Utah. He's played with me two years. [She offers me tea.] On saxophone, Brad Andrew, from New Jersey originally. He's played with W. C. and Lavelle [White]. I'm changing drummers as we speak. We'll have a new drummer from Dallas named Mark Wilson. He's been in that area a long time. Mark played with Anson and the Rockets for a long time. That's the band. Johnny Medina, our sound guy, has been with me eight years. And he's a wonderful photographer.

HUDSON: I want to see you at the Monterey Blues Festival some June. I go to the Young Rhetoricians Conference there every June.

BALL: We played the Monterey Jazz Festival this year. Quite fabulous. There's a group of films about the blues being made right now. It's overseen by Martin Scorsese. There are seven films, each directed by a director of note. The piano section is being directed by Clint Eastwood. While I was out there for the jazz festival, I was picked up and taken to Clint's place in Carmel, where Pinetop Perkins was waiting. That led to an interesting moment backstage after my set. Clint's liaison stuck his head in, saying, "Hey, Clint's out here and wants to say 'hi.'" I was talking to my guitar player's wife. She just looked at me, saying, "Clint?" It was a strange and wonderful moment.

HUDSON: So you're still having experiences that thrill you.

BALL: I'm having a ball. I read obituaries, and there was a woman today who died young with cancer. On her last good day, she said, "It's been lovely." That's exactly what I'll be saying.

HUDSON: I see a great creative writing assignment in that. Go through the obituaries and see what kind of writing comes out of that.

BALL: Yeah, note to self! You find the most amazing stories there that would never see the light of day. Their whole life is right there in a column.

HUDSON: Tell me about your involvement with Gary Hartman and the Center for Texas Music History.

BALL: We are encouraging oral history, and we need people to do field recordings, people going out and finding the people who remember. And you never know where you're going to find them.

HUDSON: How did you get involved?

BALL: Gary recruited me, and I'm happy to be recruited. I'm a bad club member. I stay so busy and enter another world when I hit the road. It's a wonderful opportunity, and it's good for the school. Having Ray Benson involved is good. We are also taking people into the future by studying the past.

HUDSON: I see a proliferation of museums and preservation organizations. I'm heading over to the Bob Bullock Texas State History Museum to see the touring Texas music collection after we speak today. What do you have to say about Texas?

BALL: Your old connections turn out to be your true connection. Sometimes, you just go home. That happens in Texas, and it happens in Louisiana too. You said you were going to talk with Betty Buckley. Well, when Betty Buckley of Fort Worth, Texas, needed a musical director, she called Stephen Bruton of Fort Worth, Texas. When Stephen was producing my record, he wanted some high-class horns, and he called Lon Price of Fort Worth, Texas. Roots do make a difference. You can go far and wide, but you do go home again.

[In September 2004, Marcia Ball added the following: Both Alligator CDs, Presumed Innocent *and* So Many Rivers *(2004), won the W. C. Handy Award for Best Contemporary Blues Album.* So Many Rivers *was also nominated for a Grammy in 2004. Otherwise, gigs go on. We're happy to be working. My bass player, Don Bennett, has been with me for twenty-three years.]*

I say to all aspiring performers, don't ever be discouraged. Don't let anything stop you from doing what you love. Even though there's no logic there, you have to be true to yourself.

Angela Strehli

BEING TRUE TO YOURSELF

I first talked with Angela at the beginning of my oral history project in about 1986. She was playing at Joseph's Foodliner on St. Mary's in San Antonio. We saw each other backstage for a few minutes and talked. I began my entire journey of documenting music by going to Antone's Blues Club in Austin as often as I could. This discovery showed me a vein of music that I loved passionately, enough to drive to Austin alone just to be at Antone's. Angela showed up then, and I loved her music. I knew that Clifford Antone also loved her music. He gave these blues players a home at a time that audiences didn't always show up. I also discovered Albert Collins, John Lee Hooker, Buddy Guy, James Cotton, Sue Foley, Sarah Brown, Derek O'Brien, Hubert Sumlin, and scores of other great blues performers during these treks of the heart. In 2004, the club branched out to showcase other forms of Americana music. But the blues is still its heart and soul. The day before interviewing Angela, I attended the debut of a documentary on Clifford Antone. The interview footage in this film was exciting and inspiring. Clifford talked about Angela in hyperbole.

HUDSON: Sarah Brown suggested that my first question be "How come you are so cool?" I also heard Clifford Antone describe you as "the best," his favorite. What do you think about these extreme comments from your friends?

STREHLI: That is interesting. For one thing, I didn't consider myself a singer for the first fifteen years I was doing this. I considered that I was learning a craft. I needed to live a little and put a lot of mileage on my voice. I was patient with myself. I feel like I've always had support, a lot of it from women. That has been a sustaining thing for me, knowing that I've been an inspiration to women. Women in general seem to love to see someone up there doing it. It was unusual back in the day. There weren't that many women fronting bands. Now it's gone the other way.

HUDSON: I remember when I first started coming to Antone's in the mid-1980s, I was enthralled with more than the music. I became aware that all the people there had stories to tell. I remember seeing you and thinking, "Yeah, that's who I want to be." I was newly divorced with a new Ph.D. I didn't really see myself as someone to document the scene, but that was my passion. I love the wisdom that keeps unfolding in myself as I talk with other women. Let's talk about Clifford's appreciation for you.

STREHLI: That's unexplainable. For someone to champion you this way, that's really important. I'll have to put it in the context that everyone thought we were either stupid or crazy to be promoting the blues. It was so "out," it was not "in." The blues was anything but "hip." And the blues purists didn't want to have anything to do with people like us because we were the wrong people. We were not qualified. We didn't have an answer to that. You do what your heart tells you. The appreciation level was not there for a really long time. The black clubs were going out of business because it was no longer being played on the radio. And the black kids did not want to learn it because this was the music of their parents and grandparents. For some reason we were drawn to the blues, and we stuck to our guns. Without someone like Clifford coming along and putting us together with the great heroes and masters, it would have been much different, much harder. In 1966 I made a pilgrimage to Chicago to hear many of my heroes. I didn't dream they would start to spend time in Austin.

HUDSON: The film on Antone's last night really captured that. What a way to live, following your heart, or your "bliss," as Joseph Campbell said so eloquently. Susan, let me hear a little from you. [Clifford's sister]

ANTONE: It's easy for me to talk about Angela. She has the sound and the rhythm that I'm drawn to. It's all about heart and soul and rhythm. I look at the world pretty much as tribes. And I feel the beat, the rhythm of the land. I think people move to those rhythms of the land and soil they are from. There are a lot of tribes and rhythms. She's from the one I'm from, so it's totally perfect from my heart. There's nothing I enjoy as much as photographing women. I don't consider myself a photographer; I take pictures. I love taking pictures of what I hear and see. If music comes out of those photos, then I'm glad. I have so many wonderful pictures of Angela and so many other women. The pictures stand for themselves. Women in music are special. They touch my soul. When I hear wonderful women, there's no sound that's any better.

HUDSON: I would love to use some of your photos in this book.

ANTONE: I'd be glad to do that. Just call me.

STREHLI: Of all the people who have taken photographs at the club over the years, none are like hers. Her backstage photos are almost my favorites. Only someone who knows the music like she does can capture the personalities.

HUDSON: Let's talk a little about the music. We can begin with your performance last night, March 12, at Antone's blues club during South by Southwest.

STREHLI: The songs I did last night are a good representation of what I love. I started out with an Eddie Taylor song, "Big Town Playboy." Eddie was maybe my favorite of all the gentlemen we had around us for all those years. I identified with Eddie. He did all of his talking with his fingers. His sons were there last night, and they'll be there tonight performing. I think I always start a show with this song. It's my signature song. It makes me feel good. It's just right. And I did an Elmore James song. He's also an incredible influence on me. I also did Albert King. So now you're hearing all of these men's names. As far as the recorded history of blues, I didn't get to hear that many women singing. The classic blues singers from the 1920s and 1930s. Ma Rainey was my favorite of all these. You might think of Bessie Smith first. But I never got to see that many blues singers. Lavelle White was one I saw, but I had already started singing. She was wonderful to run into right here in Austin. She was inspirational. Another woman who really inspired me when I started out was Ann Peebles. I always covered her material.

HUDSON: Did you end up doing some research on your own?

STREHLI: Yeah, yeah. I knew nothing about blues because I was raised in Lubbock. It was a matter of catching it on late-night clear-channel radio. Then I had to find out what I was hearing. I didn't know what to call it then. I wrote a song called "Two Bit Texas Town." It explains what happens when you don't grow up in a big city. You had to search for it or be lucky enough to find it. The big radio station on the border, XERB with Wolfman Jack, was a big influence. WHAC in Nashville featured gospel and blues. I left Lubbock when I was eighteen and went to college in Minnesota. Then I came running back to Austin. I realized the cultural differences. Growing up in Texas, I felt the Mexican and African American influences. I knew I had to get back and feel that Texas soul. When you are doing something like that, you don't think it's special at the time. That's the last thing that would occur to you.

HUDSON: Let's talk about the writing.

STREHLI: Usually what happens to me, I do think every writer gets inspiration out of the blue. It comes through you somehow, and you realize you must have put yourself in that position, and you're glad. You try to build on that and make something out of it, like a whole song. And you try to express what you deeply care about. But what has really motivated me is writing for other people, mostly women. I usually have someone else's situation in mind. It's more like coming through me but not coming from me. I knew Barbara Lynn was going to record for Antone's. I thought about her, and a song came out. It's called "Go On." She didn't end up recording it, but I did. She's close to the border in the Beaumont area. It has that feeling to it. It seems easier when I'm thinking about someone else. A recent example was Marcia Ball. I was flattered that she considered me as a producer of her current record. In trying to come up with some material for her, I ended up writing some songs. Someone else ended up producing for her. And it is a wonderful record. And I'll probably end up recording those songs. "Blue Highway" was actually about her. I still see Marcia doing a narrative and playing in the background. She's such a great storyteller. I would talk to her on the phone, and she would describe what she was seeing and feeling as she traveled on the road. I wrote a song for Lou Ann [Barton] to sing, which she didn't do either! I recorded it, but I still think she could do it so much better. It's called "Give Me Love." It was just the kind of thing that she could just nail. I did write one that was highly autobiographical, "In Spite of What You Do." And everyone can relate. You can't force love, and this was like an apology for trying to do that.

HUDSON: My Lou Ann Barton story starts back in Fort Worth, my hometown.

STREHLI: She's got so much natural talent. She's got the vibes. She's got the attitude. The kind of thing a Tina Turner has. It just turns you on. She's just tough. That's hard to come by. Etta James. Lavelle White is tough. Her voice is one of my favorites on earth.

HUDSON: What about other influences on you?

STREHLI: I've had the great fortune of traveling, mainly to Mexico, in my life. My parents were both interested in the Mexican culture. That music was always important to me. And Afro-Cuban music. I'm so much of a fan of all kinds of music. Jazz instrumentalists have influenced me. I'm not much on jazz vocalists. I think I get a lot of phrasing from the saxophone. And I'm a guitar freak. I've always had two guitarists in my bands. I think it's really great to have two working off each other. And I could never get onstage if the musicians were not just wonderful. I'm not that outgoing to think I could carry something on my own ability. I'm inspired by what I'm hearing behind me. I have worked the longest with George Rains, Derek O'Brien, Kaz Kazanoff, Sarah Brown, and Denny Freeman. That was my Austin band for ten years. I have a band now in California. It took me a long time to wean myself from this family here. We couldn't just import them, so I eventually found some great musicians there.

HUDSON: What does your week at home look like now?

STREHLI: We have a family restaurant, Rancho Nicasio, in the country in West Marin County, in a beautiful valley. I recorded a "live" record there. And in 2005 I will have a new studio recording, *Blue Highway*. I still enjoy singing because the fans are great, and my band is terrific.

I am doing some great blues festivals, and Europe is a good market for the blues. I feel so fortunate that I have been able to record. There are so many people with so much talent who don't have that opportunity. I was instrumental in starting the Antone's record label because I realized that no one else was going to be interested in the recordings he had, so I did take that on.

HUDSON: I know this is a big weekend for you. I look forward to seeing you again. Let's end by imagining someone reading this in about fifty years. What do you want people to know about you?

STREHLI: It's mind-blowing to think someone will be reading about you as part of history. I say to all aspiring performers, don't ever be discouraged. Don't let anything stop you from doing what you love. Even though there's no logic there, you have to be true to yourself.

I can remember getting the flu, being very ill a couple of different times. I was so thankful I was in a band with my mother and my sister, women who would take care of me. I can remember hearing rockabilly musicians talking about hating each other by the end of the tour. For me, it was a bonding experience.   [CONNI HANCOCK]

The Texana Dames

A FAMILY AFFAIR

The Ladies Lynching League at Luckenbach, Texas, showcased writers on May 30, 2002, including Dos Dames—Conni and Traci Hancock. Maggie Montgomery, the show's hostess, is a songwriter herself. Her interview with these women is part of a film documentary on women in Texas music. I sat in on the conversation and joined in. Maggie welcomed us to a balmy Texas afternoon, about 106 degrees in the shade. When I first met them, they were the Texana Dames, originally from Lubbock, Texas, and then they became the Supernatural Family Band, with Charlene and Tommy Hancock.

MAGGIE: Your mom has been in the music business for fifty years, and you've handed me this CD documenting her musical life.

TRACI: This CD is twenty-five songs and fifty years of singing and recording. She should get an award for all the miles she's traveled and all the gigs she's played. It begins with her first recording when she was twelve; she recorded in the same studio as Buddy Holly. She joined my dad's band when she was sixteen years old. They played for many years around Lubbock at the Cotton Club, and we became the Family Band in the early

1970s and traveled all over the country. No way to say exactly how many were in the band, because lots of friends joined in from time to time.

MAGGIE: I remember visiting your house, coming into the living room and meeting your family. It was all very formal. Then your father said, "Okay, everybody, we're moving to the music room. If you can't hear what the singer is saying, you're playing too loud." [lots of laughter] It was organized, but it was supernatural. Such fun. I'll never forget it.

TRACI: Well, first of all Kathleen's a Texana Dame. She has played her egg and her bones with us.

HUDSON: I got really interested in oral history in about 1986. My first book is a collection of interviews with Texas songwriters. Now I am focusing on the voice of women in Texas music. I've traveled thirteen days in Europe with this family, documenting their effect on audiences in Frutigen, Switzerland, and Bad Ischl, Austria. I introduced them to Rod Buckle, and he produced an album for them in England. [He also produced the Sir Douglas Quintet.] I'm fascinated by the distinction that women have in Texas. I would love to hear a comment from all three of you, describing what is distinct about being a woman in this scene.

CONNI: Well, I don't know anything else.

TRACI: You're around a lot of men. Which is fine. [laughter] We do everything in our business ourselves. We are totally self-sufficient. I think it takes a lot of strength. This may go for everybody in the business, but for a woman to be in a traveling band, you have to be really strong. There's a lot of late nights on the road by yourself. You have to stand up for what you want. You can't let anyone run over you. You have to be real clear about that. We like to have a balance between the women and the men in the band when possible. For me, as a woman in the audience, I always like to see a woman in the band. It's kind of a sisterhood there, with other women performers. We know each other and support each other. There's a real kinship there.

CONNI: For me, it's probably pretty different from lots of others. With my dad and brothers, the men in our lives have been so supportive. John Reed and Paul Mills have been so supportive in our band. And then there's our mom. She's been singing professionally since she was about ten years old. They have all made life beautiful and easy for us. It might be tougher for a woman folksinger trying to break into the business.

TRACI: Conni wrote a song that I think is really poignant and something that women need to hear. It's called "Same Taste in Men," and it's how we're not in competition with each other. Let's love each other. I think more women are starting to see the value in each other. We are not on opposite sides.

CONNI: One reason I wanted to settle in Austin is that I felt welcome right away. Marcia Ball and Angela Strehli and Lou Ann Barton made us feel so welcome when we came. We have lived in New Mexico and Colorado and traveled to Europe, Mexico, and South America. Austin felt like home.

HUDSON: I was so glad to hear that you were playing Luckenbach. Combining your family history with the heritage at Luckenbach creates a special moment in Texas music history. Historical or hysterical!

CONNI: On the way out I saw a sign that said "Thanks, Waylon." Right away I felt a connection. Waylon used to be a deejay in Lubbock and play my dad's records on the radio. He and my dad stayed in touch over the years. When he died, I felt a strange loss. I never saw him anymore, and I didn't have a personal friendship with him. But I had this connection that he supported my dad by playing his records.

HUDSON: You can't escape the line "Let's go to Luckenbach, Texas, with Waylon and Willie and the boys."

MAGGIE: Or "with Traci and Conni and the girls." [laughter]

HUDSON: Ah, the Luckenbach Ladies Lynching League.

MAGGIE: Literally!

HUDSON: What do you think of when you hear "Luckenbach"?

TRACI: First, a vision of the Willie Nelson picnic. What these people who attend look like. These buildings are amazing.

MAGGIE: We just celebrated our 150th anniversary for the fourth year in a row. We had so much fun the first time that we decided to keep it.

CONNI: When you're from Lubbock, there's a deep appreciation for the hills and the trees and the wildflowers. When I think of Luckenbach, I think of this little piece of heaven.

HUDSON: What is most important to you in your career right now?

CONNI: Just for people to know that these CDs are available. My mom's and this one by my dad and John X Reed. It has a compilation of music from each decade. It will take you back.

TRACI: We feel it's very important to get people to hear this music. I'm working on a solo project, an all-Spanish CD.

HUDSON: Will it have my favorite song on it? "Quiero Ser Solo Tuyo."

TRACI: That's a gorgeous song.

MAGGIE: I've been singing all my life. I moved from Birmingham, Alabama, when I was thirty. My brother went off to Vietnam and left me his dog and his Gibson guitar, saying "take care of my dog and learn to play the guitar." Well, the dog was killed by a neighbor's dog, so I figured I'd better learn to play the guitar. I moved to Texas with that guitar on my back, and all of a sudden there was this little child on my lap strumming [Monte Montgomery]. I was chording, and he was singing. One day he said, "I think I can play a little lead on this song, 'Someday Soon.'" I said to go ahead. He started doing my breaks, then sets by himself. Pretty soon he started doing all of my gigs. I moved into promotion and administration. And I still play and sing.

CONNI: I remember your bringing him to our gigs when he was just a toddler.

MAGGIE: Oh, he loved you girls!

CONNI: He was the sweetest thing.

MAGGIE: That's sort of my story. Luckenbach is my favorite place to play, under this tree. I've gone off in many directions, but I've always returned. Now I'm president of the Ladies Lynching League. What I'm trying to do is make sure the women know they are welcome here. There are so few of us. One woman and fifteen guys. It's fun for a while, but we need more women. Hondo Crouch also named me the Luckenbach Songbird. That's my most treasured title. We're big on titles around here. I'm also the editor of the world-famous *Luckenbach Moon*, our newsletter, so I get to write about everything. I want us to be noticed. I don't want us to have to stand in line and say, "Is it my turn? Is it my turn?" That's my story.

HUDSON: When you are traveling around the world, do you run into anything distinct about being a woman on the road?

CONNI: We're three women.

TRACI: Not many people are going to mess with us!

CONNI: I can remember getting the flu, being very ill a couple of different times. I was so thankful I was in a band with my mother and my sister, women who would take care of me. I can remember hearing rockabilly musicians talking about hating each other by the end of the tour. For me, it was a bonding experience.

MAGGIE: The noise in the background is not really noise. That's the sound of the Luckenbach pickers. It goes 24/7, and we love it. It's time to move over to the dance hall now.

[Several months later I caught up with the matriarch of this group, Charlene Hancock, in Austin, Texas. The following conversation evolved at Vinnie's Italian Restaurant on August 1, 2002.]

HUDSON: Charlene Hancock, you are a woman who has been a real source of inspiration for me. When I think of someone who has really woven all the threads together, I think about you. I've sat in Guero's on South Congress on Sunday afternoon and danced to your music with Tommy "Zen and the Art of Two Step" Hancock, your husband. I've seen the big shows and the little shows. Let's talk about the music business, relationships—you and Tommy have a unique one, choices you've made, and things you've learned about yourself.

CHARLENE: Tommy inspires me to get up and move. I'm a pretty passive person, but when you raise four kids, you lose that. I was really young, seventeen, when we married. He was ten years older than me, and everyone said, "Oh, you're marrying that older man." Some worried. We could both tell that there was something that we shared that was just meant to be. We decided to make a try of it. Over the years it has all come about and worked itself out. We've been together for forty-five years now. After we played music together for thirty years, he got tired of the music business. He always wanted to teach; he kept his teacher's license up so he could do that. He asked me to go out to Presidio with him. Conni, Traci, and I had just begun the Texana Dames band, and Conni was writing music for the three of us to sing. That was something I did with my mother when I was growing up: sing harmony. I just couldn't pass up that opportunity. I really wanted to sing with them. He and I both had enough trust and faith in each other that he could go to Presidio and pursue what he wanted to, and I could go to Europe with the Texana Dames and pursue what I wanted to. Here we are. We were together constantly for forty years. It got to the point where we didn't have any stories to tell each other. It seemed like we were stepping on each other's toes out of habit. Nothing intense. It just seemed like we needed some space. When he moved out to Presidio, we missed him badly. And the same was true for him. But he had his work teaching out there, and I had my music.

HUDSON: Isn't it great that you didn't have to call it quits? A lot of people get to that point and just quit.

CHARLENE: We couldn't. We have too much history. It's not like we didn't love each other; we were just too close. We're both back in Austin now. He has a place in town. He's in town a lot more than I am. I like staying out by the lake where it's quiet. It's a retreat for me. I need that balance in my life. I need the intensity of the music business, but at the same time, I need the balance of a retreat.

HUDSON: You seem to be really in touch with your own needs. What are some experiences that have served as a teacher for you?

CHARLENE: Moving to New Mexico from Lubbock in 1970. We lived there for three years in an isolated canyon in a log cabin with no electricity or plumbing. This was quite different from where we lived in West Lubbock with central air. Over in New Mexico we had to work with everything we had. I came from a family that did that. My mother's family moved to West Texas for free land. It was dry-land farming, and it was hard on them. I heard those stories when I was younger, and I thought, "Man, that was tough." I've seen some old pictures recently that I never saw before, and I realized how tough they were to do that. It was kind of that way with us moving to New Mexico. It looked irresponsible to everyone; they thought we were crazy. But that experience bonded all of us as a family. We had to make it through those winters. Tommy told the kids that he really wanted to do it, but he could wait until they were out of school. They were all ready to go with us. We had a simple life. You draw the water out of the creek, you make your own fire, you chop that tree down.

HUDSON: What did you do for money in a traditional sense?

CHARLENE: We still owned the Cotton Club with Tommy's parents, and we rented that out for parties. They didn't have a regular booking going on at that time. We had some income from that and some money saved. We would go back once a month and play the Cotton Club with our old band. Then the kids got interested in playing because there's nothing to do out there in the canyon. Tommy and I did the proverbial thing, saying, "These kids are good. We can do something with this." And that's how the Supernatural Family Band got its start. Also, Tommy and I are both big readers. We began to read the red-letter edition of the Bible just to see what Jesus had to say about living. And we tried to go by that. That led us to more spiritual books about all kinds of religions. We both always had these questions: "Is this all there is? Is there something better?" Someone was hitchhiking through and spent the night with us in New Mexico and told us about Maharaji. We went up to Denver to check that out. We got the techniques to meditate and have continued with that since then. It's not a religion, rather a technique to meditate to connect with yourself.

HUDSON: Is this the same person that Jimmie Dale Gilmore connected with?

CHARLENE: Yes. Maharaji is very low key. He goes around the world, and we see him when we can. That was the first time I went inside myself just to see what I want. I always knew I wanted music; that was a given. I always loved my family and knew I wanted that. It was important to me that Tommy and I enjoy each other and enjoy our kids. This is a completely personal thing for me. Maharaji is in his forties now.

HUDSON: He must have been very young when you first saw him.

CHARLENE: He was. And the things that came out of his mouth really struck me. That's the truth as I see it. He said things like "You know the truth when you hear it because it's already there." "You know the answers to your questions because they are already there."

HUDSON: I can see where that would open up a lot of space for peace.

CHARLENE: And self-reflection. I've been doing music for many years, and now I'm asking, "What else is there?" The question is answered by my love for my family. I have more time for my family this summer, but I still have the need to play.

HUDSON: I noticed that the last couple of times I've seen the Dames, it has been "Dos Dames." I wondered if you had made a decision to stop playing.

CHARLENE: For a couple of months I haven't played much. Before that I never took a break. Conni and Traci needed and wanted to go on. I understood that, and I was really pleased that they went on with their music and have done more things. I don't want any of us to feel like we're joined at the hip. I want them to have their own dreams. Maybe they are like I was. My music came from my mother. She sang and played and loved it. She would just beam when things were just right. I remember that. Everything I do, I think of her now. I always think of my mother.

HUDSON: Your new CD has all those wonderful shots of you and some of your mother. Let's talk about that. It says "family."

CHARLENE: I'm glad it does. My mother and her brother played music together. Their father played banjo, and I have a picture of him playing banjo in Kentucky. I'm so thrilled to see that thread going back a little bit further. My mother was sixty-five when she died of a heart attack. It was a sudden thing. She lost a baby when I was about four years old. He was nine months old, and at the time we were living in Dayton, Ohio. My mother would have her songbook and guitar. I could tell she would get sad and lonely, and she would sit down at the kitchen table and sing every song in her songbook and just let it out, let those feelings be soothed by those songs she was singing. She taught me some harmony. Then we got back out to West Texas, she kept getting so much joy out of her music.

HUDSON: What do you think your kids will say about their mother?

CHARLENE: I know they're going to say, "She's tough." And I am! I'm well honed by my experience. The music was the thing that kept our family together. When we moved to New Mexico, we felt we needed a little more time before everyone moved off. When we found they could play music, we started booking gigs. Tommy was big on showing them about the music business, how to run a gig on the stage. He showed them things music alone can't show you. They know how it goes.

HUDSON: I know these girls. Do you have sons?

CHARLENE: Tommy and I have four kids: Conni and Traci, and our son Joaquin, and our daughter Holli, who lives in Lubbock. Then Tommy has four other children. They are my friends, too. Tommy became such a good dad just thinking about what he wanted for his family. Holli sang with our band when we started. She was only nine then. She liked to dance. She's out in Lubbock now, married to a musician. They sing in church. His dad played in Tommy's band. Joaquin got married and didn't want to be on the road. That's when Tommy quit playing too. I still see that bond we all have from being on the road together and meeting our goals together.

HUDSON: My bonding came through barrel racing, a family affair for us.

CHARLENE: Now we all remember our time on the road fondly. Conni and Traci and I have been doing the Texana Dames Band for about fifteen years now. It seems like we just started. It's still exciting to play with them.

HUDSON: I saw the beautiful poster advertising the Broken Spoke gig next Wednesday. Tell me about that gig.

CHARLENE: John X Reed, of course, is playing with us. And Paul Skelton from the Cornell Hurd Band is playing with us. He's like John: they can do anything. The whole saga continues on. I wouldn't trade my life for anything. I'm so glad I've been able to do what I've done. Tommy always had the understanding that I needed this in my life and supported me in this. We missed each other terribly, but we had plenty of stories to tell when we got back together.

HUDSON: What's ahead?

CHARLENE: What's most important to us now is getting our Supernatural Family recordings on CD. Conni is working on the record label on a full-time basis. I want to go into the studio. I'm ready to create some new music. I feel rested enough to focus my energy on new music. Right now, I'm not into traveling. I'm spending a lot of time with Ruth, Tommy's mother. That's my priority. She's ninety-five and still lives at home. She has been going to the senior center for thirty years. She's a beauty. [Charlene joyfully greets Conni, as if she hasn't seen her in a while. The strong mother-daughter bond is evident as Conni joins us.]

CONNI: I find the Hispanic women so inspiring. In some cultures, they take what little money they have and make something so beautiful.

HUDSON: You all are part of my own learning about the value of sitting and talking to women, of certain kinds of energy.

CHARLENE: The music really makes you focus on the strength that comes from inside, from the music. And you find that you are stronger when you can learn to wait. In music, you can't jump ahead or you will miss the moment. Being a bass player, I really know that.

CONNI: Also the power and strength of female energy has to do with nurturing. I really believe that the best music does nurture us. As the Texana Dames, when we play music we are nurturing ourselves and our audience. Very rarely is a honky-tonk dance band perceived as a nurturing experience.

HUDSON: I was watching Pauline Reese play at the Broken Spoke. There is something different about a woman up there singing than a man. It's not the same.

CHARLENE: It makes you allow yourself to be more vulnerable in some way. Women can accept their vulnerability better than a man. Men seem to have to put up a front of strength at all times.

HUDSON: I love the conversation in education about nature versus nurture.

CHARLENE: My mother was a traditional wife. Daddy insisted that she not work outside the home. She set out to make our home the best home it could be. I realized something when I was pregnant and playing music. I played until I was at least seven months. I realized that the main things I got from my mother came from the womb. When she would be lonely and sit down and play music, I was there! I knew that music as comfort before I got here. I felt that in myself.

CONNI: I can remember being a toddler at their gig for the first time. I remember focusing on Mother and feeling it like a memory, kind of connecting in my mind, somehow, that this was the outside of it.

CHARLENE: Looking back, I can really see what happened. When the kids started playing with us, they followed us much better than any other players. It was easier to do with them.

HUDSON: Who are some women who come to mind as strong influences?

CHARLENE: Peggy Lee comes to mind. I always loved her voice and material. I learned much later that she was writing much of that music. Ella Fitzgerald. Any woman playing music caught my eye. There are so many. When I started singing in Tommy's band, there were no singer/songwriters around. There was the "girl singer" in the band.

HUDSON: So you were a forerunner.

CHARLENE: I remember thinking, "Why can't I do something here? My own thing?"

CONNI: I noticed the same thing. I paid attention to the women who were playing an instrument. I specifically loved blues and steel guitar, so I loved Bonnie Raitt from the beginning. What my mom experienced was transferred further with me.

HUDSON: I was talking to Pauline Reese's husband last night, and he said that Texas music today is still a boys' club.

CHARLENE: We really never wanted to draw a line around our music. You have the purists in any field, and I just shy away from that.

More anthems, more rodeos, more songs, and lots of traveling are the name of the game for us.

Pauline Reese

HONKY-TONK REIGNS

I first heard Pauline performing a solo acoustic set at the Too Damn Friendly Bar in Johnson City. Catherine Powers and Lee Duffy told me to check her out. Pauline, a fan of Freddy Powers, may be slight in her physical appearance, but her voice and performance style embody the pure honky-tonk that Texans and Europeans love. When Pauline performed at the Broken Spoke on the evening of this interview, she had an entire group of tourists from Holland up dancing a line dance. They thought they had died and gone to honky-tonk heaven, dancing to Pauline Reese at the classic Broken Spoke dance hall in Austin, Texas. James White, Broken Spoke owner and Texas music aficionado, stood by watching and smiling from ear to ear. The Broken Spoke gave Alvin Crow a permanent home for some of the best honky-tonk in Texas, and it is the perfect showcase for Pauline Reese, with its wooden floor and uneven ceiling.

HUDSON: It is Wednesday night, July 31, 2002, the night after I first heard you in Johnson City. Tell me what you're working on right now. What's exciting? Plans?

REESE: Right now we have our brand-new CD out, *Trail to Monterrey*. This is not my first piece of work. I've done a lot of demo work in the past. Right now we're trying to get radio stations to listen to the album. We've hired a promoter, and we'll be going out on a radio tour to put a personality with the album. We're playing Gruene Hall in New Braunfels this Friday. It's a well-known Texas honky-tonk. We're playing there with a friend of mine, Houston Marchman. I played there once with Two Tons of Steel as well. Basically, we're just trying to get this music out there so people can hear it. We've had a lot of good things happen lately. I'm number sixteen on the progressive country chart. Right now it goes up and down on the Texas music chart. I'm going to be on the Johnny High Show in Arlington this Saturday. It's like a modern day Opry. Bill Mack is going to meet us there, and he's certainly been responsible for many careers. He's a wonderful guy. I've been on his radio show three or four times. We're getting a lot of response nationwide from these shows. John, my husband, is the master planner.

JOHN: We're playing with David Allan Coe on August 11 at a private party. She's going to open a show with Gene Watson in September.

HUDSON: What is one of your dreams?

REESE: Got enough tape? The biggest dream would be to sing a song with Willie Nelson. I know that you can get him to play on your album. I'd like to open for him, then sing a song with him. I'd love to sing with Emmylou Harris and Dolly Parton, as well.

HUDSON: Have you been a music lover all your life?

REESE: All my life. My mom was the choir director in our Catholic Church for years. Her mother did the same thing. My grandfather was a musician who played almost every instrument. He played bluegrass and country. They lived in Argentina and all around Mexico, so I had a lot of Spanish influence growing up. They used to play 45s of Spanish songs, and they used to speak in Spanish around me. The other grandparents are city folks. He played saxophone and big band music. I was surrounded by music growing up. There are eight kids in my family, and I'm number seven. They all sing, and they all have musical talent. And they choose not to. I'm not sure why. I think it's a waste of musical talent.

HUDSON: Has there been a turning point for you?

REESE: I've always known that I wanted to be a singer. When I was in the fifth grade and my parents recognized my ability as I sang "America, the Beautiful," I see that as a turning point. In Pittsburg, Texas, once, we had an opera singer come to class and sing. She held a note for such a long time, and I was so amazed that I wanted to belt it out just like she did. I practiced all the time. The main turning point in my life was when I met my husband.

I moved to Austin when I was twelve, joined a band at fourteen, and had my own band at sixteen. I've been playing in a band for about ten years now. My husband has been helping me the last three or four years. I like that teamwork. I don't know that I could do it without him. I don't think I would get very far. It's just a lot harder on women to be in this business. Contrary to what a lot of people think, there is still chauvinism going on. The good thing about a partnership with John is that he believes in me, and he's musically gifted. He even has a lot to do with the production of my CDs. He helps me pick out songs, and we even write songs together.

JOHN: It's tough for us to be normal when all we do is music, weekends included. I think it's rare that we are in this together.

REESE: I would like to say that Freddy Powers has helped me so much with my songwriting and my guitar. Redd Volkaert has helped a lot with guitar, as well.

HUDSON: How did you meet Freddy?

REESE: Fate. I met a senator's daughter, and she introduced me to Freddy and Catherine. We went over to his house one night, and I started hanging out with him. That was six years ago. We've gotten a lot closer the last four years since John has taken over a lot of the business responsibility. I can just go over and start playing with him now.

HUDSON: What kind of response are you getting to your music?

JOHN: A lot of times I hear people say, "I'm really not into country music, but I really like Pauline."

HUDSON: Her voice is a distinct honky-tonk voice.

JOHN: It doesn't really sound like anyone else. Really. I know when I first met Pauline and heard her sing, I wondered if I were the only person hearing how special she is. I mean, I knew her voice was way above average. Well, that was four years ago, and a lot has happened since then.

HUDSON: How long did it take for you to get together?

REESE: He asked me to marry him about five months after we started dating.

JOHN: I'd never been married before, but I felt like this was it.

REESE: I was nineteen when we met. He was thirty-three. It took him about two weeks to even call me after we met.

JOHN: Right. I was wondering about the age difference myself.

REESE: I think I grew up in the music business.

JOHN: I grew up listening to music. I was the guy listening to Robert Earl Keen before others were buying his stuff. For us to be doing this now is really neat for me. We get to hang around with the people I used to admire, and still do.

REESE: Yeah, Johnny Rodriguez, for example.

HUDSON: So you all are enjoying doing the business together. And you're bound to get a lot of comments about your appearance.

REESE: Yeah, I do. I grew up around rodeo and married a bull rider. My hat is shaped a little differently than everybody else's. My grandfather was a bronco rider. I like starched shirts and jeans and square-toed boots. Most of the time people are respectful of the fact that I'm married.

JOHN: Yeah, most think I'm real lucky.

HUDSON: How old are you now, Pauline?

REESE: I'm twenty-four now; I'll be twenty-five in November.

[Several months later I talked with Pauline after she sang at a rodeo in France. They put her on a stallion, and she ran into the arena, ready to sing, and ended up doing her own bronco exhibition. She did a great job, and the French loved her. And they loved her song after the horse settled down. Not many Texas women have that story.]

REESE: You have to have a lot of faith and a lot of friends to be successful in this business. You have to surround yourself with a lot of good people in this business. You have to have family. I think that's why Willie Nelson calls his band a family. After you get to know someone well, and they help you with different things, they become your friend and a surrogate family.

JOHN: If I thought Pauline was just kind of good, I would have talked her out of it. The business is rough. I would not want to go through this as husband and wife if she did not have a good shot at being very successful.

REESE: Right. We don't have much time together, really.

JOHN: Always together, never alone. Until about three in the morning sometimes!

HUDSON: Let's talk about a song that you've written.

REESE: I've been half-assed writing for the last seven years or so. I didn't get serious until I met John. I was just a teenager and busy with other things. He helps me focus and prioritize. I don't think you can be creative when you're stressed out. Most of the songs come to me at home, often late at night. I tend to sit down on the kitchen floor. I live in an old 1928 farmhouse, with screen doors and wooden floors. I just love our house. We restored it ourselves so, of course, it is not finished. I like to listen to the crickets and feel the breeze coming in, so I often just open all the doors and windows. Turn off the air conditioner!

HUDSON: That's how I live.

REESE: One of the first songs I wrote at this house is called "Rainy Day Night." It reflects that moment when the rain first starts, you feel that breeze, and you smell that fresh smell that is so relaxing. I decided to write about that. I started out . . . it was horrible, or so I thought. I got to the end, and I decided it was awful. Then I said, "Somebody help me write a song here." After saying that, I came up with another idea, and I wrote that down in about two minutes. A lot of songs happen that way.

HUDSON: When you let go?

REESE: Yes, just like singing. You can't push it. You have to sit back and relax.

HUDSON: I heard that last night and really like it.

REESE: My brother and his girlfriend broke up. I don't know where in the hell this song came from. We were watching a movie, and I started thinking about him and his girlfriend. I said, "I have an idea, press pause." I grabbed some paper and wrote it in a few minutes. I came back in and played it for my husband and my brother. They loved it. But my brother said, "Why would you write a song from her point of view?" He doesn't really like it. The title is "Not Tonight." Recently I was thinking about Willie Nelson, and I ended up writing a song. I started a song as a waltz and wrote it in five or ten minutes. I didn't really like the music, but I lived with it for about four weeks. I was relaxing at my brother's house, and it popped into my head. This song should be a polka! "Remember November" now has a Spanish flair to it. And I thought of some of the songs my grandfather played for me.

HUDSON: So you don't have a particular writing method?

REESE: No. I do think I write better in early morning or late at night.

HUDSON: Let's end with a comment on your influences.

REESE: Kate Wolf. She is a folk musician. Her writing is phenomenal. Dolly Parton, of course. And one of the biggest influences, Emmylou Harris. I love her voice. I love the music that she chooses, and the music that she writes. Those are my top three. Kim Richey is also a great song-writer.

[I sent this interview to Pauline in September. Here are her final words.]

Wow, since we last talked, so much has happened! I have accomplished most of my goals since the last time we talked, and I've now set a whole bunch of new ones! As far as the *Trail to Monterrey* CD, it did very well for us. It got us national attention with XM-Satellite Radio. It was nominated for Album of the Year, and Song of the Year for "Trail to Monterrey," which helped me get nominated for Entertainer of the Year, as well as Rising Star, by the Academy of Western Artists. Three of the singles released got into the top twenty and one in the top ten on the Texas music chart.

Our new CD, *The Good, the Bad, and the Ugly*, is catching some attention as well. It was one of the top CDs at Waterloo Records the first week it was released. It was chosen as one of the top twenty CDs of 2004 by *Best in Texas Magazine* and Texas/Oklahoma radio. It received an honorable mention as the best in the national publication *Country Standard Time*. And the song "One Less Honky Tonk" that Freddy Powers and I wrote was awarded one of the top ten songs of 2004 by the *Austin Chronicle*, as well as climbing the Texas/Oklahoma chart to number fifteen.

Our new single, "The Cowboy Way," was released last week, just in time for rodeo season! Speaking of rodeo, we picked up a wonderful sponsorship from Bad Company Rodeo, a national rodeo contracting company. I am very honored to be part of the Bad Company family! We'll be ridin' and pickin' in a town near you!

Another sponsorship which has helped the band out tremendously is from Martin Audiology out of Waco, Texas. They make our in-ear monitors, and the show has never been better!

Some folks I've really enjoyed working with are the Anheuser-Busch family. We are currently sponsored by Bud Light and Michelob Ultra (which happened to be what I was drinking before we got sponsored).

They have helped us out at many a show, and I am forever grateful.

One more company I can't thank enough is Elixir Strings! With our hectic schedule these days, I go through a lot of guitar strings. I use the Poly Web strings, and they last three times as long as the non-coated kind, which means less time stringing my guitar and more time playing it.

My band I'm traveling with these days is great! All three of them seem to connect. We all have our sights set on the same brass ring!

As I mentioned above, I have accomplished most of my goals from last year. One of those was to do a duet with Willie Nelson, which has happened! I have become better friends with Willie as well as his band. They are the kindest bunch of guys in the music biz! They are all about helping young talent get recognized. Willie has had me sit in and sing with him as well as open for him at a number of shows around Texas, including his Fourth of July picnic, which we will be performing at this year. Look for our duet on my new album; it's called "Pick Up the Pieces," a song I co-wrote with my friend Ronnie G. Slimp. He also cut a video for his next single, "Big Booty," where I play the part of the other woman who steals Poodie (Willie's longtime stage manager) from his girlfriend. At the end of the video, Willie steals me from Poodie! It's a hilariously fun video, and I can't wait for it to come out! I would like to thank Poodie Locke for introducing me to Willie and making sure he heard my music. Poodie has been a huge factor in keeping John and me positive in these grueling times. We love him like family!

I've been singing the National Anthem at many events around the state and overseas. The biggest crowd has been at the University of Texas football games in front of 83,000! So much fun! I've sung at various rodeos, including one in France. John, the band, and I did a tour in France and Sweden. The show in France was in a small town . . . where they hold an exhibition rodeo and music show once a year. John entered the bull riding and made the U.S. proud! I entered the barrel racing for fun and sang the National Anthem on horseback—which was entertaining in itself. The horse should've been entered in saddle bronco riding! The show after the rodeo was a blast. They love country music in France; who would've thunk it?

Things in the future are a tour in Switzerland with Freddy Powers and our bands. We are headed to Chihuahua, Mexico, next month to play a huge club filled with country music fans. This will be an adventure to talk about! More anthems, more rodeos, more songs, and lots of traveling are the name of the game for us. We are currently traveling all over Texas and spreading our sights beyond the borders. Check out our new website and come honky-tonkin' when you can! Thanks to Kathleen Hudson for telling the world about WOMEN in country music.

I wanted to have a band of my own, write my own music . . . have a regular gig, make a CD, write songs in Austin, play the Fourth of July picnic with Willie . . . just outrageous things. Within eight months they had all come true.

Lee Duffy

A LIFE OF MIRACLES

I first met Lee Duffy backstage at a Merle Haggard concert at the John T. Floore Country Store in Helotes, Texas, on April 12, 2002. Catherine Powers introduced us. Freddy Powers was onstage playing guitar with Merle, playing some of those songs that Freddy wrote. Catherine heard me say I was interviewing women in Texas music, and she said, "You must meet Lee Duffy. She has a great story to tell." I became intrigued with what she told me and immediately turned on my ever-present tape recorder.

HUDSON: Let's start that story again.

DUFFY: I had a band in Austin for about ten years, about eighteen years ago. I was doing several things, and Willie gave me his studio to record in with no time limit and two engineers, Bobby Arnold and Larry Greenhill. We got about a dozen songs down, then we just shelved it. I had a four-year-old and was pregnant, and I knew I couldn't have kids and promote a recording. You could do one or the other. So I gave it up and chose to raise my own kids. I don't play an instrument or read music, but I really missed singing. I love that with all my heart. It's so hard to make a living as a musician, anyway. Even if you play everything. So, the opportunity of being hired to sing harmony was slim or none. One evening, on a new moon, I wrote down ten things I wanted to do with my friend Lana. I wanted to have a band of my own, write my own music, which I had never done, have a regular gig, make a CD, write songs in Austin, play the Fourth of July picnic with Willie . . . just outrageous things. Within eight months they had all come true. I felt like an imposter. I felt afraid to wake up. I've been very, very, very blessed. I've played Willie's picnic and recorded with Merle Haggard. I've recorded about twenty songs. I'm totally blessed every day that I wake up.

HUDSON: What do you attribute that to?

DUFFY: [long pause] Prayer? I don't know. I feel like I'm blessed and it keeps coming. Recently, I wrote a song with Stephen Doster for the Coalition Against Family Violence. For me, to write a positive song that might help other women and children was a real joy.

HUDSON: Are you familiar with Darcie Deauville and the one-woman show that she wrote?

DUFFY: Yes, and I was very proud of her for having the guts to do that. Because it takes a lot of guts to sit up there and say, "This is me." That's how we get over our fears, to face them.

HUDSON: Were you paying attention to music all those years you did not perform?

DUFFY: No. I was singing at church and for the kids. I did have a band with my group of friends, the Hormones, my girlfriends with children, and we called ourselves the "We Bad Band." We had a rule that if you could play an instrument, that it was NOT the one you played in the band. That put us all on the same level of not knowing. Just bored women entertaining ourselves.

[On June 6, 2002, I met with Lee Duffy and Catherine Powers at the Hill Country Cupboard in Johnson City at 10:30 a.m. I immediately felt the support that women can provide. I immediately felt related. Lee, a woman past the age of fifty, was beaming with excitement and love. She couldn't say enough about the blessing her life has become. Her story reveals the power of intention. After listing ten of her outrageous dreams, at the suggestion of Lana Nelson, she wakes up at the end of a year to witness the completion of this list. Now that's magic to some and a blessing to Lee. I say that speaking

our dreams and wishes is the most powerful way to create the possibility of fulfilling them.]

HUDSON: I want to weave your stories together. We were talking to Lee about her participation in the Texas music scene, and I want to talk to you, Catherine, about being a woman in the Texas music scene and where your voice makes a difference. Let's talk about what you're working on now, Lee.

DUFFY: I'm working on a project right now. I have a song on KLBJ, which has really been a trip for me. The Coalition Against Victims of Family Violence approached Stephen Doster, a songwriter in Austin, and asked him to write a song for a CD that was going to raise money for the national hotline for family violence. I would have said yes if he'd asked me to write a song about frogs or anything just because of who he is. I was so excited that he asked me to write. It turned out to be a subject that I'd never have written about myself: family violence. I was in a situation in my first marriage that was short and semi-sweet, and we had a problem with family violence. We wrote this song together. It turned out that they liked the song very much. I went to an interview about the song, and it was incredibly moving because when I wrote this song . . . it's a song about a survivor, and the first lines are "Today she's living well after all she's been through." I was basically singing this song for "them." It was not as if I were one of them. My situation was thirty years ago. That day I was sitting in their reception area. It's like a lockdown area, high security. I was sitting there, and about four feet away from me is a cutout of a woman. They have wooden cutouts of all the women that have been lost, and they are painted red and standing in the hall. About two hundred of them. They have these brass plates of Texas on them with a name engraved. As I was sitting in this area, I started to flash back to the day that I left, that I actually got out. I look over to my left and see this cutout woman, and I realize that just by the grace of God I got to be the one in the chair writing this song instead of a red cutout character. I feel so totally blessed. Then I met the women who work there. They are incredible women. All day long women call in from all over the United States and literally have just left their house or are trying to. When these women who work there met me, they had tears in their eyes, saying, "Thank you very much. This song is going to save lives." On the way home I'm listening to the song in a new way. Doster is singing the song, and I hear my own story. "You Can't Touch Her Anymore." I heard him singing that to me. I had to stop the car. It rocked me. It was very healing. It was released originally by KLBJ, on the album *Guitar Slingers*. Stephen Bruton has a cut on the album, along with Ray Benson, David Grissom, and Bill Carter, one of my favorites. Sales on the first 5,000 copies go to help the hotline. Then after that they are going to release it nationally. Each performer donated a song to the album. I think our song is the only one written specifically for this project. They've asked me to perform at their national conference in October, and I feel very blessed to be able to give something back.

HUDSON: I hear you addressing the power of writing to reveal things that you don't even know are there.

POWERS: Music can change lives, destroy lives, and save lives. This is a good thing Lee is doing.

HUDSON: Tell me about the co-writing process with Stephen.

DUFFY: It was very interesting to me. Let's go back a bit. I have a weekly gig at the Texacalli Grill. Let's go back more. I raised two kids. I had a band in Austin in the 1970s to mid-1980s called the Leonard Mitchell Band. And I also sang backup with the Geezinslaws. I made a living playing music back then. It was easier. We played the Armadillo and emmajoes. I got married and had two children. You can either have children or have a band. You can't have both, really. It's the way I saw it. I had Angela when I was thirty, and I had Colin when I was thirty-four, and I knew that it made a difference to put time in when they are little. For other people it might be easier, but for me, I could not share my time. My husband had a night gig running his martial arts school. I did the mom thing until the kids were older, and now they are twenty-two and eighteen. They need me in theory, but they don't need any mothering right now. I was totally devastated and at a loss for who I was in my life. I did the mom thing; I was head of the PTA and did the dance lessons. I was totally into what they were doing and into my husband's career. He went from brown belt to seventh-level black. I knew what they were going to do with their lives; they were moving on. I realized that I had no life. My life had become their life. I had chosen this, and it worked well at the time. But now I was taking up space at the house. I loved music, and I missed it. I don't play an instrument, and I don't know anything about music theory. I just sing from my head. I'm number eleven of thirteen children.

POWERS: You sing from your heart!

DUFFY: Right. There were always teenagers in my family. I went through every form of music that came in. I was born in Oklahoma and raised in Arkansas. I moved to Dallas when I was fourteen. I was happy with the way my life had gone. I felt very good as a mom and a wife, but I did not feel like I was living my life anymore. Two things happened. One, I met Freddy Powers through Rattlesnake Annie and became an immediate fan of his. I got to go to a pickers' circle and hear Freddy do all these songs that he'd written for Merle [Haggard], whom I love. Freddy had moved back to town. I reconnected with Freddy and Catherine. Two, Kimmie Rhodes called me about a play she was doing out at Willie's with Joe Sears. She asked me to sing harmony with her on this song she had written called "Our Father's Face." I had absolutely no idea; I didn't get the Joe Sears connection; I'm dumb as dirt. I had no idea what they were doing, or I'd never have had the guts to go out there and sing. So, I show up out there, assuming there would be a small group. It turned into this thing called "Stone Soup." Kimmie selected her friends to share their talents. It turned out to be a gourmet dinner with everyone putting their part in. It turned out to be a play Kimmie co-wrote with Joe Sears called "West Texas Heaven," named after one of her CDs. It's about her life. Catherine and Freddy live right out there by the location in Luck, Texas. Catherine was there to be with Freddy. She was very kind and encouraging.

HUDSON: Yes, I always knew that about Catherine. She is the voice of encouragement for lots of people, myself included.

DUFFY: I was petrified. She was saying, "You're doing great. Don't let them see you sweat. You look good." She helped me out, and we really connected again. After that play, they wrote another play called "Hillbilly Heaven," and they wrote a part for me. I played Tammy Wynette, and I got to do a damn solo. Go figure. I remember looking at the invitations that said "Starring Joe Ely, Freddy Powers, Kimmie Rhodes, Jimmie Dale Gilmore, Lee Duffy, Maryann Price." It felt like *Sesame Street* with "One of these things just doesn't belong here." Freddy and David Zetner were in the band. To have them both on the same stage was incredible.

HUDSON: Let's talk about that writing.

DUFFY: I was in one of my desperate moments. I was whining to my girlfriend Lana Nelson, saying, "I want to sing, and I'm not. Wah . . . wah . . ." She said, "What would you do if you could do anything?" I couldn't come up with anything. Lana suggested that I write down everything I might want to do. It was a new moon, so I wrote down these ten things that were just outrageous. I wanted to have my own band. I wanted to write songs. I wanted to have my own CD. I wanted to sing with Freddy Powers. I wanted to have a weekly gig, which is so rare in Austin. I wanted to sing with somebody famous. I wanted to do some recording.

POWERS: She did every bit of the list the first year. Including singing vocals with Merle Haggard.

DUFFY: I was afraid to wake up. It just kept falling in my lap. I went from that play to a session with Freddy and Merle when they were working on a CD. It turned out at that moment they were doing "Motorcycle Cowboy," and they needed some harmony singers. So, of course, Catherine and Freddy suggested that I sing. My heart was beating so hard. I thought, "My God, you're going to record with somebody famous." I could see the next thing on the list coming true. It was a wonderful night; Merle was fabulous. I got to see him record in the studio, and I think he's one of the top two singers in the world. Right up there with Willie.

HUDSON: I asked Catherine to recommend a woman I needed to interview for this book. She said, "Absolutely Lee Duffy. Let me tell you about her." She provided so much support for my first book by inviting me to her house to visit with Darrell Royal and Willie and Freddy. She made me so comfortable there. I really see Catherine as a woman weaving many threads together.

DUFFY: That's because she's my best friend. She didn't just open the door for me. She opened the door, put me in the damn car, and drove me there. Freddy invited me to Coach Royal's golf tournament with all the best singer/songwriters in the world. Freddy is his sidekick. Freddy runs the pickin' part of the show. He knew how shy I was, and it's hilarious to see that at other times I can't shut up. But, if I'm in front of a microphone, I can't speak. I was petrified that I wasn't good enough. Freddy was in the middle of singing "Riding High," from his country jazz album. The first line is "They told us we would never reach the top. They told us we would probably not." I love it. I had jammed with him a few times at his house because he was just pulling it out of me. I would show up there everyday. He leaves his guitar and microphone out 24/7. He would get up early and play until lunch. I would just ask for every song I knew. Catherine found this satchel of a couple of hundred songs that he had written, which they found under a bed in Tyler at her mom's. He would just sort through them; he'd forgotten about five hundred of them. Like diamonds. So Freddy knew I would never sing out loud in front of all these people. He's in the middle of his show, in a room of singer/songwriters, trained professionals, and I'm minding my own business talking to Coach Royal, so excited that Freddy is singing "Riding High." I heard him introduce me as this wonderful singer and friend of his. I was melting. He doesn't play this in the same key I sing, and I heard him say to the band, "We're going to change this to the key of A." He just looked at me and smiled. You can't say no to Freddy. What could I do? I had to sing.

POWERS: She kept her back to Coach all the time.

DUFFY: I couldn't look at anyone I knew. There was this younger guy about five feet way. He was lifting me up with his smile. I just tagged him and sang to him. He turned out to be Matthew McConaughey. He was darling, a wonderful guy and a great drummer! He liked my singing, so I kept singing to him. They asked me to sing a couple more songs. It was a night I will never forget.

HUDSON: Where are you going now with the singing and recording?

DUFFY: I have in my possession my first CD. I'm going to turn it in this afternoon. I wrote twelve songs, and Gabe Rhodes, Kimmie's son, produced it. I don't play guitar, and I've thought that it was too late for me to learn. Catherine gave me one of Freddy's guitars to learn on. I was a nervous wreck having this guitar with me, so I gave it back. I went to Gabe Rhodes and asked for a guitar lesson. I had this song stuck in my head that I'd written. I played it for Catherine at the Luck gig, and she said, "That's a great song." I got my nerve up and sang it to Joe Gracey, one of my heroes and Kimmie's husband. He said to change one word, so I did. I sang it to Gabe, and he asked if I had any more. I have lots of songs that I hear in my head. I can tell you what the music is doing, bass and horns. I can hum or whistle the song. It's hard to tell someone what music is in your head if you don't play. Gabe, by the grace of God, had been playing with Kimmie so many years that he listens in a certain way. He played it back to me, and it was gorgeous. He actually was hearing the music. He went on tour with Jimmie Dale Gilmore to do the Jimmie Rodgers thing in New York. He came back after learning about forty songs on that trip, but he still had my song playing in his head. It was very empowering for me. I had another song by that time, and I gave that to him. He called the next day saying,

"My mom's out of town for a few days. Let's go in and use the studio and record some of your songs." I went over there, and it was like magic. It was first takes. I'd make the coffee, and he'd set up the mikes. We just did it. Now I have twelve songs on that CD, and I'm working on my second one, for kids under thirty, called "You Have to Be Present to Win."

POWERS: She's going to Europe again this year. Her CD will debut at the Col-des-Roches music festival in Switzerland on June 22. The album is called *Lee Duffy,* and Gabe Rhodes produced it.

DUFFY: Freddy took me last year to sing at a festival. It was pretty much magic. He took me as a backup singer. He's been doing this for fifty years, and he plays with top musicians in the world. I got to meet Sonny Throck-morton, Sonny James, Aaron Barker and, of course, Merle. I got to see them work and meet the other musicians. Things I would not get to do in this lifetime, Freddy and Catherine made possible. Freddy is seventy years old, and I'm like a youngster around him. I saw Freddy help lots of people, including Bill McDavid. I pay very close attention to what Freddy says; he taught me a lot about basic things like "People aren't going to hear your songs if you don't sing them." He also said, "If it sounds good to you, if you like it, it's good! It's for you." Now my whole approach to music is not whether or not I'm good enough. I'm not for everybody, but if it sounds good to me, it's all good. When I see other performers, I don't think if it's good or bad. I just notice whether it's for me or not.

HUDSON: Both of us call Catherine, the red-headed stranger there, our inspiration. Freddy and Catherine are a beautiful couple. I love the way they take care of each other. Catherine, let's talk about your story as wife, friend, and lover to Freddy.

POWERS: I grew up in a family of wannabe musicians and singers. Every time my father would start singing, we'd go, "Burn it, burn it." And we weren't talking about CDs. I took some piano lessons and sang in the school choir. I've learned a lot about music being with Freddy. He's trained my ears. We've been together sixteen years. I know a lot about the guitar. I can make chords, tell you the circle of fifths and explain that to you, but as far as playing it, I can't. My right hand has no rhythm. I love to sing. Give me a shower, and I'll sing my heart out. I had shows at Lake Tahoe where I deliberately sang off-key—part of the jokes in the show. I was an auctioneer. Freddy used to come see me at my shows and bring other girls. Then they would tell me, "He's crazy about you." We ended up getting together. Actually, he stole me from his son's best friend. We didn't want anybody getting their feelings hurt, so we had a secret affair for about a year and a half before we came out and said, "Hey." We were together about six years before we got married. I also booked him. I learned about the business that way. Freddy's the third musician in my life. I guess in some ways I was bound to be with a musician, and it's a real honor to be married to one of the best in the business. I'm always ready to help. I like being involved. And sometimes I get frustrated when I know how badly Freddy wants to be singing. Being married to a top-notch musician has its own set of challenges. It's hard to watch him come back from a tour and know he wants to still be out there performing. Handling the down time. There's a lot of work in Austin, but there's no money. Freddy might be glad to work for no money, but he can't ask his musicians to do that. We end up doing a lot of picking parties at our own house with other musicians, just so they can pick and perform.

DUFFY: She's making everything work for Freddy, and I think it's hard for her to see that there's time for her in there. That's not part of what she sees as her role and her life. She's got ten thousand stories! They know everybody in the damn world. Some of the stories are hysterical. Both Catherine and Freddy have a great sense of humor.

HUDSON: As we get to the end of this tape, let's share a favorite story.

DUFFY: One of the sweetest little moments was one night when I got to go on the tour with Freddy and Merle. Merle had us up to his room, a handful of us. Freddy was playing rhythm, and Merle was playing lead. I had to pinch myself to believe this was happening in front of me. I got to see Freddy do some songwriting, and I got to experience Merle working on a couple of songs. Incredible. I've had so many beautiful moments in my life. I've been around Willie's studio for thirty years through my association with Lana, his daughter and my best friend. Everybody has recorded at the Pedernales studio. For that to be in my life and be so cool is part of the blessing of my life.

HUDSON: What's something you like to remember? First thought, best thought.

POWERS: The mornings waking up with Freddy Powers when he would sneak our houseboat out into the middle of the lake and serve me coffee. Waking me up with "Peg of my heart, I love you." That's my life with Freddy.

HUDSON: How would you like to be remembered, Lee?

DUFFY: I hope they say that I was a good wife, a good mother, and a good friend.

POWERS: And a good entertainer.

DUFFY: And a total entertainer.

POWERS: That I was always there to help anybody I could. Between my admiration for my husband and grandkids, I couldn't have had it any better.

[In September 2004, I asked Lee to add a postscript to this conversation.]

Since the interview, I have continued to be blessed. My first CD came out, and I have a second one that is almost finished. On both of those CDs I wrote all of the songs. Then there is another CD I am working on that Freddy Powers is producing, which consists of pop standards. We have four songs recorded so far.

I became·involved with the Austin Songwriters Group and was voted their president for 2004. Through my association with ASG I have been involved in a number of projects: I produced the cable television series "ASG presents Austin Songwriters in the Round" for the Austin Music Network and taped two seasons of shows (approximately thirty episodes). I planned and produced ASG's 2004 Fall Songwriting Symposium and brought in instructors Jim Photoglo, Freebo, Kimmie Rhodes, Joe Gracey, Stephen Doster, Bobby Arnold, Monte Warden, and others.

Aside from the ASG I produced several music DVDs with artists such as Freddy Powers, Sonny Throckmorton, Johnny Rodriguez, Deborah Allen, and Bruce Channel.

I sang harmony on Merle Haggard's song "Motorcycle Cowboy" and have had the opportunity to sing harmony with him on several of his live performances.

I performed in two musical plays co-written and starring Kimmie Rhodes and Joe Sears [of Greater Tuna fame]. The plays were *Small Town Girl* and *Hillbilly Heaven*. I also worked with both of them as a production assistant in their musical play *Windblown*.

I played the Col-des-Roches International Country Music and Bluegrass Festival in Col-des-Roches, Switzerland, with Freddy Powers in 2002 and 2003 and am returning to play it again in 2005.

As I said, my life continues to be blessed and I look forward to whatever opportunity the future holds for me. It's all good.

If you want to be negative and waste your time, it's a choice. Mostly I feel blessed and focus on that energy.

Shemekia Copeland

A WILD, WILD WOMAN

I had spent some time with the late Johnny Copeland, the Texas Twister. He had served on the founding board of the Texas Heritage Music Foundation in 1987. I first met him at the Navasota River Bottom Blues Festival. His love for Texas was surpassed only by his love for his family. I had heard of his young daughter. When her first CD came in the mail from Alligator Records, memories of her dad flashed through my mind. In 2002, after the Young Rhetoricians Conference, I made my way to the Monterey Bay Blues Festival to hear Shemekia Copeland. I gave her a copy of my first book, which included an interview with her dad. The next year my sister, Carolyn, accompanied me on this California visit. She was just getting out of a thirty-two-year marriage and experiencing some of her own freedom and energy. The sister energy now present in my life informed the interviews I was doing with women. I was glad she was with me for this conversation with Shemekia at the Carmel River Inn on June 26, 2003, before her Sunday show. Shemekia strutted across the stage, challenging all women to stand up. We had the following conversation before her show.

COPELAND: My dad had this ability to look right into a person and know whether their heart was good or evil. I think sometimes he thought maybe he could change how he saw a person as well. I certainly didn't approve of all the people around my dad. Now this guy [pointing to the man with her] came to see my dad in a club when I was about fifteen. I didn't know where the dressing room was, and he pointed it out to me. He, Damon, became friends with my dad and friends of the family. Now I'm stuck with him. I just can't get rid of him. [laughter]

HUDSON: I appreciate the way Damon kept in communication with me as I set up this conversation.

COPELAND: Well, it's been a long time now. I'm not trying to get rid of him.

HUDSON: Every time I saw Johnny he encouraged me to keep up my work in Texas music. I know you have been performing for a while, and you are quite young. You have three albums behind you right now. Let's talk about the challenges in your young life.

COPELAND: From when I was a child until I was fifteen, I lived right in the middle of the ghetto. For the first thirteen years of my life, I was kept in the house, enclosed. Oh, I traveled to Europe with my dad, but my life at home was enclosed. We weren't stoop kids. I wasn't allowed to do that. That's where kids just hang out around the porch of a building. My parents always said that my friends could come into my house, but I could not just hang out outside. I had a lot of friends that just got killed. Murdered. It wasn't the bad kids that got killed. It was the good kids, the ones trying to do something with their life. That bothered me a lot. We moved to Jersey when I got older. When I was about sixteen, my father got really sick. He went from okay to drastically ill in a matter of a couple of months.

HUDSON: Fathers have such a strong influence on a young woman.

COPELAND: He was strong. I grew up with him. I couldn't look out the window without his knowing it. He wasn't there every day, but he called and checked on us every day. My mom would let me go to a party because she trusted me. I had three older sisters by a different mom. They were all pregnant by sixteen. I think Dad had that fear for me. My mom kept telling him that I was different; I wanted more for myself. My best friends now have four kids each. I didn't know I wanted to sing, but I knew I didn't want that. I had traveled at a young age. I was nine and in Spain. I knew I wasn't going to be in the ghetto my whole life. I knew I was going to get out of there. I didn't want any little brats tagging along behind me while I'm doing my thing. Oh, eventually, one day, I'd like to be married and do that whole thing. Not now.

HUDSON: What is your biggest challenge now at your age?

COPELAND: The music business is hard. I see all this terrible stuff going on, and you can't do anything about it. I try really hard not to put energy toward things I can't change. Seeing someone without any talent becoming very successful is hard for me, but I don't want my energy going there. It's a waste of time. I can put my energy into my own career.

HUDSON: I don't think people really realize that we have a choice where we put our energy.

COPELAND: Exactly. If you want to be negative and waste your time, it's a choice. Mostly I feel blessed and focus on that energy. I've come a long way in a short time. I'm twenty-four now.

HUDSON: It would look to most people like you have already achieved your goals. You're playing huge successful festivals, like the Monterey Bay Blues Festival. You've traveled around the world. You have great label support. What's left?

COPELAND: I want to take blues to another level. You know what I mean? I don't want to be the type of artist that gets away from the blues because the money isn't there. I want to be the one that takes blues to that next step.

HUDSON: You mean a wider audience base?

COPELAND: I'm not singing, "My man done left me." I'm singing, "I'm a wild, wild woman."

HUDSON: We need that!

COPELAND: We're not oppressed. We're strong and talented. We run this world. Everybody needs to know that. We're powerful now. I like to put women in a position of power. Don't get me wrong. I love men. I don't want to be on this earth without them. I think they were made for us, and we should all have one. [All three of the women laugh at this.] Or two or three! It's not about bashing men. It's about making you confident. Some of the compliments I get are from women who are larger than they want to be. They say, "You make me feel confident and happy about who I am, seeing you up there dancing around in your miniskirts. When I see you being happy with who you are, it makes me happy with who I am." I love hearing those comments. That's important.

HUDSON: That's deep wisdom.

COPELAND: Don't get me wrong. There's days I wake up thinking, "Oh, I need to lose fifty pounds." I'm not always accepting myself. Then you realize what you have. I'm not going to grow. I'm five foot nothing. Wishing to be different isn't going to bring me much happiness. Accepting myself as I am now brings me peace.

HUDSON: I guess everyone who interviews you talks about your age.

COPELAND: They do, and to me it's not that big a deal. All these women, Koko [Taylor], Etta [James], Ruth [Brown], Irma Thomas, all started early. Maybe it was more common back then for a young black woman to be doing blues.

HUDSON: Let's talk a little about your label.

COPELAND: I've done some really great things with Alligator. I think I came as a shock to Bruce, being as opinionated as I am. Shemekia's going to do what Shemekia wants to do, or there's nothing going to be done! You know what I mean? I choose my own songs and music. I pick out what I want. My latest album, *Talking to Strangers,* includes some really hip songs. The first album was a lot more bluesy. I felt like a rock-and-roller on the second album, *Wicked.* I wanted to do the Tina Turner thing. I wanted to rock. My last album I wanted to do the New Orleans funk thing, R&B. My manager, John Hahn, has his name on a lot of the songs. We collaborated. He knows me, and he knows my mind. I met him when I was eight years old. He produced my father's records. It was funny, because my father was dealing with a person who wasn't helping him do anything. I won't mention any names. He was a Grammy award–winning artist who didn't even have a record label. So John hired him to do a commercial. He asked Dad why he didn't have a label. Then John went to work on finding him one. That's how he got with Verve. John wrote me my first blues tune when I was twelve. When I was eight, I used to say, "This is John Hahn, my manager." He's been with me sixteen years now. That's a long time.

HUDSON: What about the writing for you?

COPELAND: Yeah, at this point I am writing. I wasn't before. I wrote very little on the first two albums. I was not so much scared to write, as I was scared of what I might say. You know what I mean? I still have that fear. Right now I pick smart songs. I think that's as important as picking the right songs. I don't do political or insulting. I want it to mean something to me. And I appreciate humorous. Sometimes I'm nervous about what I might say! This business is political, and you have to say the right things. And I'm honest, but I believe there's a way to say things that don't hurt people.

HUDSON: Have you ever been criticized in a way that hurt you?

COPELAND: I got one bad review that I can think of. I was a lot less mad about it than he [pointing to Damon] was. We were in Seattle, and Damon asked me if I had yelled at the people at the radio station. Seems the criticism was that I was up there having fun.

HUDSON: Sounds like the thing to do!

COPELAND: I'm onstage. We're not a funeral here. It was obviously a more jazz guy who was used to a laid-back show. There ain't nothing laid-back about what I do onstage. He's just at the wrong damn show. I was playing at a club called Jazz Alley. They didn't book me because I played jazz. They heard my albums. I try not to let it bother me. Of course, it did. We're only human.

HUDSON: I talk to a lot about people who live life out of their center rather than out of their circumstances. I can tell that you do express who you are.

COPELAND: I just do what I do, and it comes naturally. I didn't learn it. It wasn't taught to me.

HUDSON: Any regrets?

COPELAND: No. I'm comfortable enough to say I've done it all right. I've done the right things. I've taken care of myself. My performances are all consistent. I work hard to make it that way. I haven't abused myself with drinking and drugs. There's a lot of things I live without so I can have a good show. I'm talking about little things too . . . like ice cream. I know the dairy is not good for me.

HUDSON: What do you imagine for yourself at fifty?

COPELAND: The same thing. Even more comfortably. I'd like to become a musician at some point and learn instruments. I'd like to take six months off and learn piano or guitar. I want to learn how to do the studio work so I can make my own records someday. At some point, I want to be making enough money where I can take time off. Hopefully, I'll have a husband of a few years and a family. Maybe I'll learn how to put up with a man for more than twenty minutes. [All three women laugh again.]

HUDSON: That is still something I'm learning!

COPELAND: I love it in Pennsylvania right now. It's beautiful, quiet and nice. I like the people there. I love traveling. Switzerland is great, but I can't imagine living there.

HUDSON: Do you still have family responsibilities?

COPELAND: I don't know what I would do without my mom. She's great. I remember all the sacrifices she made for all of us. I remember a time where my mom worked, and my dad did nothing. She believed in him, and she knew that he would make it someday. It took a lot of time for that to happen. So she supported his art. I've grown up to be a strong, supportive person. I'll tell you a story. My father used to go on these long tours. He'd come back with nothing. He paid the band and tried to get his name out there. One day I passed him on our stairs, and he asked me where I was going. I told him I had to borrow some money from one of our neighbors because we needed bread and a pack of cigarettes for my mom. That was the day he decided that he'd never go to work and come back without any money.

HUDSON: That's hard in the arts.

COPELAND: We were struggling. We were on welfare, and my mom totally believed in him. She raised both my brother and me. She went to college and had a four-point average. I felt bad for her. As soon as she went to work, she got sick with lupus. Now she's only fifty, and she has some heart trouble. You wouldn't know it by looking at her. I'm really happy I get to take care of her.

HUDSON: Does she ever get to travel with you?

COPELAND: If I'm going to go to Europe and stay in a place for a week, she'll go with me. Mostly she stays home now.

HUDSON: Do you ever play the smaller venues?

COPELAND: I do. Sometimes we play clubs. I have a great booking agent, Monterey. They have been really good to me. My drummer played with my dad for five years, Barry Harrison. On guitar is Arthur Neilson, a New York musician. On the keyboards, a young man named Jason Ladanye, who's the same age as I am. He's been with me about four years. I almost didn't hire him because of his age. On bass, Jason Langley, from Boston. All these guys are from New York. Of course, Damon Eppley, my road manager. I haven't killed them, and they haven't killed me.

HUDSON: Let's talk about favorites.

COPELAND: There are so many, and a lot of them are male. O. V. Wright is one of them. He has a great voice. As a kid, I wanted to sound like a dude! Sam Cooke and Joe Tex and Marvin Gaye and Al Green. I can't wait to see him today. I actually opened for him once with my dad years ago. I was about sixteen.

HUDSON: Favorite songs?

COPELAND: "I'm A Woman" by Koko Taylor. That song got me in trouble when I was a kid. I had my friends over when I was in elementary school. We went to school singing it, talking about making love to crocodiles. The teacher called the parents.

HUDSON: Have you had a Texas gig?

COPELAND: Not in a while. We did play that Dallas festival recently. There are no venues in Houston, unfortunately.

HUDSON: Who inspires you?

COPELAND: I really like Lou Ann Barton and Lucinda Williams. Lou Ann sounds like a slut when she sings. I think that's so cool. She's so sexy and so attractive.

HUDSON: I've known her since my Fort Worth days. I grew up with Ray Sharpe, Delbert McClinton, Juke Jumpers, and Lou Ann. We were in Montreux, Switzerland, together one year at the jazz festival. She has that something that women want.

COPELAND: I met her while I was doing Austin City Limits with Jimmie Vaughan.

HUDSON: "You can have my husband, but please don't mess with my man." That Texas twang.

COPELAND: And that's a lot different than a Southern twang.

HUDSON: What words of advice do you have for other women?

COPELAND: Be happy with yourself. That is such a hard thing to do at times. I see a lot of women hurt themselves and hurt their bodies. Stay away from the diet pills and all that stuff.

HUDSON: What is the key to that?

COPELAND: It's here. [points to her head] It's a mind thing. That's what I'm working on now.

HUDSON: I think it's about a gentle acceptance of life.

COPELAND: It's tough. I'm still learning how to do that. I just recently found out how young and impressionable I am! I listen a lot, and that's where the learning is for me. I just want to be happy about me. [We three women laugh again at the examples she gives.]

HUDSON: My granddaughters are mixed, and they are exotic and beautiful. I want the same for them.

COPELAND: My motto is if you can have a baby, then it was meant to be.

If God thought mixed races were not to be, then we would not be able to cross over and have these children. We're all human beings. We all belong together. In the next hundred years, we're all going to be mixtures. No one will be one of anything. People look at me and see African heritage. That might be true on my dad's side. My mom's heritage is all Indian. My great-grandparents had gray hair in braids that went to the floor. They were Blackfoot. I know I have Indian roots.

The truth might get me in trouble, but the Lord will set me free. . . .
All things are only what the Lord allows.

Jewel Brown

PRAYERS AND JOY

Roger Wood, author of Down in Houston, *recommended Jewel Brown to me as a "brilliant, charming storyteller." I met up with her at a restaurant in Houston, after an engaging phone conversation. She carefully tied a turquoise scarf around her head, matching the turquoise silk pantsuit she was wearing. I later found out that her brain surgery last year affected her otherwise thick hair and the scarf served as more than just a dramatic fashion statement. Born in 1937, this woman has many stories to tell, and she wants to tell them. At times she did say, "I'm not going to talk about this part," referring to some unpleasant business moments in her musical life with Louis Armstrong. We immediately bonded, our stories of faith and the importance of a spiritual foundation creating the closeness of sisters sharing life. Jewel's life as an insurance agent provides her with a frame for her music. She takes care of business and continues to honor her own creativity. She does not perform on a regular basis, but she does participate in conferences and most recently the 2004 New Orleans Jazz Fest.*

HUDSON: I appreciate your taking this time on a Sunday evening to talk with me about your life. Let's talk about why Roger recommended you so highly.

BROWN: I can't tell you. A man like Roger knows many, many people. I'm not a person to brag on myself. It's a privilege to know he feels that way. I know I have longevity; I've learned quite a bit in this life the hard way, on my own, by seeking wisdom from a higher power. Martin Luther King once said that longevity is a great thing. I agree. It can give you the time you need to "get it right." And at the same time it can also give you time to share what you've learned with others to help them along life's highway. We make the choices in how we live our life. I'm grateful as I fulfill my purpose.

HUDSON: My appreciation for the power of stories came from time spent with August McClary, my grandfather. Where did that start out in your life?

BROWN: My dad taught me from childhood to always listen, observe, and analyze. In doing so, that's how I think I've been able to see the truth in what I have been told. I attribute a lot to my father. I always say, "Thank God for Jesus, and thank Jesus for my father." He also taught me that the truth might get me in trouble, but the Lord will set me free. I believe that is good guidance. I'm not saying I'm an angel or a saint. I have found that no matter what you do, if you're living in truth, love, and peace, you can live a better life. My days are much further behind me than ahead of me. There comes a time to 'fess up so you can clean your mess up. You got to get real so you can heal. I just prefer to be real.

HUDSON: And how does music fit into this?

BROWN: The gospel and blues I heard led me right into the jazz I ended up singing. In my house, if you didn't go to church and perform in some churchly activities, you didn't get a chance to participate in other things. I'm glad my father forced this participation on us. It is a "raising" that affects your life. My father says, "You can stray away, but with the proper teaching you'll always stray back." My father was Baptist. My mother was Methodist, but when she married, she went Baptist.

HUDSON: I loved the music I heard in the Baptist church of my childhood, North Richland Hills Baptist Church.

BROWN: I asked my father once why he hadn't become a minister. He said the Lord never called him. He was deacon, president of the usher board, and treasurer. Everyone respected him. We had six children in my family, three boys and three girls. Praise God we are all still here. That's a blessing, and there's a reason.

HUDSON: I'm blessed to also have my parents with me. They are eighty and eighty-one now. I just spent three days with them, sharing breakfast each morning.

BROWN: I just did that with my dad. He passed on at age ninety-three. My mom had eight strokes and passed at age seventy. She played piano and would sing a little. I have a brother, Theodore, who has a great love for music. He is in the hospital. They have a piano on the seventh floor of the hospital. He pushes his IV stand and goes upstairs to play that piano twice a day.

HUDSON: I read about your singing and saw that picture of you with all that wild curly hair singing around a piano.

BROWN: Which they cut out when I had brain surgery last year. Everything so far has gone well. It was a brain tumor on the pituitary. I have God to thank, my Savior, my Keeper, my All. They say only two percent of all people make it through this. And I did not know this before I went into surgery. I know that all things are only what the Lord allows. I always relate to people who are troubled. I always take them back to Job. He was a perfect man, and the Lord allowed the devil to touch his life but not his soul. When my father spoke of this story, he explained it briefly. He said that God asked the devil where he was going one day. The devil said that he was going to Earth to see who he could devour. My father stopped and said, "He'll devour you and me and anyone else who will let him. You got to let him." In other words, it's a choice. Then God said, "Have you tried my servant Job?" This was a test of the time. Job hadn't done anything to deserve this. His wife and friends said, "You must have sinned. Just cuss God and die." Job said, "No, but for all my appointed days, I'll wait my challenge." People are saying, "Lord, why me?" Why not say, "Lord, why not me?" He uses us as he needs to. You know, I sell insurance. The manager of our staff said, "Keep it simple." I added that I like selling life insurance because it's just like life. I said all of that to say this one statement: Life is very simple. It's because of our greed and disobedience that it becomes difficult. If we just work on the simple truths of life, life becomes simple. I had to come to the realization at a late age that worry belongs to the devil. You can also say it like this: It's what you allow God to allow. [We continue to talk and agree philosophically.]

HUDSON: How does this attitude affect the way you've been in the music business?

BROWN: Anything I do, I look at what the Lord allows. I never went to school for music for one day. My brother taught me breath control. The entertainment business can be hard, but I know my limits, and I know my capabilities. I don't go outside my realm to try and prove to someone that I can be like them.

HUDSON: What are the challenges you have faced?

BROWN: [pause] I can say that what I was allowed to have fell in place for me. I had a drug dealer come up to me once, saying that he had something that would make me feel good. I told him no thanks. He then asked me, "Don't you want to sound like Ray Charles?" I said, "No, I want to sound like Jewel Brown." Here's why I was that adamant about being able to fluff him off. My father advised me, when I left home, to do good and remember that I had a home to come back to. He also said that if I got on drugs, I did not have a home anymore. My father was a man who said what he meant and meant what he said. He was a parent with tough love. I think a lot of our youth don't have enough of that. I think our youth need that. There is a song, "I Won't Complain," that I really like. My father is one of the main reasons that I won't complain in my life. I remember when my father had a bad back at fifty-three years old. After all his examinations, the doctor asked him what he did as a young man. My dad, with his Louisiana brogue, said, "We hardly et." Most of what they ate came out of a truck patch [garden] and they ate whatever they had. Ear of corn, head of cabbage. They just ate it raw. The doctor told him that he was eating lots of nutrients. He told him that his bone structure was that of a thirty-year-old man. Let's tie this in. My father was a very poor man, but he didn't complain. Now he has six children who also have strong bones. We don't question God. He's showtime.

HUDSON: Let's talk about the music.

BROWN: There are pitfalls in the music business. I leave what I want to leave where it is. Now, insurance is my priority. That's what takes care of me. I told my agent in New Orleans that I needed to keep this as a priority so I couldn't go out on long tours. I played piano early on. During my coming up, if you sang and played the piano, you got a musician's salary. If you just stood up and sang, you got a showgirl's salary. They were very different. You might get $10 or $15 for doing the gig, but you got $50 or

$100 for doing a show spot. That kind of discouraged me from wanting to be a musician at that time. I was asked in one interview, "Jewel, what has the blues done for you?" I said, "I'm not ashamed when you call my name." I grew up in rural conditions. I sang my way out of those conditions. As a little girl, we lived in a shotgun house. All eight of us were in one bedroom. But there was a whole lot of love in that house. I used to pray that I would find something to do to help them to get along. My father was illiterate but very wise. My mother was an educated woman but extremely modest. It turned out that one day in elementary school, the principal wasn't there and neither was my teacher. All the kids had gotten very unruly. Back in that day the teacher could whip you, your mama could whip you, your daddy could whip you. So, I just put my head down on my desk and went to sleep. As the assistant principal came in to corral the children, I thought I heard somebody say, "What do you want to be when you grow up?" But the real question was, "What is the young lady's name with her head on her desk?" I raised up quickly and said, "A singer." Where I got that from, I don't know. I was about nine. Just like I asked for something, I got it. My dad taught me to pray my most sincere prayer when things got to a place of choice. He also taught us not to borrow. If we need something, we can substitute or go without.

HUDSON: I know you played with Louis Armstrong from 1961 to 1968. How did that happen?

BROWN: I had worked with Earl Grant in Los Angeles, California. I was his featured singer. I had gone to California to see my sister, who had been in a car wreck. Her husband was a saxophone player, and he had friends in the clubs. We decided to go out and jam. An organ player named Louis Rivera really liked me, and he recommended me to his friend, Leroy Baskerville, and Earl performed in his club. Louis said, "They can afford you." I don't know what he meant by that, but I let that comment guide me in what I was going to ask for. When I got there, he introduced me as Jewel Brown from Houston, Texas. I did some numbers with him and some on my own. Earl went to the proprietor and said to hire me and give me whatever I wanted. In that era, "Looking Back" was strong. "Send for Me" was strong. Sam Cooke was hotter than a firecracker back then. And I did some of the blues songs. I did torch numbers. Then I ran into a guy named Jim Dolan who was over AGRA, the American Guild of Race Artists. He had this friend named Jack Ruby, and he wanted to change his club from a burlesque house to a nice supper club. They called me. I worked seven nights a week for over a year. I sang with Joe Johnston's band. After I did this, and Mr. Jack and I fell out about an "issue," I went to the Chalet Club, owned by Mr. T. J. Jeffers. In the process of all of this, because of a writer for the *Dallas Morning News*, Tony Zoppi, and Tony Pappa, head of the Dallas Booking Organization, I was in the paper every day. Across the street from the Sovereign Club where I was playing they had an entertainment room called the Century Room. The bellman would say to people, "Have you heard that little girl across the street?" So our place, the Sovereign Club, would stay packed every night behind a lot of people's recommendations. Velma Middleton, the female singer with Louis Armstrong, had passed on, and I guess they needed another feminine act. They started contemplating singers, and there were about 500 singers who wanted the job. I don't know who told who, but the word was out on me. I got this call, saying, "Girl, Louis doesn't really want another girl singer, but if we put anybody with the band, it will be you." I said, "Well, if you decide upon me, give me good advance warning." He called me one morning in Dallas and told me to be on a three o'clock flight out of Houston that same day. Therefore, back on that day, in June of 1961, I drove from Dallas in my little '57 Ford convertible at 100 to 120 miles per hour. I was stopped once by the state trooper. I told him I was going for my chance of a lifetime, and I started crying. He believed me and told me to go ahead and be careful. When he said that, I sped off again in front of him. I believe I made it in about two and a half hours. I got home and started throwing my best stuff in the suitcase. I gave my car to my brother, saying, "From now on a 707 is going to be my transportation." I got to the airport in less than ten minutes. I had just that little time. All the skycaps had been coming to Club Ebony to see me, and I asked them to hold that plane. "I've got to be there. I'm going to New York to join up with Louis Armstrong." They helped me find a back way, and I ran up the stairs to the plane. I slept from there to New York. When I went down the stairs, my first step was on the first step of the tour bus. Our first show that night was for George Weir at Storyville. Those guys played for me like they had been working with me for thirty years. I played in a lot of honky-tonks, and I learned a lot about the behavior and attitude of musicians. I think I was gracefully guided through all of that.

HUDSON: Do you write music?

BROWN: I wrote music with my first husband, my son's father. He was a very vain and egotistical kind of person. He didn't put my name on anything. That's life. There's a reason for that too. Now that he's passed on, my son gets the returns, so it still doesn't matter.

HUDSON: Do you have some songs recorded?

BROWN: We wrote an Eddie Fisher song, "Song of the Dream." [She sings it for me in the restaurant.] He wrote "It Should Have Been Me" for Ray Charles. I have a contract to sing November 14 with the Houston Blues Society at the Eldorado Ballroom.

HUDSON: Let's talk about how it was those years singing with Louis Armstrong. Were you aware that you were doing something big?

BROWN: I should have been. Do you know what it meant to me? Making a good living to take care of my mom and dad and my son. That was really where my head was. I did the *Shindig* show, *The Mike Douglas Show*. I went through Europe, Asia, and Africa. One night when I was not sleeping on the bus, Louis said, "What's the matter, baby, you can't sleep?" I said (and this was good therapy for me), "Pops, just thinking." He asked me what I was thinking about. I told him I was thinking about my family. He asked me if I was worried about them. I told him I was worried that they couldn't reach me anytime, any place. No cell phones then. I did always send them an itinerary. He said, "Let me put it to you like this. Where are we heading? What are you gonna do when you get there?" I told him I was going to stretch out my body and get some good sleep. Then he asked me what I was going to do when I was sleeping. I'm wondering where he's coming from, and I'm trying to answer as best I can. I said, "Well, I'll take a good hot soothing bath. Then I'll go to a bank and deposit what I can." He asks, again, what I am going to do. I tell him I'm going to send some money home. He said, "As far as I'm concerned, that is what you ought to do. And since that is what you do, don't worry about it at all!" You see what I mean? He was pointing out that I'm doing all I can do, so why worry and stay up thinking about it? What else can you do? So, go on and relax and keep doing what you're doing.

HUDSON: I know it was hard to be away from your family.

BROWN: I came home one time, after sending money for air conditioners, and saw them sitting up in the house sweating. What's going on? I asked them what they were saving it for. They answered, "You." Lo and behold, when my mom had that stroke, I found out they had all that money stuck in a bank. I wanted to stop working to be there for my mom, and I was able to do that. Then my father turned all the accounts over to me. He even asked me to be responsible for all the other children, saying, "I know you'll see to it." All things are only what the Lord allows. When I was fifteen, I helped them buy this home. I didn't think I was doing it for me. I thought I would run into a man someday who would take care of everything for me. My prince charming. It didn't happen for me that way. That offered me a certain strength too. I found out what I need to do for myself to have a good life. I look around now, and in my most needy times, everything came back to me. I could live a good life without having to struggle to pay rent. I was alone at the time I took care of my parents. I didn't stay married to my son's father very long. He didn't feel godly to me. A lot of women stay in bad marriages maybe because the gentleman is making lots of money or buying a house. A lot of scenarios to that. My father equipped me not to fall into those traps.

HUDSON: Sounds like you were closer to your father than your mother.

BROWN: I was close to both of them. My father taught my mother everything she knew. She was extremely naïve. Her parents died when she was a child, and her sisters didn't treat her well. My father was the best thing that happened to my mom. His name was Preston, which means to press on. Before Mother passed on, I can recall her in her bedroom thanking the Lord for the husband that he gave her. She prayed that he would live a long life, and he lived until he was ninety-three, which was nineteen and a half years after her death. He never wanted another woman after my mom passed on.

[In 2005, the Texas Country Reporter ran a program that included my interviews with Jewel Brown and the next interview, with Trudy Lynn.]

I tell people I don't want that recognition after I'm gone. Give me my flowers while I'm living. When I'm gone, I don't give a shit.

Trudy Lynn

DIVA OF SOUL AND BLUES

On October 26, 2004, I drove to the edge of Houston to visit with Trudy Lynn. I knew of her but had never met her. She met me at the door, with cropped blond hair (like a cap) in a black headband and long black earrings. It can be awkward entering a person's house with a tape recorder in hand, but Trudy treated me like an old friend. We immediately started sharing stories and music. The stack of eleven CDs that she put in my hand revealed a woman with focus. Trudy Lynn has known since the age of thirteen, when she was invited to share the stage with Albert Collins, the Iceman on guitar, that music was her life. She now lives in the family home with her sister Mary. The walls are covered with photos, music, books, and memorabilia. Most interesting are the collections of figurines—black musicians, instruments in hands, blowing sax and playing guitar. The bookshelves are full, and various types of recorded music surround us. After we talk, after Mary joins us, we decide to go out to eat at a nearby Luby's. Trudy changes into a sleek black outfit, black headband stylishly adorning her cap of very short blond hair. After looking at the various Trudy Lynn promo shots, I laugh, knowing we share a tendency to invent our appearance in new ways from time to time. She even has a gift for me, one of her sequined and fringed "sweat" rags that go to the stage with her each time she performs. That band of gold on her front tooth is also part of this statement.

HUDSON: Let's talk about your first time onstage.

LYNN: I was thirteen. They used to have a Sunday matinee at Walter's Lounge from 3:00 p.m. till 7:00 p.m. It was one Sunday when Albert Collins was playing, right before his first hit, "The Freeze." He played there with a band, Big Tiny and the Thunderbirds. They told me to come up there onstage, and I did "Money." We used to go to these places just to dance. I even carried some little fold-up dancing shoes with me. My mother told them I could sing. I knew three songs, "Night Time Is the Right Time," "Change Will Come," and "Money." I always looked older. In fact, my older sisters would tell me what to say to get in, and then I would be the only one they let in! I also did a lot of singing in high school with choirs and little groups.

HUDSON: You have known a lot of people in the music business.

LYNN: Honestly, when I first started I was working with Clarence Green here in Houston. He was known as the "Best little band in Houston." Whatever was on the radio, we were on it. The first real artists I met, other than Albert, were Ike and Tina Turner. I opened a show for them. Bobby Milton and I still do shows together. Bobby Rush. My goodness, you name them, I'll claim them. I've worked with all of them. Etta is still number one on my list! My sisters and brothers and I would do talent shows on our front porch. I used to do "Tweedlee Dee" by LaVerne Baker. What did Ruth Brown do? I used to sing some of her songs. She's a master. She did "Mama, He Treats Your Daughter Mean." I tell you another lady I was impressed with when I was a little girl: Fay Adams, "Shake a Hand." We listened to lots of music on the radio; I was the only one bold enough to step out there and do it. Nobody else in the family sings, just me.

HUDSON: So you knew pretty early on that you wanted to sing?

LYNN: Always. I always said I was going to be a singer.

HUDSON: What gave you the courage to do this?

LYNN: I've never been scared. Girl, I'd step out there in the front and that would be it. Something would just turn on in me. I feel like I was always doing what I was supposed to be doing. I was with a group that became big after high school, Archie Bell and the Drells. They were well known for "Tighten Up." Before he even got with the group, he and I used to go on talent shows and do Ray Charles and "You Are My Sunshine" by Jimmy Davis.

HUDSON: I was reading about Fifth Ward in your bio by Roger Wood.

LYNN: That's Fifth Ward, TEXAS. Put that TEXAS in there.

HUDSON: Where does that term come from? Ray Sharpe told me about Third Ward in Ft. Worth, Texas.

LYNN: The wards are just different areas of the city. Houston is spread out all kinds of ways. Wards became known for their schools and for the people who lived there. Fifth Ward is known for music, that's for sure. And for the Club Matinee. Third Ward here is also known for the many musicians who lived there. Both wards were home to diverse ethnic populations. Back in the 1960s the Club Matinee was on Lyons Avenue. The hotel in the back was the Dixon Hotel, where all the black entertainers stayed. At that time you couldn't stay anywhere else in town. This is where you would see all the black entertainers in the Fifth Ward, and they would go out and perform other places. This club would stay open twenty-four hours. It would never close . . . and served food twenty-four hours. I had never been in that club, but around the corner my mother had a beauty shop. The high school I went to was right across the street. We would walk by there to see who we could see. [laughter] I saw Jackie Wilson, Bobby "Blue" Bland, and many more by peeking through that fence. Everybody would leave Duke and Peacock and come down the street. Duke and Peacock were on Erastus. That's where everybody would hang out. There was another club called La Joya. The first year I came out of high school, I went on a vacation to an aunt's house in Lufkin, Texas. I did "Tell Mama" at a talent show in school. I got kicked off in Lufkin when I got to stand in for a singer who did not show up. I think she was alcoholic or something. I have this long letter from my mother telling me to come home. I was supposed to be going to college to be an X-ray technician. I got up there on that stage, and that was it! I came back with a new name and all. Trudy was a stage name. I was at a club called the Cinderella when I used this name. When they asked me my name, I looked up on the wall and saw "Trudy." I said "Trudy Lynn" because I wanted two names. My name doesn't sound like a stage name. My real name is Audrey. Lee is my first name. I wanted one of those quick names. [laughter] I heard about Gloria Lynn and Barbara Lynn.

HUDSON: Let's talk about your career in the world.

LYNN: I've been all over Europe—France, Italy, Switzerland, Spain, and even Japan. A lot of people say that people in Europe appreciate blues more. I say that a lot of people in the States appreciate blues; you just have to go where they are. When I'm in Europe, the people who love the blues come out, so it seems like there might be more appreciation. We work where the blues are appreciated. I don't think people there appreciate it more.

HUDSON: Let's talk about an occasion that was special and exciting for you.

LYNN: When I was in Tokyo. Lowell Fulson was on this show. I came on before he did. The place was jam-packed. There are a lot of people over there, you know. I was so surprised. I was on the stage, and I saw the people coming in carrying a long row of lights. Then I saw that the lights spelled out my name. I couldn't believe it. I said, "Nobody is going to believe this!" These were the fans who did this. I've been to a lot of places where people had posters for me, but I was so impressed with those lights. That seaweed almost killed me, though. We ate that seaweed over there. It looked like spinach one morning at breakfast. It was good. It looked like greens of some sort. I might have eaten too much. That evening before the concert they had to call a doctor for me. Now it might have been something else, though. Lots of fans brought me gifts.

HUDSON: What about challenges for you?

LYNN: I feel like my biggest challenge is right now. A lot of record companies have shut down. You catch a lot of entertainers today doing their own CDs and selling their own CDs. I've been writing now, and I'm going to do this CD on my own. The Internet really changes things for the artist. I call it "the mark of the beast." Them numbers. Pretty soon everybody will have to have that thing in their house. Just like a phone. Once you go in there and put something in there, you don't have any business. But you can't live without them. I'm going to work with Theodis Ealey. He's got a number-one hit in the soul charts now called "Stand Up in It." He says, "You ain't done a doggone thing until you stand up in it." Like Clarence Carter says, "Stroke it."

HUDSON: As your music has evolved, your persona has also evolved. Right now, are you deliberately creating a new direction or are you building on what you have?

LYNN: I'm in the soul/blues arena. Sometimes I'm damned if I do and damned if I don't. The music that was kickin' when I grew up was soul music. Then I heard the blues music. I can do both. I can work the white circuit and the black circuit. A lot of black artists can only work what we call the "chitlins" circuit, the black circuit. I can do traditional blues and soul blues. To make it on this "chitlins" circuit, you have to have one of those songs we were talking about. You've got to be stroking it or standing up in it! Now it seems that black audiences like the urban blues more than any traditional blues.

HUDSON: I have been to many blues shows that do not draw a white audience.

LYNN: I'm gonna tell you why. Because black blues is traditional blues, Muddy Waters and Howlin' Wolf. The older people like them. But if you say blues to a youngster now, they resist going, saying, "I don't want to hear any slow music." People sometimes say to me, after hearing me for the first time, "I didn't know blues was like that." I will say one thing. There are more young people overseas that are interested in the blues.

HUDSON: Some people say that music crosses all barriers and invites us to join together. Are there still any racial issues around the music today?

LYNN: I don't think so. Ever since different races started crossing, it changed all that. It depends on what's in you and what you are feeling.

HUDSON: Ray Sharpe told me that when his hit "Linda Lu" came out in 1959, he got booked for many gigs by people who were surprised when he showed up. They thought he was a white man.

LYNN: I didn't know that about him either! I know the song because many of the groups I played with did that song.

HUDSON: Let's talk about some of the songs you like.

LYNN: When it comes to music, I listen to all of it. I like some of all of it. I like R&B. I'm just in love with that little kid, R. Kelly. He reminds me of Marvin Gaye and Al Green. I'm an Al Green fanatic. Saw him the other night, and he's gotten chubby. I wanted to walk up and pinch him on the butt! He just released a new comeback, doing all R&B. He did a great job on all that gospel music as well. My favorite is Etta, of course. She's changed a lot, and we've all changed a lot. She has a new album doing Chicago blues artists. Her voice is real, real low. She sounds like a man. You don't hear that push and that fire like in the last one. When I was raising my kids and doing music with Clarence Green, we had to do some country. Being from Texas, we heard it on the radio all the time. To me, country and blues are the same thing with different flavors. Blues has a little more grease in it, a little more seasoning. Country music tells stories just like blues. When a country song is sad, you cry. When a blues song is sad, you whoop and cry. You feel it differently. I like country.

HUDSON: What do you want people to be saying about your music when you're gone?

LYNN: I tell people I don't want that recognition after I'm gone. Give me my flowers while I'm living. When I'm gone, I don't give a shit. When I'm gone, I'm through. I mean that from my heart.

HUDSON: Tell me about Johnny Copeland.

LYNN: We were close. When I started writing songs, he wanted to see them all. One time he was looking at them, and he saw "void" written on one. I told him it wasn't right. He said, "That is the one that is right. Don't put that on songs you write. Never void anything you write. Just leave them there. Someone can do them." We did a lot of shows together, including one at Antone's in Austin.

HUDSON: Tell me about your life.

LYNN: I was married to a musician, but we weren't compatible. It's hell being married when you are an entertainer. I've got friends who say, "Why don't you stay home? I'll give you the money." I tell them it's not about the money. It's what I do! This is me. I've had men try to make choices for me. I say, "Don't pick for Ms. Trudy." You know, they're all just the same—black, white, red, or green. And when the hard drive goes out, they all complain just the same. One guy told me he took Viagra and saw blue spots. He had high blood pressure. My mom used to tell me that a bullshitting man ain't nothing but a pile of shit. Just chunk two eyes on it, and you got a man. My mother and I were just like sisters.

HUDSON: My daughter and I are also best friends and have many great conversations. We have the United Nations at our dinner table. My daughter married a black man, my brother married a Hispanic woman, and my cousin married an Asian woman. What a beautiful rainbow of colors.

LYNN: My husband was with the best big band, and I was with the best little band, Clarence Green. He was ten years older than me, but he just wasn't sharp enough. We could have really helped each other out. He could have almost molded me.

HUDSON: Let's talk about mothers.

LYNN: All my lessons came from my mother. She didn't bite words. Just like we're sitting up here talking, that's how we talked. There's three girls, and we all talk. I remember when they were telling them about the birds and the bees. She just sat my butt down and said, "I'm going to tell you right along with them." Our mother said, "Keep that dress tail down and those drawers up. Don't come home with any babies." And I didn't. I never had any problems with my daughter. She has her own salon with about twenty booths leased out. She married her high school sweetheart, and they are doing good. She had poodles for so long, I asked her if those were my grandchildren. She was about twenty-seven when she had her first child.

I am not a blues singer! I sing blues because that's what people want.
I also sing funk, soul, country, and spiritual. I'm all of that.

Lavelle White

STRUTTING HER STUFF

Lavelle White is a name that has always been synonymous with good blues.
Since I was familiar with her recordings and her association with Antone's in
Austin and with Marcia Ball, I chose to showcase her at Schreiner University
on February 20, 2002. She arrived, dressed in style as always, with David
Webber to accompany her on keyboard. What a duo! His use of those ivories
and her voice and style combined to present Texas music in a way that both
educated and entertained. When she invited me to join her at her house some
weekend for some of her good cooking, well, I knew then that we would be
good friends. She won Best Blues Band at the 2006 Austin Chronicle *Music*
Awards, and her performance was wild, soulful, and colorful. Everyone loves
Miss Lavelle White.

HUDSON: Let's talk about a time in your life when you had an extraordinary moment, when everything was clicking, when you were having
lots of fun.

WHITE: From about 1959 to 1984 everything was fine. There were lots
of places to play; I had the hot album out. There were lots of clubs and

music. We all went together. I was on shows with James Brown, Gladys Knight and the Pips, Aretha Franklin, the Isley Brothers, and Sam and Dave. We went to Hollywood and did the Hollywood Bowl. This was the time of the biggest highlights of my life. It was just great. I was on the road touring. This is who I've been with, and this is what I've done.

HUDSON: I noticed in your bio that you've also received awards in France.

WHITE: I received the Otis Redding Award. I always did "The Dock of the Bay" and other songs by him. He was one of the main artists that I liked. I loved Otis Redding. I also loved the Drifters, Gladys Knight and the Pips, and the Isley Brothers.

HUDSON: You were always received well in Europe, right?

WHITE: Still am. They really do appreciate what I do there. They treat me like a queen.

HUDSON: I ran into Calvin Owens once in France, and he had the same story to tell.

WHITE: Oh yes, that's my guy. I love him. You know, there are a lot of lady singers in Houston that you haven't reached yet. Like Lady D. But you will, though.

HUDSON: I think that women have a distinct place in the history of Texas music.

WHITE: We do. But we just haven't received the recommendation yet. For some reason, women are put on the back burner. This is one thing that I really do not like. We need to be more recognized for what we are doing. It is certainly more than it was, but it is not up to what it should be. Right now they are recognizing the younger musicians in Austin. They don't recognize me like they should. When I'm there and perform at a club, they don't call my name like they should. We older musicians need the recognition. And there's still racial stuff going on.

HUDSON: I announced to my students that your performance captured some pioneer moments and they needed to come hear you, even though they don't know who you are.

WHITE: That's it. That's it. Often you don't get any recognition until you get old. . . . I mean real old. [We laugh.] We're not that old yet, Kathleen. It just makes you feel so doggoned angry because of the things you know you are doing, and you don't get anything for it.

HUDSON: I noticed that beautiful necklace you're wearing, a hologram of an angel. I have one just like that with the hologram of a dragon on it. I guess that makes us sisters!

WHITE: Yes, I pray for people all over the world. And I always say "I love you" and "God bless you" to everybody. I love the people in the world. I don't even know their names, but I pray for them. I also pray for peace all over the world. We need peace in every corner. We need peace among ourselves. We are sisters under the skin. If I cut you, Kathleen, you are going to bleed the same blood I bleed.

HUDSON: Family of man.

WHITE: We're all from the same bag!

HUDSON: You started off with our dear friend, Johnny Copeland. I loved his spirit, and I'm sad he's no longer with us. His daughter, Shemekia, is carrying on, though. And she is one tough woman as a youngster! I know you loved Johnny too.

WHITE: I sure did, Kathleen. He was on the first record that I did for Duke Records: "If I Could Be with You," "Teenage Love." I'm going to get this thing and send it to you so you can hear it. It's called "Teenage Love." He was so sweet about things. He and I did a record together some years ago. Huey Meaux had it. You know him, it might be in the back of his car somewhere. We went on the road together, Johnny and I, and we worked together for a long time. When I recorded and got the little record off, I went to Atlanta, Georgia, and I was working for Henry Wynn. This is where I met the Isley Brothers and all the other people.

HUDSON: I see in your bio that you've spent some time in Chicago. I'm going there next week. Any suggestions?

WHITE: Yes, the Kingston Mines and across from that the Blues. I played there for eight or nine years. Also I worked for Buddy Guy. Go to Buddy Guy's club, he's a wonderful person. He's marvelous. He's beautiful.

HUDSON: Is there a difference performing in Chicago and performing in Texas?

WHITE: There sure is. People appreciate you more there than they do in Austin or anywhere else in Texas.

HUDSON: Well, it is the home of the blues.

WHITE: Listen. I want to explain something to everybody. I am not a blues singer! I sing blues because that's what people want. I also sing funk, soul, country, and spiritual. I'm all of that. When I first started singing, it was rhythm and blues. I didn't just do blues. When I recorded for Robey, I did rhythm and blues. When I recorded for Antone's, they wanted blues. When I played the Kingston Mines, they wanted blues. Buddy Guy's is kind of versatile. With me, it's funk, soul, blues, jazz, and a little rap.

HUDSON: How do you see the influence of Houston on your music?

WHITE: Those people in Houston were sort of age-oriented, like, "Oh, she's too old." I definitely want you to put this in the book. A guy in Houston says, "Oh, that's Lavelle White. She's too old." God has blessed me to live and keep singing.

HUDSON: Imagine a conversation about you after you're gone. What would you love to have people say about you?

WHITE: Just everything good. As a person, a musician, an entertainer, and a good friend.

HUDSON: What is the biggest contribution you've made to the history of Texas music?

WHITE: I think that I have inspired a lot of people. I have uplifted a lot of people, although I've been downgraded by people. I have saved a lot of people from destruction.

HUDSON: Who are some women you have worked with?

WHITE: Marcia Ball. She's wonderful. She's beautiful. I wrote a song for her. And Angela Strehli and Lou Ann Barton. Lou Ann did my song "Stop These Teardrops." I think they are wonderful. I worked with Big Time Sarah in Chicago. Lots of different ladies that I've enjoyed working with.

HUDSON: I want us to get together again. You need to start this gig. Let's end by talking about your beginning.

WHITE: The beginning was when I was a kid about twelve years old. I started singing spirituals in Hollandale, Mississippi. I was born in Jackson, Mississippi. My mother was a piano player in church. After that I came to Houston. I started singing around with Clarence Holliman, and I couldn't carry a song in a paper bag. My people were farmers, and we moved from town to town. I stayed in Louisiana when I was small. I came to Houston with my brother. I went to the clubs singing, and I couldn't carry a tune in a paper bag. Clarence taught me my timing. He played on both my CDs. He was an excellent guitar player. His brother Sweets Holliman was an excellent piano player. He sounded just like Charles Brown. I'll send you a tape of this music. Come visit me in Austin. Come to my house, and I can cook you some soul food. I love it that I met you. You are down to earth and ordinary. I like that.

HUDSON: How do you describe yourself?

WHITE: Ordinary, down-to-earth, country person that loves people and loves to be with people. I love soul food and all kinds of music. I want to spread out, and I want to come out here again!

HUDSON: You have a real story to tell.

WHITE: I want to go around to schools talking about my times growing up. I used to ride around on a cotton sack with my mother. I'm trying to find the money to do my biography. I know I have an important story to tell.

This is the way we used to do this in the swamps 'round Lafayette, Louisiana. We didn't have any big systems. . . . They had little bitty amplifiers, and the piano had no mike. . . . Sometimes I would play until my fingers would just bleed, having to pound so hard while everyone was dancing.

Katie Webster

SWAMP BOOGIE QUEEN

Katie Webster played Antone's in Austin on my forty-third birthday. My daughter and I had gone to Austin. We visited a club that appealed to my young daughter but not to me, so I left this crowd of young people at a crowded disco and went to Antone's, a soulful blues club on Guadalupe. I was in the audience, standing alone and listening to the blues. I noticed that I felt a spirit of celebration rather than sadness. I realized that Katie's words inspired me to be a sassy, free woman. Then I wondered why I even needed that inspiration. I believe I had allowed the culture to tell me things about being a woman rather than allowing my own spirit to shine through. What a breakthrough for me! I had to have similar breakthroughs along the way, each one opening me up a bit more. I am fifty-nine now, writing this introduction five years after her death. I'm remembering how it felt that first time on October 2, 1988, my forty-third birthday, suffering from another broken heart. What she gave me was a story about being a woman. That's what I carry forth with me into my life.

HUDSON: Let's talk about last night.
WEBSTER: When we first left the hotel, it was raining. I told the band

not to get too comfortable. Sometimes in Texas storms do some different things. When this rain came up fast and swift, they said that maybe it would stop when we got to the club. I said, "Not in Texas. Maybe in California, but not in Texas." While we were getting there, this little song was running through my mind. Well, when the electricity went off at the club, I thought of this little song. I realized that the packed house came to hear Katie Webster. The marquee can say "Silent Partners" tomorrow night, but tonight it says Katie. I felt I owed these people something. I know I am a trooper, and I know I've saved the day before. I was in the dressing room, and I made up this little song. "When the lights went out in Austin, Texas, and I was on my way to Antone's Club, the people were sitting around by candlelight, wondering what was going to happen next." I just came out of the dressing room singing that song. The people started applauding, and a chill went over my body. I realized I'd better finish this. I walked up to the piano and told the crowd, "This is the way we used to do this in the swamps 'round Lafayette, Louisiana. We didn't have any big systems and amplifiers. They had little bitty amplifiers, and the piano had no mike. I had to sing through this amplifier and play this piano raw like that. Sometimes I would play until my fingers would just bleed, having to pound so hard while everyone was dancing. It really brought back memories of the late 1950s and 1960s to me. At that time I was playing with a blues band in Louisiana. From age thirteen to age eighteen I played on 78 and 45 records for Excello Records and for Goldband Records, for the Gin label. I was the session pianist for J. D. Miller and Eddie Shuler from Louisiana for fifteen years. I played on everything that came out of there: folk, blues, gospel, and country. Everything. Last night brought back these memories. I had the whole strip of Broad Street in Lake Charles where I played each club on a different night. The crowds would follow me. I did this for six or seven years, playing solo before I even organized a band. Then I organized one and called it the Uptighters. I had a big band then. I had four horns, two drummers, a bass player, two guitar players, and two more singers besides myself. And I had a group of guys called the Soul Steppers.

HUDSON: I know this album on Alligator Records marks another turning point for you.

WEBSTER: That's right. I've been recording albums in Europe. I've done twenty-three tours of Europe since 1982. I've been back three times this year. I went from May to July 26. Then I went back to Switzerland for the month of August. Then after this tour is over in November, I'll go back to Europe for another month. I play France, Italy, Austria, Australia, Norway, Sweden, and Amsterdam. I have two managers over there: Ralph Schubert and Ziggy Crisman, who is also the owner of the record company over there producing solo albums for me. I've done five solo albums over there. And I have two reissues of earlier work on the Flyright Label that is based in England. I have two albums on Goldband Records. Charly Records picked up that old material. I also did an album on Arhoolie Records. I used a group called Hot Links, a group very popular in San Francisco. I call this recent album my baby. This is the first time I've gotten this kind of company to give me a contract. They knew that I had the talent, but many times they weren't trying to push female singers so much. They had Etta James and Ruth Brown and Laverne Baker. I think they felt like the market was crowded with female vocalists, so they were focusing on male vocalists. I got the job playing piano because there was no one else in Louisiana who played the blues this way, an old time boogie-woogie sound. The males played soft and feminine-like. I blasted them on out! So I played piano on albums with Lazy Lester, Slim Harpo, Silas Hogan, Clifton Chenier, and Rocking Sidney. I had quite a track record. There was a slump in my career at one time because when my mother and father became ill in California I spent a lot of time with them.

HUDSON: Let's talk about your Texas roots.

WEBSTER: I was born in Houston, Texas. When I was living there with my parents, I was not allowed to play jazz, blues, rhythm and blues, or rock and roll. My mother was a classical pianist, and my father was a minister. I had been singing since I was about three years old. When I was six, I did my solo in church. When I was about eight, my mother wanted to give me piano lessons. No teacher would take me, because my fingers were so short. I taught myself to play what I would hear on the radio in Houston. Fats Domino had a record out called "They Call Me the Fat Man." That piano was different than any piano I had heard. It sounded like Professor Longhair, but it was Champion Jack Dupree, who is seventy-eight years old and has lived in Europe for fifty years. I had a chance later to meet him in Europe. He still looks like a man about fifty years old. It fascinated me to hear the way he played the piano. This is how I got interested in Louisiana music. A little later on my parents decided to move to California because of my mother's illness. I didn't want to leave the South. They knew I would have more opportunities there, less racism. I did play with a group of mixed children when I was growing up. My mother would cook fried chicken and mashed potatoes with brown gravy. The white kids in the neighborhood would come over, amazed that the gravy was brown and not white. My mother would not let us use slang, so we had to speak correct English at all times. I think that made most of the white people in the neighborhood a part of our family. We weren't illiterate. We had manners. I've never had any problems relating to other races. I always had all kinds of friends. Then music really opened some doors. I moved to Beaumont with an aunt of mine. My godfather, Clarence Garlow, who passed away a couple of years ago, discovered Johnny Winter. He wrote "Bon Ton Roulette." He discovered Clifton Chenier and Barbara Lynn. Johnny Winter used to come out and sit in with my band when he was young and I was just starting out. I enrolled in high school and was part of the Glee Club, the girls' choir. I could do a little more things there. My dresses had to come under the knee with my parents, but with my aunt I could have a poodle skirt. I could sing and play any kind of music I wanted to. At home, it had to be gospel in the morning and gospel in the evening.

HUDSON: I came in late last night. You were singing a song about seeing a man packing his bags. I heard you say, "You can't see me in the dark, but you don't want a man who goes like this!"

WEBSTER: I told everybody to take lessons. I wrote that song. It happened one time in my life. This man came into my life, and he didn't have very much. He wanted to go on my jobs with me. And hey, I've always been the Elizabeth Taylor of the blues. I didn't want anyone up there who didn't look really good. I took him out and bought him some Stacy Adams, some silk underwear and a diamond ring, a beautiful suit and a hat. One day he told me he was tired of being a kept man. He said he wanted to get out and do something for himself. Then he said he would come back to me after he accomplished something. Later on we did get back together. It was beautiful. But I wrote this song at a time when he would go out and be with other ladies. I was always on the road. I asked him to be a little more discreet. "Don't come home with that heavy makeup on your shirt." I used to always tell him that he could stay out there all night long, but when he stepped through that door, he'd better not fail me!

HUDSON: We need more women telling it like it is!

WEBSTER: I have two more songs that I do. One is called "Red Negligee." I am telling the woman how to look when the man comes home. Let him smell that steak from outdoors when he gets out of the car. Put those children to bed, and put some candles on the tables. There's nothing he can do, like we say in Louisiana, but get gumbo, get go go and then go do do. That means to eat your dinner, make a little love, and then you can go to sleep. That's what those words mean.

HUDSON: It sure takes two.

WEBSTER: In the same song, I tell the men to listen up. Just because you got this marriage license on us, you think we should stay home pregnant and barefoot all the time. You used to take us out to nice restaurants. You never want to talk about anything with me. You come to my breakfast table and bring a newspaper. When your secretary comes and brings you a cup of coffee, she can sit on your lap.

HUDSON: I think Barbara Lynn said it well: "If You Should Lose Me, You'll Lose a Good Thing."

WEBSTER: I wrote a song about a young woman who lived on my street. She was put out of the house with no money or clothing. I took her in, fed and clothed her. She told me when I had to leave, she would take care of my house. And that's what she did. She took care of everything, my dog, my cat, and that man in my house! I write about true things that happened to me in my life. It seems that a man cannot be faithful to one woman. He believes that he can still be Mr. So-and-so even if he goes out with a bunch of women. But if we women go out, we're just whores. Double standard, for sure, I say. But this is 1988 now. That does not still stand. Society does still say a man can have a younger woman, but a woman with a younger man is still a crime. If I can please a man twenty years old, and I'm forty-eight, well God bless me. I say this to a man, and if he doesn't like it, he can get to steppin'. Not half-steppin', but whole steppin'.

HUDSON: Mark Twain wrote about this in "Letter from the Earth." He said that biologically a man cannot take care of a hundred women, but a woman can biologically take care of a hundred men. I think the fear of what women were capable of might be part of why this "ownership" of women developed.

WEBSTER: They've got to prove to themselves that they can still please a woman one-half their age. If I felt like I wanted a younger man, I had one. I can please them from eighteen to eighty. If I can stand my ground, what's the deal? And I have a song that says that. I've played jobs where guys didn't even realize that I have kids their age. I'm forty-eight now. Four years ago I was playing in Europe. There were three guys between twenty-one and twenty-five that showed up at all my gigs. They absolutely thought I was in my thirties. They were coming around, trying to spend time with me. I told them I had kids as old as they were. Once in Louisiana when I was twenty-seven, I was confronted with a guy who told me he was twenty-five. He absolutely fell in love with me. I found out later he was only eighteen. I could not shake him at all. He was working as a foreman at a rice factory in Beaumont. He would bring in his entire check and give it to me, asking for only $5 for cigarettes. I found myself getting into a deep situation. His mother and family didn't tell me anything. His name was Jimmy. I wrote about him on my Arhoolie album. I wrote a song called "Jimmy, Jimmy." I met his mother, and we talked. I told her he seemed immature at times. She said, "Well, he's only nineteen now." We had been going together a year. I was the first woman he'd been with in his life. He always said he liked someone with experience. I had to get away from him because he did get jealous at times. I moved out to San Francisco. A week after I was there, he came out and found me. He rode a Greyhound bus to get to me. And he said he would do whatever he could to help with my parents. Only two of us were there to take care of my parents. I live with her now in San Francisco. I write songs about incidents in my life. It always touches someone else. Back to Beaumont. Clarence had this club called Bon Ton Drive Inn. I used to stand up on top of these big garbage cans and listen to Clifton Chenier. I fell off one night, right into all that barbecue sauce. I was screaming and hollering. I started beating on the sides. I was short. Clarence and his wife took me into the place. His wife gave me a dress to put on. I went into the club and started dancing. I thought it was a strange music. It was zydeco. I could not erase that from my head. I was a bold little girl. I didn't know but fifteen songs, but you couldn't tell me that I wasn't bad. I knew three songs by Sam Cooke, six by Fats Domino, four by Little Richard, and one by Phil Gunter. Now I know over three thousand songs.

HUDSON: You're in a unique situation being a female piano player. We both know Marcia Ball.

WEBSTER: Yes, she's great. Most women are strictly jazz around New

York and Chicago. Most of the ladies are great blues singers, but they don't play an instrument. Etta James once said, "If I could just play the piano like Katie Webster and sing at the same time, then I wouldn't have to put up with these other musicians." I can play solo or with a band. I think that intimidates a man. Like last night. I jumped up there with no mike and just a piano. You've got to have a big mouth and strong lungs. Just be sure you've never used any drugs in your life. I'm drug-free, and I don't smoke or drink. When you want to bring me something, you bring me a shot of orange juice. I've been tempted to do these things over the years. I've been out here thirty-five years, and I have a daughter who's thirty-three. She was two years old when I got out here. I couldn't get a babysitter, so I put her in a dressing room. Most of my shows in Europe are mostly solo. I play on a grand piano to fifty thousand people. As far as you can see, they are jumping. If it's raining, they have their umbrellas. Looks like a parade of umbrellas. After I decided to stay in Beaumont, then there was a guy who came from Lawtell, up where Rockin' Sidney is from, Ashton Savoy. He discovered me when I was playing at this club in Beaumont. I did jazz with this band as the featured vocalist. One night someone asked for some R&B. That jazz band did not play any R&B, so I asked to play something alone. It got to be something that the people wanted. Ashton said he had a blues band in Louisiana; Roosevelt Griffin played drums, and Sidney Rainard played sax. He said he needed a piano player because he played guitar and sang. I told him he would have to talk to my aunt since I was only fifteen. They had to get an affidavit for me to play at this club where I was known as Big Mama Kat. I later became the Swamp Boogie Queen. Another name was Two Hundred Pounds of Joy. I weighed 230 pounds when I started going to Europe. I want to make it clear how I began to go to Louisiana. I knew I had the Texas blues down. I wanted to be able to do other styles. I fit right in. My early influence was my father. He played piano, and he had a left hand that would not wait a minute. I used to pray for a left hand like my father's. He played just like I wanted to. He played real hard, and I wanted to do that. My entire family played instruments. My brother had a band in Houston called Three Wigs and a Wiggle. I was the wiggle! Now he's playing in church. I had brothers that could really sing, but they all went back to church. I've got my kids in Texas, of course, but my family is out in California. All four of my girls live in Missouri City, outside of Houston. One is a nurse.

The other is a supervisor for ATT. She stays home with the other three girls.

I got to Louisiana with Ashton Savoy. I am so happy with this Alligator record. It's the first time I've had this much publicity spread out on me. I played the San Francisco Blues Festival after meeting Tom Mazzolini in Germany while on tour.

HUDSON: Let's talk about your new album.

WEBSTER: One of my favorites on the album is one I also did last night at Antone's: "Who Will the Next Fool Be?" And "On the Run." There are songs I wrote from the heart. And the dedication to Otis Redding. He was a dominant figure in my life in the late 1960s. When he had that tragic accident, it was like a piece of me went away with him. He gave me opportunities that no one else gave me. He had given me the opportunity to go out on the road with him just as he was in his peak. He didn't need me then. But he said his singers didn't push enough. He wanted someone to get the audience going for him when he came out. He paid me my salary and then their salaries. I'm on one or two of his albums. It's like he's guiding me right now. I do have conversations with him in my dreams. He comes to me when I'm depressed or down. He always encourages me. "Do not let people intimidate you. Forge ahead, even if you have to do it alone." Sometimes when I'm working with a group, I notice that even though I'm working hard to promote the entire group, they are not working with me. If I was not in front of them, they would not be where they are. Before the night is gone, it's complete serenity. My kids have walked in to see this big smile on my face while I am sleeping. Sometimes I just laugh out loud, and they wake me up and ask me if I'm okay. They tell me I'm talking and singing in my sleep. I tell them I was talking to Otis.

Louisiana has been real good to me. I left Houston at an early age. Everything I've accomplished began on Goldband Records with just my piano. In 1975 J. D. Miller released an album of me in Europe with Flyright. I was the "Unknown Swamp Boogie Queen" in the stories that came before my first performance in San Francisco. Most of my touring was in Europe.

I'm singing from my soul, so I want to move people. Whenever you hear me sing a song, I try and make it my song.

Wanda King

BLUES FOR FREDDIE

I first heard of Wanda King from Ray Sharpe, the man who wrote and took "Linda Lu" to the top. He reminded me that her father, Freddie King, not only was a phenomenal bluesman, but also influenced a host of guitar players, including Stevie Ray Vaughan. Wanda was working on establishing a non-profit organization to honor her father's contribution and to help create possibilities for others interested in the blues. A performer herself, Wanda took the stage on December 25, 2004, at a club in North Dallas, Django's on the Parkway, after all her guests had performed. I left fully satisfied with her performance and inspired by our conversation. Her face holds a beauty that she sheds on others like light.

HUDSON: Let's talk about what's on your mind right now.

KING: Let's start with this. The Freddie King Foundation was a concept I came up with a couple of years ago. I had been so busy working my day job, trying to reestablish my own music career, taking care of my father's estate, that I needed to take a break and really get the ball rolling. I had the opportunity at the first of the year to produce a tribute for the Freddie King Foundation. We raised enough money to hire an attorney, Jack Calmes, my father's ex-manager, and founded a non-profit. From there I want to start having some small festivals. We are trying to have a statue of Freddie King commissioned and placed in the Dallas Metroplex. That costs from $30,000 to $50,000, so we have our work cut out for us. That's not pocket change. We might be talking with Eric Clapton, but I also want to get lots of people involved. When I had to sue several recording companies for copyright infringements, other people started calling me, asking for help. So I want part of the foundation to assist people who might have similar problems.

HUDSON: And your career?

KING: I have a CD out. I'm currently working with a label in Europe that will distribute my CD in a new format for people on home theater. It's a way to reissue music for the consumer to purchase again. It's like Dobie sound in a theater. We're negotiating a two-record deal. I financed the first project, *From a Blue Point of View*. I have made a commitment to have at least one Freddie King song on each CD I put out. I want to honor his legacy, and he was a great writer. I'm a fan of his music and his talent as well as his daughter.

HUDSON: What did you inherit from him?

KING: I think I inherited his talent. Not the guitar part. My ability to get along with people. He had this great personality in his life, gregarious and outgoing. People loved him. And he could really go bad on you if you pushed him too far. I think I'm more business-savvy than he was. I learned by watching. I was young when he died, about eighteen. He was a character. He kept us laughing all the time. He wasn't a stay-at-home dad, and he toured a lot. Sometime around 1970 he really became world-known. When he created "Hideway," he created a whole new genre, blues-pop. Then he signed with Shelter and created his blues-rock. He put some thunder behind the blues. I am writing my own music, inspired by life, joy, and disappointments. You know, things that happen. I tend to do jazz, blues, R&B. My father's vocals really inspired me. I love listening to jazz artists, and I love Julie London and Sarah Vaughan. Ella, of course. Aretha and Gladys Knight, Billie Holiday, Patti LaBelle, Dionne Warwick. There are certain sounds I listen to, and I've tried to develop my own style. I'm singing from my soul, so I want to move people. Whenever you hear me sing a song, I try and make it my song. In the beginning, when I was younger, I sang like my heroes. Then I noticed that tempo and voices can make a difference, so I make a song my own. I can hear a song, then swing it to jazz, and that's my favorite song. Then another night I might take a song and bebop it. I like to interpret a song as I go along. My biggest challenge right now is sidemen. When you are a vocalist, you have to rely on them for the music. Sometimes they try to bully you, but I have an ear; I grew up in this music. I can hear a bad note a mile away, and I can hear when a guy is out of tune. Then you have egos to deal with. I think that's part of the creativity. It's difficult for a guy who is talented to be criticized. I have to use certain techniques to let them know what I want. It's diplomacy. My band is all male, and I love it like that! It's all a work in progress with the band. There's not a lot that can surprise me now.

HUDSON: Do you run into any issues connected to the fact that you are female?

KING: Yeah! As I get older, even more. That's all I want to say about that. In this business a lot of times men don't take women seriously. We often come off like "eye candy" until we come on so strong that they can't deny us. I'm a big girl, but I'll tell you right now. I turn them away left and right. When you come into this business, you soon realize if they're listening to you or looking at you. I think we all have fifteen minutes. If we work at it really hard, we all get our fifteen minutes. And it's great when you get listened to and looked at. I know I'm a big girl, some say I'm cute, but the music is what matters to me. Don't get sidetracked. If you're serious about the music, you need to focus on the music. Looks will abandon you, but the music won't.

HUDSON: You sure look happy tonight.

KING: I'm finally getting back to my first love, the music. I lost my mother in August 2004. I had already told her I was going back to the music. She was so excited for me. I had taken off many years to take care of family matters. It's tough losing your family, but these things will happen to all of us. My faith keeps me centered. I think that things happen for a reason, and God is an all-powerful being in control. I think our lives are already planned, and we also have choices. We can go left or right or stay in the middle. The choices we make create a long or short path in terms of the end. It's all about what you choose to do. Am I spiritual? Yes. I am spiritually grounded. I let God lead me.

We ate dinner, sat on the porch, and played music. . . . I'm a big believer that this is how we pass stories down.

Karen Abrahams

PAYING HER DUES

I first saw Karen at the Old Settlers Reunion in 2002. I had heard of her for a long time, often from my pal Johnny Krause as he said, "Come on out to Luckenbach this Wednesday. Karen is coming down from Austin to play with us." At that time, a weekly gathering including Roger Moon, B. B. Morse, Doug Davis, and others occurred each Wednesday under the big tree. Johnny was always there with his mandolin, ready to join in. Karen and I finally talked at the 2002 Kerrville Folk Festival after her powerful performance on the Threadgill Stage. I was drawn to her energy, her willingness to just let it flow. I thought of Janis Joplin without all the angst. Karen rocks and enjoys it.

HUDSON: Let's talk about your Texas roots and about your writing.

ABRAHAMS: I grew up in Taft, a little town near Rockport. I guess I don't know anything else to do except write and perform. That's who I am, and sometimes it takes a while to find that out. After spending time in Taft, we moved twelve miles farther out into the country. I was adopted very young, but I had lots of time on my hands. No time was spent with television, so I spent most of my time outdoors. I can't really remember when I wasn't making up songs. My parents bought me little toy pianos and stuff. Even very young, I was memorizing songs. So it was in my blood, I think. As I got older, I was pretty much of a loner, not really popular, because I was pretty wacky, like a lot of musicians. [laughter] Playing guitar was really what saved me. I wrote and I wrote, and when I played guitar at a church camp, I was suddenly popular for the first time. My parents were very religious. Everybody just loved me. I saw there was something more to it. I made friends, and I didn't have to talk. A lot of time musicians are socially inept, and we talk through our music and our songs. The scary part about writing songs is that you wear your heart on your sleeve. Everybody knows what's on your mind. It gets kind of crazy sometimes.

HUDSON: We were talking earlier about writers who look for the "hook" and write to an audience.

ABRAHAMS: I have some good friends from Nashville, David MacKenzie and Adie Grey. Dave is a great slide blues player and plays all around. He came down here and he said, "You Texas writers. You need to learn how to edit yourself." I understood what he meant. A lot of us just say what is true in the moment for us. We talk stories about our home, our ma and pa. We love to tell stories. Of course, I also know a lot of writers in Texas can't understand the Nashville mentality of going in from 9 to 5 and writing about these three subjects today. I can't write that way. They have to be real to me, personally. Either I know them, or they are me, the subjects of my songs. I can write about historical events, lots of angst and pain. I can write about tragedy, things I know well.

HUDSON: What are some of the things that have been said about you over the years?

ABRAHAMS: Let's see. Gutsy. Ballsy. A wailer. I've won lots of songwriting awards and lots of vocalist awards, but I think I'm known more for my voice than the writing. It depends on when you hear me. I've played with blues bands, rocking out, and I've played with bluegrass bands. Sometimes I hear a comparison with Janis [Joplin]. I think I'm versatile. Mostly I hear "Karen rocks!" I hear that more than anything else. As far as all roots music, it still has a bit of an edge. I grew up in the 1960s and 1970s. Hendrix and all those people influenced me. I opened for Johnny Winter once in Florida. I used to have a seven-piece blues band,

and we would open for John Lee Hooker, Winter, and others. I was also a mother raising kids, so I didn't have a chance to do as much performing as I might like. I played with Edgar Winter one night right before his dad died. He went ahead and did the show. I thought of that last year when I had to play after my mom died. I also read about Rusty Wier playing his gig right after his mother died. What else could we do? Our mothers know that is what we do. Growing up in Texas, I think we have a history of songwriters. As long as I can remember, we ate dinner, sat on the porch, and played music. Even though I am adopted, I went back and found my birth parents. It turned out that my great-uncle and grandfather had played fiddle at barn dances all over Texas. Seems to be in the blood as well. I'm a big believer that this is how we pass our stories down. I used to write poetry and little novels when I was in school. Then it became an issue of discipline. I don't have enough to write books, but I can write the story in a song.

HUDSON: It does take an enormous amount of courage to do what you do. When I'm in your audience, I feel like you are really present, not hiding behind anything.

ABRAHAMS: That's another thing I've heard people say, "What you see is what you get." I'm able to just be there with the audience. In fact, I'm affected by the audience each time I perform. I have lot of other interests, as well. I'm a mural painter, and I do faux painting. I've always been an artist; I love painting walls and floors. Art, to me, is sometimes deeper than music in some ways. You become so lost in it. I have kids and grandkids; I have family. And I'm glad. I see a lot of friends my age who gave that up along the way. I can name quite a few people who wish they had kids and family. I think jobs are harder to get as you get older if you haven't attained a certain status. That's just the nature of the music business.

HUDSON: I'm thinking about all the roles I play as a woman.

ABRAHAMS: It is difficult when you do have kids. Music is important, but you're still a mother first. I find as much joy with my children as anything else. The hardest part about being a woman is trying to do it all. I don't think you really can do it all well. But we want to! I think back on a trip to Kansas I took, visiting all those Swedish relatives who came over here and moved on to the plain. Here they are in a sod shack. I think about how lonely and hard it had to be. Women got up earlier to cook for the men who were going out to work in the fields. At night they were still doing that. I think it's no different now. It's all about priorities. I think I could have gone further with my music had I delved in with that single intention.

HUDSON: I heard you were a young mother, too.

ABRAHAMS: Yeah, sixteen. I really never had any freedom. I didn't even do my CDs until I was forty. I was really amazed at how much response I still get. It's a hard business for women when they get older.

HUDSON: I have to share this Tanya Tucker comment I unearthed in my research: "It's lonely business being ballsy."

ABRAHAMS: Well, it is. I've had bands for many years. Even if I'm one of the guys with my guys, there's still a loneliness when a woman is in charge in this business. It's very hard, because if you start to demand or want things a certain way, you become "the bitch." No matter how nice you are. I've known lots of nice women who get chewed up and spit out of this business. Most of the club owners are male. Most festival promoters are male. Things change as we get older. Even with lots of talent, women could play on their looks a little. Then the looks go, and things change. I've heard middle-aged women say that they become invisible. I see that it takes a lot when people meet me for the first time and hear me play music. They see me as a soccer mom. It takes a shift in perspective for them to take in the musician that I am. It changes after I get up on stage. I do have a young audience.

HUDSON: We are in a culture where there's so much emphasis on appearance and youth.

ABRAHAMS: Small butts are in! [laughter] If you're over twenty-five now, things are different. I was offered a label deal last year for my two CDs. I turned it down, after talking with people. I realized that I am approaching fifty, and a record company wants another four or five years. I felt like they wouldn't promote me, so I kept my own CDs. I didn't want them lost with a label. I do think men are allowed to become characters as they get older, carrying a certain mystique. Women have a harder time with aging in the business, being that character.

HUDSON: I'm counting on this "character" thing. Don't burst my bubble.

ABRAHAMS: That's why I wrote "Howling at the Moon." If you're out there playing long enough, people will go, "That's really cool that you are still out there." I call it the Don Walser factor. Some call it persistence.

How many women do you see out there playing that are over forty? You just don't see them out there playing. I travel a lot, and I can't tell you how many places I go where I'm the only woman on the bill. It's because I'm rocking. They say, "We have lots of great guys. We need one female to rock." A woman who really plays "like a guy." In all the stories about Americana music, I see a lack of representation by women. I think people like Jimmy LaFave and Lyle Lovett are great, but women have a harder time getting an image.

HUDSON: Who are your heroes?

ABRAHAMS: Etta James. Koko Taylor. This is another thing. Black women are allowed to get older and fat and are still respected in this business. White women aren't. Look at Mary Chapin Carpenter or Wynonna [Judd]. All critics do is write about their weight changes. Just an observation I've always had. They don't write about Garth [Brooks] with a pudgy stomach. I'm not a feminist, but I believe we should treat everyone as a human being. I believe women have to try harder in this business.

HUDSON: Yeah, my research on Janis Joplin uncovered many, many comments about her looks, her skin, her weight. That seemed to always be part of the story.

ABRAHAMS: I know that sometimes I'm not hired because of my appearance or my age, but that's okay. That's life, and it occurs in all fields of business. The older I get, the earlier I get put on a bill. I used to rock out late at night.

HUDSON: What are your regular gigs now?

ABRAHAMS: I do Gruene Hall on one Monday night per month. Monday is female vocalists' night. Of course, the music producer is a woman. Let me tell you a story about Rod Kennedy, the producer of this festival. I met him at a party once where I played one song. He said I was hired, and that floored a lot of people who knew how long it usually took to get onstage at the Kerrville Folk Festival. He hired me on the spot to play the blues project, and I've been onstage here ever since.

HUDSON: What is your attitude about music?

ABRAHAMS: I'm serious about it, but I don't take myself so seriously. There's a lot of good writers out there. I do it because I have to write, and I'm lucky some people like what I write. I'm so lucky to do what I do. I'm the world's worst promoter, and my husband now helps me a lot. If he hadn't made the brochures, I wouldn't have any promo material.

HUDSON: Tell me about relationships and the business. Cliff said the sweetest thing coming over. He said, "I'm the guy behind the scenes."

ABRAHAMS: We've only been married eight years. I first got married when I was sixteen and was divorced at twenty. I stayed divorced a long time. I had two kids, and it was too darn hard to bring another person into the family. I was engaged twice and broke it off at the last minute. They were both musicians, and it's absolutely crazy for a musician to date another musician. They always like you for playing music, but once they get you, they don't want you to go out and play music. That was my experience. I know some others have made this work. I never had any luck until I met Cliff. We're two separate people, and we have fun. It's the only way a marriage works. And he helps me out. It's real easy with him.

HUDSON: You don't have the sense of giving up anything?

ABRAHAMS: Right. This is my work. It's what I do. I didn't think I'd be able to do it. I was so used to having an empty house when the kids were gone. Now, having somebody there in the same house can feel difficult. He doesn't care, but I feel like I should be doing something else. That mama mentality kicks in. I feel guilty for taking the time to myself. Isn't that funny? He doesn't care!

HUDSON: I think Virginia Woolf got it right, saying everyone needs a room of her own.

ABRAHAMS: That is important. I also love to travel. I don't sing too much about the sweetness of love. Most of my songs are about pain and loss and death. I think that theme might separate some of us older artists from the younger crowds. I've always done things a bit early.

HUDSON: What are you working on right now?

ABRAHAMS: I'm working on new songs. I've been going through a lot of turmoil. Last year my mother died of cancer. Then I had my own cancer surgery two weeks later. Then 9/11 happened. We lost Champ Hood. All of a sudden, the songs I had written seemed so trivial. I talked with some other writers. Then I was in a slump for a long time, some kind of depression. How can I sing about this when all of that is happening? I'm just now coming out of that process. It's okay to talk about loss and the people who have left. You know, that's just life. I think mothers absorb all of the things that happen to their kids, more than men do. I want to see my grandkids happy, and I often wonder what I can do.

Perfection is not the answer. Good music comes from the heart.

Barb Donovan

SERIOUS ABOUT TOWNES

Harold Eggers and I met with Barb on June 10, 2003, in Austin, Texas. Harold Eggers took me to Barb Donovan's house for a conversation. He knew I loved Townes Van Zandt, and he knew Townes loved Barb. Nice connection to have with someone. Our conversation was relaxed and, although I had not seen her perform, I had listened to her albums. We immediately connected through our love for Townes, and her DVD performance in a 1988 Townes hotel room concert produced by Harold Eggers and Hank Sinatra captures a moment in time as she plays tribute to Townes. That DVD also captures an important moment in Texas music history: Townes Van Zandt talking about his songs, playing his songs, and sharing his life with the camera and an audience of two.

HUDSON: Harold Eggers recommended that we talk, based on your own songs as well as your relationship with Townes Van Zandt. I find your music haunting. And I loved the duet with Townes on your CD. Let's begin by talking about influences. I know I cut my hair off after hearing Lucinda Williams, just to look a little more like her.

DONOVAN: And I dyed mine to match Bonnie Raitt's at one time! When I was growing up, I had the radio on by my ear, and I fell asleep to music. At that time it was Emmylou Harris, Dolly Parton, Buffy Sainte-Marie, Linda Ronstadt, and more. Emmylou and Linda came from folk, did country, and could also rock. That was a huge influence on me. My musical influences were Creedence Clearwater Revival, Motown, Steppenwolf, Three Dog Night. I was in Detroit at this time. The lyrics mattered, so Paul Simon was also an influence. Now I'm a fan of Lucinda Williams, Shawn Colvin, Ruthie Foster, Terri Hendrix, Shelley King, and Betty Elders. Lyrics matter, and presentation matters. I don't like to be pigeonholed, and I don't enjoy music that was designed for airplay. I want music that is about the artist, that comes from within them. I want to go into a show and leave different than I arrive. Townes Van Zandt did that to me every single show I attended. I shed tears I didn't expect, I laughed when I didn't expect to, and I left a different person. What I want to do as a performer is make you feel something. When I perform a song, I go back to the place in me where I wrote it. I might even shed my own tears performing it.

HUDSON: I love artists who speak what is true for them.

DONOVAN: Yes, I write down my feelings to share with you. I did not write them for you. "Sometimes When the Morning Comes" is a song that people usually connect with and come to the stage to tell me their own story. I know the song can also mean something else depending on who's listening. "Angelina" is one of those songs.

HUDSON: I know that we all listen through a filter, and we all create our own story of an experience. Music does affect the brain in a way that is measurable, but the words, although they are sounds, create different responses in each person.

DONOVAN: "Angelina" is about a selfish person I know. She's always dreaming about something different. I wrote the song to say, "Look right here. You have it all." People come up and share so many stories of their own about that song. It doesn't have to mean the same thing to everyone. Townes Van Zandt and I became fast and furious friends because he just put out his feelings, often raw and unmanageable.

HUDSON: I've been a Townes fan forever.

DONOVAN: We kind of met in stages, gradually, through music. He came to some of my shows. I opened a show or two for Townes. We had a mutual admiration for each other. Harold was also in the mix as a friend of both of us. Sometimes Townes would call me from the road, saying he needed to talk with someone sane and grounded. Ha. I was surprised he was calling me. I would respond that I wanted to be where he was . . . in the craziness. [laughter] That was our relationship. He loved just sitting back and being a fan when I would open shows for him.

HUDSON: I could feel that dance of female and male energy in that duet you sing with him.

DONOVAN: He had that way of just tapping into you. It was pretty scary and pretty amazing. That friendship did lead to some writing for me. I really became friends with him after my father died. I stopped playing then. A lot of my songs were about communicating with my dad. I quit writing for a while, then I met Townes and started again. He was kind of a surrogate father with me. I was under his wing. I may not have come out of that hole if I hadn't met Townes.

HUDSON: Let's trace the story of one song, your choice.

DONOVAN: "Factory Town" is very Townes-inspired as well as Paul Simon and Bruce Springsteen. I went home for Christmas to Detroit, and the car companies were closing down the factories. They were letting people go right before Christmas so they didn't have to pay a Christmas bonus. I was angry, and that's where the song came from. "Broken Heart" is the last song on that CD. It's very personal to me; it makes me cry every time I sing it. It came from a series of failed relationships.

HUDSON: Do you have a particular discipline that you follow when writing? A regimen?

DONOVAN: I wish. That would really be nice. But it doesn't work like that for me. I dream some songs. I dreamed the setting for "Angelina." I got up the next morning and wrote the song. I write it when I feel it. The biggest prolific time in my life was during the heyday of the Chicago House in Austin. Will T. Massey, Jimmy LaFave, Beaver Nelson, Betty Elders, Tish Hinojosa, and more. It reminded me of what I imagined about Greenwich Village in the 1960s with Paul Simon, Joan Baez, Judy Collins, and Bob Dylan. It was like a competition among songwriters. It was very inspirational. There was nothing else in your world but writing that next song. That atmosphere produced a mountain of these songs.

HUDSON: We often think of the songwriter being alone with her writing. I'm glad to hear you point to the value of community as well.

DONOVAN: Chicago House was it. I don't think a club has matched that energy again. It was not about how much beer you sold to the patrons. We were all poor, and Peg [Miller] and Glynda [Cox] were always on the verge of closing. They would even hush audience members who were talking during a set. It was totally about the original song. Chicago House and Kerrville are the reasons I moved from L.A. to Austin. Los Angeles was not about creating; it was about selling. You had gigs to industry representatives, not to people. I went there to move into the business. Then I realized I didn't want that. I met Lucinda [Williams] then. She said she was from Austin and going back. I came to the Kerrville Folk Festival and heard David Halley, Michelle Shocked, and Buddy Mondlock around campfires. Oh my God. This is where it is. I've been here twelve years now. This is for me. I moved here that first October after being in Kerrville in June.

HUDSON: Now what inspires you here?

DONOVAN: It's the individuals that I met at the Chicago House. I still play with Larry Wilson and Beth Gallagher, people I met at the Chicago House. That's the trio. Larry has five or six projects going at a time. He's a fruit fly of energy! Beth is playing with tons of people.

HUDSON: Do you have a roadmap for what you're doing now?

DONOVAN: I'm pretty much enjoying the opportunities right now. It's not an ongoing thing. I do meet with Larry regularly to write. We are heading in the direction of rock and roll. Just another place to go. I also want to have a totally sparse acoustic album. I want it all, baby!

HUDSON: And what would be a dream for you right now?

DONOVAN: I'd love to play Telluride, just for the beauty of the whole thing. I don't see myself in the folk scene at the Kerrville Folk Festival, but it is becoming more interesting as they open up to new forms of music. I'm spending time now concentrating on me and who I am. Family is in Michigan. No distractions. It's going to be all about the writing for the next year. I go out to Larry's studio on Thursdays. When I feel like I have something to say, I'll put out an album. That's another thing I like about Lucinda. She doesn't say she's going to put out an album in a year. When the child is ready, it will come out!

HUDSON: A great quotation on timing.

DONOVAN: I also want to play music in Europe. They have been playing this CD forever. They seem to be a fertile ground for this trio. Maybe just follow in the footsteps of Townes. That is next.

HUDSON: I hope to join you someday! Right now every classroom I lead is a fertile ground for the creative process to emerge. I see my day job, teaching, at the heart of all that I do.

DONOVAN: So do I. I design magazines. That comes from a different side of the brain than playing music. My schedule is my own. I like that. I do end up writing more at night. I seem to get real creative at night. The worst part of the day is two or three in the afternoon. Creative rhythms instead of biorhythms.

HUDSON: Is there something distinct that women bring to the stage and to writing?

DONOVAN: Absolutely. The women I follow have a real sense of independence. Look at Lucinda and Terri Hendrix, controlling their lives by controlling what they record. These women are bucking what happens when you go with another company. You get told to change your wardrobe, your hair, your songs. I follow the women who say "No" to this. Ani DiFranco is another. Betty Elders and Whistling Pig music, working right out of her home. Mary Chapin Carpenter always has that independent message as well. She might begin with "You done me wrong," but she ends up walking out the door doing just fine.

HUDSON: So you think maybe women bring a certain kind of strength to the music that men don't bring? They bring something else, for sure.

DONOVAN: Look at Dolly Parton. She knows exactly who she is, and it comes out in her writing. You don't mess with her.

HUDSON: The key is getting in touch with who you really are, not who your culture says you are. I know this has been my journey as a woman. We're always uncovering.

DONOVAN: It's being willing to admit the challenges and then share them with other people. Often an audience! There are blue skies on the horizon, and I'm going to find them. My voice is always optimistic in the end. I am also hearing that from other women.

HUDSON: I look at the stories of women through my mythology class. One of the connections that women have is with the natural world. A connection with an organic way of being. We seem to know better about birth and death because our bodies experience it monthly. Cycles and rhythms prevail, and we seem to be more aware of that.

DONOVAN: We also talked about that with the creative process. Terri Hendrix and Lloyd Maines are incredible. She is holding her own with him, and they appear as partners in the performance. I'm seeing this all over the place. Lucinda takes control of her career even as she plays with musicians who have done it all.

HUDSON: Do you know any younger songwriters that you encourage?

DONOVAN: No. I haven't been hitting the clubs in the last few years. Do you know of someone?

HUDSON: I think of Pauline Reese. She is working hard, bringing her honky-tonk music to new audiences.

DONOVAN: There's not much on the radio inspiring me these days, for sure. The country music I hear is predictable and not interesting. I hate to sound like an old folkie.

HUDSON: How do you relate to other areas of the arts?

DONOVAN: I love books. See that Steinbeck over there? I have all the Steinbeck books, including his letters and diaries. I'm a huge Steinbeck fan.

HUDSON: Next week I'll be in Monterey, California, with his son, Thom. That will be an inspiring moment for me.

DONOVAN: Wish I were going along. You'll find my book collection as eclectic as my music collection. I just went to Italy last year. Venice and Florence really inspired me. I want to live in another culture for a while. Something is drawing me to Italy. I think it's the slowness of the life. They take two hours for dinner. It's not just about the food; it's about the conversation and the company. The waiter will join in, and the table next to you. I see different values in this culture.

HUDSON: I look around and see this photo of you and Townes. Tell me that story.

DONOVAN: Townes had a show in Leon Springs. He had lost his voice, and Harold called to see if I could do the show. I did the show, apologizing to his audience. This is the time when I finally got time with just Townes and not all the craziness. I was honored that he chose me to do this.

HUDSON: When he showed up later at the Jimmie Rodgers tribute, I heard this story! He told me he was saving his voice for this songwriters' tribute that also included Guy Clark and Tish Hinojosa that I was producing. What a connection that is for us.

DONOVAN: I love doing some of his songs. He just sat on the front row, listening to me. We talked afterward.

HUDSON: What are some questions that you would like to ask?

EGGERS: Let's talk about the album *Thin Line* and the relationship with Bob Johnston.

DONOVAN: You tell that one!

EGGERS: I was working with Bob Johnston on several projects. He would stay at my condo when he came to Austin. We'd go out to Willie's, and I'd watch them talk and visit. Bob went through Willie's entire catalogue mastering them to DAT. While all this was going on, Bob would come over to the house and talk about the mixing. He asked me about my work with Barb, and I told him that Townes's favorite song was "Factory Town." I put it on for him to hear. Bob said, "I want to produce her." We didn't have the money for this. But he worked with us. Watching Barbara recording down at Fire Station and Pedernales was a joy. I noticed one of his wonderful abilities was to pump up Barb, telling her how good she was.

DONOVAN: The album came out great. I was trying to get him to do one more track to take to Europe. Bob was gone. The engineer said, "I can do this." We tried and tried. We finally figured out what Bob did. It became clear that a producer can do something that we can't put a finger on. What Bob did was let us play our music. He didn't interfere. I was expecting more interference. He explained to me that he hated perfection. He said that when Johnny Cash would strive for perfection, he would throw a chair into the room, just to throw him off his game. Perfection is not the answer. Good music comes from the heart. We keep the track if it sounds like you mean it. He comes into the room like he's nothing special. He's so humble. I had control of the songs I wanted on the album. He recommended a couple, and they worked. The album is called *Thin Line*.

EGGERS: Townes and I would travel for ten months out of the year. We did a tour of thirty-five cities. I put on Barb's CD at the beginning of one of the last shows. The road manager was thrilled with it, asking me why I hadn't given it to him earlier. He forwarded the music to the booking agent. We later heard from the agent that they wanted Barb to tour the next time with Townes. We stopped by and told Barb. She took me in the other room, saying, "I don't want to do this right now. I don't want to look like you guys." Meaning the wear and tear of the road was taking its toll. Townes was fine with that. Then he passed away, and it never happened.

HUDSON: We've come full circle now. Beginning and ending with Townes. We both love him. And your own story is a powerful statement of an independent woman.

DONOVAN: I would recommend that anyone writing original music go out and look for a community. It is possible to be independent and learn from a community. Don't do it alone. It becomes too introspective.

People ask if I'm the wild one in the family, and I answer, "No, that would be my mother."

Neesie Beal

SURPRISE IN THE PACKAGE

When I first met Jim Beal, music writer for the San Antonio Express-News, *he quickly became my hero as I started out in the business of writing about music. I saw him at many of the same shows. I admired everything about him, from his beret to his writing. Oh yes, I noticed the persona of Jim Beal. And I knew he had a wife who played music with him. Over the years I joined them at the Corpus Christi Jazz Festival, Jazz and Heritage in New Orleans, and the Cajun Festival in Medina, watching all the versions of music they performed and getting to know them as a couple, a rare couple of people really in love. I also knew that Neesie was a schoolteacher, elementary school at that. When I heard that blues growl in the throat of a woman who looked far younger than her years and experience, I was intrigued. Now I had two heroes, for I had always, in some tiny way, wanted to be onstage. Neesie and I finally took time to talk one Sunday afternoon at Casbeers on Blanco in San Antonio in July 2004. Downing that great Mexican buffet in between questions and answers, we had the following conversation.*

HUDSON: Let's talk about the present. You've always been a hero of mine, putting all these pieces of your life together with such grace. How do you have such grace and ease in all you do?

BEAL: That's really an interesting perspective. I never even thought about it. I guess ease is a good word, because I don't think about it. I taught for twenty-nine years, and I've been retired the last two years. People would ask me, "How do you do that, blend the careers?" I find it a nice balance. My entire life is about balance. I don't consciously try to balance things, but that is a perceptive way to look at it. Thanks for that question! Glad you asked that.

HUDSON: What's at the source of that ease and grace?

BEAL: Not having a partner who is exactly alike is a start. And honoring the difference my partner brings to the relationship instead of fighting with it. My parents were like that. I feel that what I love and what I do don't necessarily seem to go together. And I can easily make them fit together. I'm one of those people who make the best of each situation. I think it's a waste to be negative. Even with the recent tough diagnosis of my dad having Alzheimer's, what good does it do to create more negativity?

HUDSON: Have you had a turning point that created this perspective, or have you always been on this path?

BEAL: Jim kind of helps me with this too. He's very much this way, even more than me at times. I've always had a kind of spiritual grounding. I'm not talking about church, although church has always been part of my life. Jim's even more spiritual than I am. We tend to accentuate that with each other. It's a shared grounding. We help each other, rather than feeding off each other like I see in some other couples. Everybody goes through tough times, of course. As you well know. I know some of your tough times! We're not going to wallow in self-pity. I was raised Catholic, and Jim was raised Lutheran. That's pretty close. We are still involved in a Lutheran church right now. I'm not going to preach, but I feel that being spiritual is an important thing.

HUDSON: When did you decide to play music?

BEAL: The core members of the band, a group of five, have been together over twenty years. Jim and the accordion player grew up in church together. Jim and I were in high school when we met. On my first date ever, my husband, now, drove the car to take my date and me on the date. Jim's date stood him up. I love that story!

HUDSON: Let's talk about songwriting.

BEAL: I'm not much of a songwriter. Most of the Ear Food music has been a collaboration with our drummer, Ollie Morris. He's the natural poet. Allen Elsasser is the guitar player. Ronnie Biediger is the keyboard and accordionist. Of course, Jim plays bass. I do vocals, and when we do the zydeco thing, I play scrubboard ["frattoire" in Cajun] as well. We do have a horn section for the gospel brunch. Mike Davis is the trombone/harmonica player. And most of the time we have Rich Tellez, who plays trumpet. Other horn players sit in. The recording in your hand now was recorded at Sam's Burger Joint one night. The sound guy recorded us without our knowing it. It's the real performance, *au natural*! This is our first CD. We do have an Ear Food cassette. Take a look at the shrine on the piano. You'll recognize parts of it. And our CD is called *Enshrined*. You're even on the shrine somewhere. Ollie, an art teacher, periodically adds things. We evolved into the Ear Food configuration. When we first started, we were Anarchist Convention.

HUDSON: Let's talk about the women who have influenced you.

BEAL: At first I was a folksinger. Joan Baez was one of my heroes as a kid. When I was in college, I discovered Bonnie Raitt. I resent people saying, "All women want to be Bonnie Raitt." She's an influence on many women, for sure.

HUDSON: I first heard Bonnie at an Austin festival when she had Sippie Wallace join her onstage.

BEAL: My biggest blues influence is Koko Taylor. I really love blues: Denise LaSalle, Etta James.

HUDSON: I know you've heard lots of comments about your voice — big voice, small girl stuff.

BEAL: I've heard I sound like a 300-pound black woman or the mouse that roars! My dad's very quiet and peaceful. My mom speaks up loudly. People ask if I'm the wild one in the family, and I answer, "No, that would be my mother." I love moms like that.

HUDSON: Let's hear you describe how you feel singing and playing that music. I love the rhythm.

BEAL: It's a lot of different kinds of musical genres. One of the songs that I love is "Jerusalem," by Steve Earle. We are not doing it today, but it's a great song. Steve recently studied the children of Abraham, and the three major monotheistic religions of the world; we are all children of

Abraham. It makes me sad to see all the fighting. We're all family here. Jimmy Carter said, "We don't have to be killing each other." I feel all that. Steve Earle says, "I woke up this morning and none of the news was good. Death machines were rumbling across the ground where Jesus stood." That's a sad commentary on the state of the world.

HUDSON: Is there a part of your involvement with music that feels like sharing a message with the audience?

BEAL: Ear Food agrees with the Rolling Stones: "We don't always give you what you want, but we give you what you need."

HUDSON: Let's talk about one of the songs you're singing today that you really love. I love "You've Got to Move."

BEAL: I also love "Nobody's Fault But Mine." We'll do that in the next set. Those are songs that make you really feel something. No matter what you believe. Jim does a gospel hour on the radio each Thursday on 90.1 FM. He says, "It doesn't matter what your religion is, just move to the right lane and chill out a little bit."

HUDSON: I have this sense of expansion inside me today with the music. I'll carry that out with me.

BEAL: That's right. You carry it out into the world. Pass it on kind of thing.

The challenge . . . is being more in control of the business we have created.

Christine Albert

THE FRENCH CONNECTION

Christine and I first met in about 1987 at Midem in Cannes, France, the first year Texas had a booth at this worldwide music conference. I was representing the Texas Heritage Music Foundation, and she was promoting her music to the world. Her French heritage adds a further flavor to this music that she sometimes calls Texafrance. Her beauty is both physical and spiritual. Her songs reflect a woman who is centered and clear about her goals in life. She has been down the road of dealing with a major record, writing, performing in Europe, and performing at the Kerrville Folk Festival. We met at Artz Rib House in December 2004 for a birthday party for Caryl P. Weiss, a folksinger we both know and love. Christine currently records and tours as one-half of the acclaimed Texas duo Albert and Gage, with her husband and partner Chris Gage.

HUDSON: Let's talk about where you are right now and look at the roads that led you here.

ALBERT: The challenge for me now is being more in control of the business we have created, embracing that role rather than resisting it. I am looking at this as an integral part of what I want to do. It is the vehicle for the projects that come up for me, and I am learning to use these tools and keep the creativity alive. The challenge is how to keep the creative aspect alive while managing databases and answering phone calls. I am fortunate in my partnership with Chris. We started a professional relationship eight years ago, and we got married about a year and a half ago, thus merging my professional and personal life. We merge well. We each have strengths we bring to our relationship, and we run these companies together. We have a record company that has our releases and two outside artists, twelve releases in all. We manage our distribution totally through the Internet, and the Internet has really changed things. Remember when we heard this discussion at Midem? I remember hearing the comment that the Internet would put power back into the hands of the artist. I think we are seeing that now. I couldn't envision that at the time. It is now an incredible tool. We also have a recording studio, digital and state of the art. We have all the facets of the business under our roof. We have the label, the studio, and we still tour. We've released records of a couple of artists we really believe in. One is Cowboy Johnson. He has done a complete album of the music of Mickey Newbury. He has a warm and incredible voice. This is his first album. Two days after the CD release, Willie Nelson heard it and booked him for the 2004 picnic. Mickey's family heard the CD and love it. They really embraced him. He has such a soulful quality to him. That record has a life of its own. Michael Austin on clarinet is the other artist. Chris produced both in our studio, and they're on our label.

HUDSON: I know you're looking forward to going back to Europe.

ALBERT: Chris and I go to Europe every year or so. We have been there fifteen times together. We have an agent in Germany who keeps us going back. Butch Hancock says, "I have played to hundreds of people in isolated pockets of good taste all over the world." The European audience loves the rootsy and soulful quality of Texas music, and audiences are so knowledgeable about the albums. They know who plays bass on what album, where it was recorded, and in what year.

HUDSON: How does your French background show up?

ALBERT: We weave the songs throughout our shows. I have two French albums: *Texafrance*, the first one I did, and *Texafrance-Encore*, a follow-up. What I worked on all day today is a project with a French teacher. She has written a book of exercises that go along with the albums! Her students listen to my records and then do some exercises around the songs. She has had requests from other teachers for this material, so we are putting together a book. We're going to market it through organizations of French teachers and the Internet. This gives students some hands-on reasons to develop their French. We are going to publish this through our own business. Now we have a structure to support our creative endeavors.

HUDSON: Texas music is so rich, with many threads weaving through this fabric. The French thread is unique with you, and there are also the threads of the songwriter, the soul, and the roots music.

ALBERT: My mom is from Europe, and I grew up with the French language. All the women in my family spoke French, and at a molecular level, it feels right to sing in French, but I also love to write and to sing Ray Charles's songs. I started out singing in honky-tonks in New Mexico, so country music will always show up in my sound.

HUDSON: Many women in Texas are staying in control of their own music.

ALBERT: I had a record deal in Nashville with Columbia. I made a record that didn't come out because of change in management of the label. I also had a publishing deal with a major company. I learned a lot, but it is not in my nature to sit and write on demand. I am too much of a live performer and too much of a Texan to just write and wait for that major cut. I need to be in front of a live audience every week. I grew up in New York and then moved to Santa Fe. I spent twelve years there before I moved to Texas. The first time I came to Texas with Eliza Gilkyson, Gary P. Nunn showed us around. He took us to hear Lucinda Williams at the Alamo Hotel when she was playing in the corner of the bar. We both knew that this was a community that would feed our muse.

HUDSON: Let's talk about the women who have influenced you.

ALBERT: I have a lot of close women friends. Musically, Eliza Gilkyson is the main one. When I moved to Santa Fe, my brother was playing music with her. I was fifteen, and she was about to turn twenty. She was the first woman I'd seen go onstage and perform. I had been doing that in my bedroom as a teenager. We became close friends. I took care of her babies while she was on the road. We're still really good friends. It's been thirty-four years since our paths first crossed. She e-mailed me last week, saying, "I'm so tired. Is it still worth it to you?" We cheer each other up. We're still hauling our CDs around and loading up at the end of the gig. We have no choice. This is what we do. As a writer, Eliza is incredibly gifted, and I am thrilled to see her finally get the recognition that she deserves. My mother, my aunt, and my grandmother were really strong.

My aunt was an artist in New York City. She was single her entire life and had a creative drive.

HUDSON: It sounds to me like you and Chris have really woven a life together.

ALBERT: Sometimes when we get home from the road, we pretend like we weren't together. He'll turn around and say, "Hi, how was your trip?" Just to have someone welcoming us home. My son is sixteen now. He stays with Ernie, his dad, when I'm on the road. It works out well. We are fortunate that we are able to raise him together, even though Ernie lives across town.

HUDSON: You have such a clear statement about center and balance. What personal practices do you have that support you?

ALBERT: I walk and do yoga. I also meditate. Lately, I've been writing more each day. That's been hard for me. The further away I get from those practices, the more off balance I get. I'm a Virgo; I can run the business well. But if I sacrifice the creative and more intuitive parts of me, I get resentful of the business. A daily practice is so important. The further away I get, the harder it is to check back in.

HUDSON: Let's talk about one song before you go back to that plate of ribs.

ALBERT: One of my favorites is called "Tumbleweed." It was written about a creative dry spell. The first line was "I can't stay in a barren place for too many years." It was a gift for me when I realized that the thing that broke the creative dry spell was to sit down and write a song about it! Now that's ironic. Whenever I sing that song, I remember that lesson.

[Christine added a final comment upon reading the interview.]

Since our conversation I have embarked on another journey. After twenty-four years in Austin, I felt like it was time to give back to the community that has supported me for so long. I have created Swan Songs, a 501(c)(3) non-profit, which organizes private concerts by a favorite Texas musician for individuals with a life-threatening illness. We will bring the requested performer to their home, hospital, or hospice facility to fulfill their musical wish. As executive director, I will act as liaison with the music community and match recipients with the artists. I am excited to be realizing a dream I've had for many years.

When I sing and play the guitar, no matter how scared I am, something happens spiritually around me.

Sara Hickman

MAGIC ON STAGE

We sat down for a conversation at Flipnotics Coffeespace Cafe in Austin, Texas, on December 15, 2002. Sara had decided to step away from the music business as she had been doing it and look for other ways while being with her children. Our conversation was so forthright and genuine that, after admiring her rhinestone horseshoe necklace, I found myself the proud recipient of this gift. I promptly took off a string of small amber pieces that I wear and gave it to her. We grinned and shared like sisters. Sara is totally self-aware and expressive, hiding nothing. At least that was the perception I left with. We looked into each other's eyes, no averting or ducking. We had a real conversation about things that matter.

HUDSON: After knowing of your association with the Hill Country Youth Ranch, and after seeing you at the Kerrville Folk Festival for years, I know you have a distinct story to tell. Let's start with the past and look at three times that were magical for you, turning points or awakenings.

HICKMAN: [long pause] The first thing that comes up for me is having this teacher, Pat Bonner, at the High School for Performing Visual Arts.

I had been making music since I was six, so it was just something I did as a child. It felt natural to write songs, make up stories and pretend I was Carol Burnett. I even wrote a eulogy when I was seven or eight that I wanted George Burns to read at my funeral. I rolled it up and carried it inside my guitar for years. I grew up in a very creative household. There wasn't ever any "No" or "Why." I heard "Yes," "Try that," "What made you think of that?" "Here's some art supplies." It was always very supportive, and I feel very blessed. I thought that was how the whole world was. When I got to the performing arts high school, I realized that, for a lot of the kids, that was the first time they had lived in a creative environment. And I appreciated my background even more. It was really mind-blowing.

I was in the vocal department there. My parents had just gotten divorced, and I was experiencing a lot of confusion. Miss Bonner, my teacher, would set up performances for me. People would call the school needing someone for a wedding or some other event, and she would set it up for me. I got a little money, but mostly I got experience. One day she came to me and said, "Would you like to go sing at a psychiatric unit?" And she told me it was for kids my age and I might even know some of the kids there.

So I went to this lockdown unit. I had never been in a psych unit and had never done any therapeutic work at all. So I was a little unprepared. I went in, and they locked the doors behind me. I remember this boy Jay. He came up to me and he said, "Hi, Sara, We went to school together." I had instructions to deny knowing any of these kids. That was hard; it was hard for me to lie to that kid. I had been told this would protect the kids from worrying that people on the "outside" would find out they were in the unit. But that was the beginning of my awareness that I had a gift. When I sing and play the guitar, no matter how scared I am, something happens spiritually around me. That was really moving for me. I remember leaving that unit and thinking, "I want to do more of this." That was a turning moment in my life. That led to doing volunteer work with music and joining Arts for People later in Dallas and being involved with them for about seventeen years. I would go into hospitals and work in burn units. I worked with the first case of AIDS in Dallas County. I worked with MHMR [Mental Health/Mental Retardation], homeless people, suicidal people. So I learned a lot about people, and I learned about compassion, about letting things be. How music can heal.

HUDSON: Well, you're making me cry at the beginning of this conversation. I am so moved by this story.

HICKMAN: My heroes have always been Mother Teresa, Jesus, Buddha, and other people on a higher plane. I can't ever hope to be as great and selfless as these people, but when I am out working, that's what I aspire to. It's amazing now, all these years later, that people still come up and remind me of a hospital visit I had with them. One woman reminded me that I made her sing an Elvis song and made her laugh. She said, "You saved my soul that day. I was so lost. You made me laugh again." Then I started weeping, and she was weeping too. Her son came over and hugged me. It was an amazing moment. Something I think of as a very simple act [singing in a hospital room] can really alter something for someone else in the world.

HUDSON: Some of us have always known that music operates at a spiritual level.

HICKMAN: Yes, physiologically, something happens to the synapses and memories come up. Sometimes people even remember smells when they hear a certain song. Music is in film and TV because it can cause such a real reaction. So, perhaps those of us who perform are also responsible, in some way, for what happens with music. It makes you feel alive, and it makes you feel pain. The music in the movie *Schindler's List* is what makes you suffer with those people. You can feel that pain in the music. It is like this universal pumping of the heart. That goes back to the rhythm of the drum. It is an amazing fact. Like Bob Dylan's voice, for example, isn't the easiest voice to listen to, but many people want to hear him. What does that say?

HUDSON: Hard science is bringing forth information that links back to the work of early mystics and sounds. I can see the gift working both ways, with the giver also being blessed.

HICKMAN: I ask every musician who asks me for advice, "Do you volunteer? You will be amazed at what you get by your giving."

HUDSON: Where is that leading you into the future?

HICKMAN: I've gotten to the point where I don't really like what I see, and it's a very big "what I see." I'm not sure I can describe it, but I've always been a highly emotional person. I was in church this morning listening to a cantata, and I felt my own heart again. I guess that could be called tender-hearted, and I'm glad I'm tender-hearted. There is so much beauty in the world. I think that is why I'm stepping away for a while. I've always believed that I have a purpose and that I'm making a difference. God made me and gave me this gift, as all of us have been made and all of us have gifts. I really started feeling this calling to step away and be quiet for a while. I've done this for thirty-two years, and I'm physically and spiritually exhausted. I'm at a place in life where I really love being at home, in the earth gardening and being with my family. Walking my kids to school, making the cookies, or teaching in their classes—all these things call to me now. There was a part of me feeling kind of hopeless about people and nations—how people are responding to each other in the world. It's an overwhelming feeling to imagine how a little CD can go out there and make a difference. I don't want that to be my life's purpose, getting the next CD out. I don't want to try to fix the world anymore. I want to be in the world and of the world. Right now I want to be quiet and see what my next calling is. That might be working in smaller groups with women. I really like to do motivational speaking. I've thought about being a musical doula, where I go and sing to women's bellies. The fetus does respond to music, especially with someone who's trained as a musician.

HUDSON: A musical doula? I've never heard of that term.

HICKMAN: It's something I made up. There aren't any, but I would love to be the first one! It's a concept where I would place my hands and mouth on a woman's belly and sing. Just to watch the body move and respond is evidence that something is happening.

I love doing children's music. I've won some awards for these, and those CDs sell well enough to support my little family. There's such a joy in singing for children. They don't know about the world yet. They know about their mommy and daddy, their family. I love sitting with a group of kids and teaching about art and music. I could do it forever. So, I don't know if my calling is this direction. I've always been one of those people who "know." Now I'm willing to be with "I don't know." I feel like I've had a whole career, and I'm ready to try some different things.

HUDSON: Everything you're saying addresses where I am right now in my own life. Yesterday I attended a writing workshop here in Austin with Thom the World Poet. There were just four of us in a library, and we sat and wrote for twenty-five minutes, then read to each other. I realized that I haven't been quiet in a long time.

HICKMAN: I feel like there's a movement toward being quiet. I've just come out of a system that is very Western in thinking. Pushy. You have to make so much money in order to be successful, be in the public eye, get a Grammy. Shifting from it is like going through withdrawal in a way. I feel like I was always trying to be myself in that system [the music business], and I'm quirky. You can't really box me in or put me on a shelf. I think that's something to be celebrated. After a while I realized that the system does not work for me, and that's okay. It's very hard to get away from that system without everyone responding with their own fear. You know, that was a moment in my life and very exciting. That quiet is something missing, though. People will buy second homes to go find a place to rest. Then they fill that home with stuff. You don't need another home or place to be quiet. You just need to be quiet where you are. A lot of that is listening more and choosing your words with care. That's where I want to be. When I was at Rod Kennedy's farewell party, I thought it was weird to go up on a stage to sing to Rod. I don't want to be on a stage; I wanted to go sing to Rod. [So, Sara did just that. She walked up to him, sang to his personality, and sat in his lap.] I leaned in and talked to him. Getting on a stage, in some ways, is the antithesis of what my music started out to be. I would get my guitar, close my eyes, and sing to my mom and dad. It was this great big connection. I'm not saying it isn't beautiful to watch U2 and see thousands of people connect, but I know that I can also connect with people from stage. It's incredibly moving to just use your voice and your guitar and look someone in the eye and really love them. I wanted to give that to Rod. He's always supported me and believed in me.

HUDSON: I remember nights at the Kerrville Folk Festival listening to your beautiful songs and your beautiful voice. Even then, when I didn't know you, I had the impression of this centered woman who knows who she is.

HICKMAN: And I've always inspired people to be who they are. People are neat. It goes back to the joy. Where is that joy? It's in the quiet.

HUDSON: How did you get involved with the Hill Country Youth Ranch?

HICKMAN: Tony Young called me. He and Gary Priour were putting out that first *Broken Wings Can Fly* CD. It was such a gorgeous idea to have children write poetry about their experiences and have professional songwriters put music to it. They had already finished the music, but they wanted me to sing a song. I chose three of them. That was an honor.

Once, after a performance, a woman walked up to me, saying, "I really want to support your projects. I believe in you." I gave her four proposals of different projects, and one was the CD *Newborn*. She cut the check and said, "I don't want to have the money back. Just give my part to a project in Washington, D.C., that I believe in." That inspired me. I ended up giving all the money from the CD to Hill Country Youth Ranch. I really like all the work they are doing out there. Powerful work transforming the lives of children.

HUDSON: Let's talk about your relationship to family and how that has evolved.

HICKMAN: Look at someone like Trout Fishing in America. They are on tour about 270 days out of the years, and their wives are running the business. That seems very enviable. I don't have a wife but I feel blessed, that Lance, my husband for the last two and a half years, has been a stay-at-home dad. This has worked really well, and my kids have benefited from having one parent home all the time. I would go out for three or four days on tour, then stay home five or six. I started getting tired of being on the road. Especially after 9/11. The airports got harder to be in, and people seemed traumatized. I'm the kind of woman who always ends up talking with strangers, so I really heard a lot of fear. I didn't mind, but I was worn out from it. I realized that I didn't want to be trapped somewhere, stuck somewhere away from my family. What is most important to me right now is my family. Least important to me is saving the world. Actually, I can save the world by staying at home with my family. I can save the world by going to my child's school and teaching once a week. These are kids hungry and thirsty for art, for music. The world is really a big place. I always thought it was small. Eventually, I might want to be involved in a city council or be an ambassador. I don't really know where that will go. I can feel that coming on.

HUDSON: I'm putting together some workshops in San Miguel de Allende where I teach each year.

HICKMAN: San Miguel must be a special calling. A woman I'm working with is going down there in January. The calling to go there seems very strong.

HUDSON: Let's discuss your writing and your own creative process.

HICKMAN: [She pulls out her latest CD, *Faithful Heart*.] Do you have this one? I saved a place to interact and write your own stuff inside. It celebrates human sexuality and love. It's a collection of songs that have made a difference in my world, some written by me, some by other people.

HUDSON: This is beautiful!

HICKMAN: I wanted it to be beautiful. I used my own painting on the cover. Last year when I was making a Christmas CD, I went to my five-year-old and said, "I would really love it if you would do the artwork for this." She said, "OK, what do you need?" I answered, "Angels and Christmas trees." As she walked around the corner, she told my husband, "I have a job to do." She came back with these drawings. [We look them over.] How empowering for a child to be asked to contribute. Now she's asked for her autograph! Lily is her name; it's an acronym for "Lily I love you." Lily Blessing Hickman-Walden. My new baby, my two-year-old, is Iolana Rose Hickman-Schriner, and Iolana is Hawaiian for "heavenly bird."

You were asking me about my writing process. I have always kept journals. In that way you document your life and keep moments you might forget about. I keep journals with about ten different people. We draw and write to each other. That is an awesome way to write, and it keeps you connected to people in a very beautiful way. There's also the mystery of putting it in the mail, knowing you might never see it again. That is so symbolic of how life is. That's one way. I try to find ways to journal with people. Even when I teach classes, I bring in a fresh journal. I give it to them, saying, "Write in this and mail it to me."

Another way is that I'm still very open . . . this is hard to explain. I grew up in a house with a weaver and a painter. I became aware of tiny things, like the thread being used when my mother would sew. It's almost like I'm feeding all the time, feeding on texture, light, movement, space, sound . . . you name it. As we sit and talk, I'm noticing the different colors in your hair, your eye makeup, the glitter in your face, how your teeth fit together. [laughter from us both] I can't stop noticing. What I notice eventually comes out in a story or a song.

I do have discipline. I have to write a lot. I've started writing more stories. I've found out that I really enjoy writing without the music or the poetry. There are moments in my life that I make the effort to write at the same time every day. The biggest thing for me is spirit. I can be in a car, something will happen, then I see the chords and the song all comes at once. Or I will be running in a race, and the whole song comes to me while I'm running. Walking seems to be such a mind-blowing experience. I don't carry a tape recorder. I think there is something about the breathing when I walk that relaxes my brain and frees me up to be creative. I also read everything, from milk cartons to the *New York Times*. It's like I have this addiction to the word. I am interested in what other songwriters are saying. That reveals their soul more than the music, for me.

HUDSON: I have a favorite expression: "Your choice of words is your choice of worlds."

HICKMAN: I have people come up to me a lot, saying, "I wish I could do something like this with my life." I just want to put my arm around them and say, "Just do it." It's that simple. Just start doing it. I don't know how or why I do it. I just know I have to do it. It's exciting to me to think that I only have this much time on earth, and I don't know how much that time is. I feel really blessed to be here.

HUDSON: What's your favorite song that you've written?

HICKMAN: "It's Alright." It's on *Newborn* and is a song from God. I didn't write it. It came through me in a moment of great despair. It was a God thing.

Tibetan Buddhism brings in the concept of "crazy wisdom," sudden enlightenment . . . it's the moment when you just know certain things.

Melissa Javors

SERIOUS ABOUT WRITING

I met Melissa Javors on a Sunday morning, September 8, 2002, before she recorded a set for the Greg Forest TV series at the YO Ranch Hotel at the Folk Alliance conference. We sat facing each other on a big leather couch. After years of knowing each other, teaching together, doing gigs together, we just talked. She was part of a writers' workshop I created at Schreiner—joining Kinky Friedman, C. J. Berkman, Becky Crouch, Naomi Nye, Carrie Cogan, and others. She played my favorite, "Wild Horses." I met her Irish producers when attending Midem, and I knew TVA, the bluegrass group her former husband belonged to. Melissa and I always had much in common.

HUDSON: It's a rainy Sunday at the end of Folk Alliance. It's September 8, 2002. Happy birthday to Jimmie Rodgers! I had to say that. I'm thrown back into a memory of years ago when Guy Clark and I sat in that restaurant and had a long conversation about writing. Also, my association with you, which started at the Kerrville Folk Festival and grew into an association between educators. Remember when you came to the Lions Club? We were a duo. I came to your classroom and gave a presentation on Greece. We've gone back and forth on many projects. We've got this really wonderful history woven together. Now you've moved to Nashville. First, I want to mention this training that we have in common. We both studied at Naropa in Boulder, and we've both participated in programs with the Landmark Education Corporation.

JAVORS: I was always encouraged by my family to think for myself, and I've always been interested in philosophy and religion. I would always follow these little trails of people getting into new things, and I would always bail out at the point when you were supposed to say, "This is the right way." It really disturbed me and disrupted me. In 1979 I found out, at age twenty-nine, that I had type 1 diabetes. I had just moved to Texas with my husband and my little girl. I was pretty freaked out at this point in my life. I had always wanted to be a musician. I married a musician, but in his case it was like a hobby. I had put a lot of things on hold to have the babies. After I got sick, it suddenly hit me that I wasn't going to be here forever, and if I wanted to do something, I'd better do it now. And then I did the training [est, at that time] in October 1980. I came to Kerrville in May 1981 and won the New Folk contest. So, it gave me the clarity that I needed about what I really wanted to be doing with my life and my time. It has also given me some ways of dealing with my illness and things that have enabled me to function without being a victim.

HUDSON: What a huge tool that you took advantage of. Over breakfast you mentioned that you had been to Naropa.

JAVORS: I was living in Boulder in the 1970s, and when [Chögyam] Trungpa came there and founded Naropa, we went to several different lectures at that time. Now, when I go back and read the writing this guy was doing, I guess I wasn't ready then to hear what he was saying. It is a thread of Tibetan Buddhism, and if you look at all the influences on Werner [Erhard] when he started the est training, I think you would find this same thread. Tibetan Buddhism brings in the concept of "crazy wisdom," sudden enlightenment.

HUDSON: You get it.

JAVORS: Right. There's no other way he could have found that concept. Some of the weird Sufi stuff, like [G. I.] Gurdjieff, has a similar take, but it's definitely a strain of Tibetan Buddhism.

HUDSON: When you think of all the women you know, how would you see your voice as distinct?

JAVORS: [silence] I think that, first of all, I write as a human being. I'm only a woman second to that. And the attention is not on sexuality and gender. It's a different focus. Maybe the focus for me has been that I want to write songs that address the realities of human relationships. Not according to some consensus, or a collection of mythologies about the way things are supposed to be. I can write things that have an edge to them. I'm trying to reconcile the notion and the lyrics of popular songs that I listened to as a kid with the truth of relationships.

HUDSON: You're a mother, a daughter, and a grandmother. A lot of female energy there.

JAVORS: I read an interview with Bob Dylan one time, and he got in a lot of trouble for saying this one time: "Women who got up on stage were prostituting themselves." The interviewer said, "What about Joni Mitchell?" Dylan replied, "She's like a man." That's what he was saying. He was saying that her music was not about being a woman; she was just delivering her essence.

HUDSON: What are your reading and other influences?

JAVORS: I've been doing astrology since 1973, at a pretty in-depth level. That has afforded me an opportunity to understand things I've never been able to understand about people. Metaphysics and philosophy and religions are important. I read a lot of fiction. I love John Updike, and Martin Amis, the son of Kingsley Amis. He wrote one book that I just love that you would flip over. It's called *Time's Arrow*. It's written backwards. It tells the story of a man's life backwards. The conversations are backwards. This guy finds himself going over to the wall, takes a picture off the wall, backs up across the room, takes wrapping paper out of the trash can . . . the insights have to do with the fact that it doesn't make any difference which direction things happen. The point of power is in the present. The middles of all relationships are the same, and at the beginning and the end you're like strangers. It's a kind of inventive and creative way of approaching our situation that gives us a different way of looking at things.

HUDSON: Was the move to Nashville a big shift for you?

JAVORS: I was never happy in San Antonio. I grew up on the East Coast, met my husband in Boulder, and we came back to his home in Texas. It was not my choice to be here or to stay here. When my youngest daughter was through with high school, I wanted to go somewhere else. I noticed lots of the people I knew at Kerrville had moved to Nashville. I got a job teaching music there. It's been really good.

HUDSON: What a rich place for you to work.

JAVORS: The school district in Nashville is extremely interested that I write songs and have a foot in several worlds. Here in Texas nobody would have cared that much.

HUDSON: Yesterday we got to talk about the opportunities we create in education. I loved the ones you talked about with the Country Music Foundation.

JAVORS: I've found that people who have been brought up to do every-thing perfect, as in classical music, are not comfortable with inventing and spontaneity. There was a move to give people that sense that they own music. There are a number of music teachers here who do both. It works out well for me to be on committees who work with creating some new opportunities.

HUDSON: Tell me about this latest project.

JAVORS: The title is *Crazy Wisdom,* which is the name of one of my songs. That's a term that comes from Tibetan Buddhism. It refers to the moment that you just know certain things. There's a quote on the back of the CD from Trungpa: "You could say that seeing things as they are is not quite crazy enough. It's like you have to be a realist, but you also have to be able to have this other kind of vision that is not based on evidence. In that sense, it's crazy.

HUDSON: Tell me about your recording history.

JAVORS: My first recording was when Gary P. Nunn paid for my first recording in San Antonio with his Guacamole label in 1983. Then Greg Forest took my music to Midem one year, and this guy from a British record label picked up my music and really liked it. Dave Bulmer's Celtic Music had a label called Making Waves. It was a Celtic label. I did a CD for them in 1990. They were a tiny, tiny label with no advertising or promotional budget. I have considered my albums and CDs also as song demos. I haven't had anything major cut in Nashville, but a few artists from Kerrville have recorded my songs. I've also done a lot of co-writing since moving to Nashville. I've loved that.

HUDSON: What's a big dream for you right now?

JAVORS: I'd be really happy to have anybody else record my songs and walk around places that I don't go. I really enjoy performing, and I'm not interested in driving around the United States doing house concerts. I'm past wanting to do that with my time. I enjoy going out to writers' nights in Nashville, but I'm really more of a writer than I am a star. It's taken me many years to understand those different hats to wear.

HUDSON: You have so much to offer in being able to articulate what you are doing and why.

JAVORS: I think one of the practices of teaching is that you have to learn quickly that your first way of saying something is not going to get through to everyone.

HUDSON: Tell me a story about a time when a lot of rich and wonderful things happened in your life and that evolved into a song.

JAVORS: I'll tell you the story of "Crazy Wisdom." I moved to Nashville in August 1998, and I found out three months after I got there that I was going to have to start dialysis; my kidneys were failing. My brother offered to give me one of his kidneys, and I had to wait a period of time. I was meeting so many amazing writers at this time. One of the people I met was Alex Call. He wrote a lot with Huey Lewis. I was meeting people who were the sources of music that I'd been listening to my whole life. Being in an environment with so many artists was so important to me. I was watching CNN, and I was up to here with news anchors announcing something else to worry about. So I wrote this song that begins, "Talking heads on CNN . . ." The chorus is "Sing me your dreams, paint me your vision." It was addressed to artists. Artists are drawing their own conclusions. Wrapping things up in their own bows instead of adopting the consensus interpretation on the news. That gives me strength. I have to function from that other space.

To us, she was just a mother who took care of us. . . . She washed our clothing, ironed, cooked, and did the housecleaning. . . . She would not let us into the kitchen. . . . Sometimes she would be sewing and singing at the same time.

Lydia Mendoza Davila

HER MOTHER'S DAUGHTER

My love for Mexico, my many trips to San Miguel de Allende, heightened my appreciation for music in the Spanish language. The voice of Lydia Mendoza is a presence in the world of music. Her life is a golden thread in the tapestry of Texas music. Since her health prevented an interview, I requested a conversation with her daughter, Lydia Mendoza Davila. She was generous with her time, and we talked several times. The book Lydia Mendoza's Life in Music, *by Yolanda Broyles-González, captures Lydia's story in her own words, her own language. It is a poetic work of art. After reading this book, I knew I had to meet Lydia Mendoza, be in her presence. One afternoon I sat quietly with her at a San Antonio nursing home. I went to the Witte Museum in San Antonio to hear Dr. Gonzalez speak, and I bought the book and accompanying CD. It is a perfect piece of oral history, including the music. The recordings of Lydia Mendoza capture her distinctive voice.*

HUDSON: I have a great relationship with my mom, who just turned eighty. We talk several times a week. I cherish that opportunity. It's a privilege to talk with a daughter about her mom. And the Mendoza family is such an important part of Texas musical history. I was at the Witte Museum when Yolanda Broyles-González gave a presentation on the wonderful book she wrote about your mom. I bought the book and accompanying CD. I loved the fact that the book was written in English and in Spanish.

MENDOZA: Yes, it was a great idea. I enjoyed that presentation as well.

HUDSON: The book, which gave your mom a chance to tell her own story, revealed the challenge for a woman being both performer and mother.

MENDOZA: Yes, my mom, for the longest time, stopped singing, when she started having us. She stayed home. It was during the war, I believe. We didn't really know she was a big star. We were just going to school. When we were about thirteen and fourteen, both my sister and I realized that she was somebody in the world. The first time we went to Los Angeles, we stayed near the theater. My father would always travel with her. He took us to the theater to see her, and I was amazed to see the long lines of people waiting to get tickets. I had never seen so many people. We were so impressed. We realized that people liked her.

HUDSON: What are some of your memories of her as a mother?

MENDOZA: When we were growing up, my mom would play the guitar and sing a little. She wanted us to start singing too. We were not interested in singing. We thought, "Why does she sing all the time? I guess she likes it." We would see her get some students for guitar and voice. We would look and wonder why she was doing this. She enjoyed it. We enjoyed seeing her play the guitar at night for us. Sometimes she would just practice. She was a very loving person. A lot of people liked her, and we liked her too! I remember once when I was in junior high school, we had a play at school. One of the teachers, who knew who my mother was, asked if my mom could come sing for us. It was so funny. I went and asked my mom. It happened to be that she was going out of town that day. I was so disappointed. I wanted the whole school to see her. She was a very pretty lady. To us, she was just a mother who took care of us. She never made us do housecleaning. She washed our clothing, ironed, cooked, and did the housecleaning. We never knew how to cook! She would not let us into the kitchen. *Arroz* and beans with Kool-Aid was my favorite dish. She knew how to sew very well. We always had new dresses. My father was a shoemaker, so we always had new shoes. We were not rich, but we had new things handmade by our parents. Sometimes she would be sewing and singing at the same time.

HUDSON: I'm sure my kids remember me as an English teacher, always grading papers and reading books. I wanted to encourage them to like school because I liked school. We have four generations of women in our family. And my new relationship with my sister is very meaningful to me.

MENDOZA: I had two sisters, Nora and Yolanda. One passed away with diabetes. Yolanda and I were very close, always doing things together. Then we had a misunderstanding. We don't talk to each other anymore. It's kind of sad for me. My mother is in between. She always asks me if I've called Yolanda. She knows I don't. Sometimes it can't be done. You try, but no. Yolanda is a little younger than I am.

HUDSON: This is a sweet picture of the two of you with your mom in the book by Yolanda Broyles-González.

MENDOZA: I remember being in Chicago. I remember going to a store that had Shirley Temple dolls. My mother bought two of them, one for my sister and one for me. I don't know why my mother bought those dolls. She never left us home. We always had a nanny who traveled with us. Mom traveled a lot, and she would always take us with her. Then when we got older, we wanted to stay at home with our friends. We would stay with our grandmother, our father's mother. I remember one time when we were about fifteen. We were in Los Angeles. My father told us that he was planning on staying in L.A. with my mother. I was so upset because I had a boyfriend then. I didn't eat for a whole week. My mother was so worried. She told my dad that they'd better send us back to San Antonio. We came back to San Antonio by bus. And when we got home my mother had already called many times to find out that we were okay. We spent summertime with my grandmother. We used to like the traveling when we were younger.

HUDSON: Did you speak Spanish in the house together?

MENDOZA: Yes, my mom never speaks English. She understands it, but she cannot speak it. My father, too, you know. He would speak to us in Spanish. When we went to school, we started speaking English. We mix it in my house now. It's Mex-Tex now. All my kids speak English all the time. In fact, they don't know how to speak Spanish.

HUDSON: Did you ever visit Mexico with your mom?

MENDOZA: Mom had some contracts in Mexico. We stayed here with our dad and grandmother. A long time, maybe six weeks. She always called us! She talked with us every day.

HUDSON: Did you work with Yolanda Broyles-González on this book?

MENDOZA: I think she talked with Manuel, my uncle. He's already passed away. I think she talked to my aunt Juanita. She always wanted to write her story, but she never did until Yolanda came by with this book idea. There's a man who wrote another book. . . . What's his name? Chris Strachwitz. He called my mom very often. He's a very good friend of my mom. He has several CDs of her music.

HUDSON: He's a very important person. He came from California to San Antonio to document the conjunto festival. He knew that music was important to the history of this state and to the history of American music. Why does it always take an outsider to notice these things?

MENDOZA: He also had a video that documents her [*Chulas Fronteras*, by Les Blank]. It's just a little part that my mother has in it. We all went to Houston for Christmas, and my mother was making tamales. She always did this at Christmas. We were all married at the time [1975–1976]. She's a very good cook. But she never wanted us in the kitchen. She would also wash my grandmother's clothes. She lived about two blocks from where we lived, and she would always go there in the morning, get her clothing, and wash them in the tub at our house. We didn't have a washing machine, so she would hang them outside and dry them. Then she would press them and take them back. She was very close to my grandma. Her mother. Every morning she would go to see her. Then in the afternoon. She was always there at my grandma's house.

HUDSON: What was it like when you decided to get married and leave the family?

MENDOZA: I wanted to get married right after I finished school. My mother was happy about it. I was nineteen when I got married. I had just finished high school at Sidney Lanier High School. It was and still is all Spanish kids. It's just like a family. I was a cheerleader for three years there. My mother is so funny. When I asked her if I could try out for cheerleader, she said, "Fine." But she didn't know what a cheerleader was. So, when I made it and had my uniform, she suddenly told me I could not wear that to the first football game. She saw it and said to go take it off. I told her, "I can't, Mom, you signed the papers." It was not short or anything like today. She let me go ahead. She knew it was my duty. But the funny part is that she never bought any shorts for us. We never wore shorts in the house, and we never had a bike or skates. She was always afraid that we might get hurt. She was old-fashioned too. When we started wearing shorts at school, she didn't like that.

HUDSON: Yeah, times change. Now we have other issues about clothing.

MENDOZA: It was so different when I was in school in 1952–1955. Our sponsor would not let us wear long hair, so I had to cut mine. I remember my mom got angry because I had to cut my hair so I would look like the other ones. She never did go to any of the football or basketball games. She was not that type of mother. She was just interested in her housework.

HUDSON: Let's talk about the music. I know you like music; I can hear it playing now in the background. Who are some of your favorites?

MENDOZA: I like Joni James. She was a very popular lady in the 1950s. In Spanish, it's Mazz. I play this music every night. I hear it every night before I go to sleep. I just love the way he sings. Also Gary Hobbs.

HUDSON: Were you ever interested in the folk music of Mexico like your mom?

MENDOZA: I like the groups that come up from Mexico. I wish I had learned how to sing. I don't have the voice to sing. Now that I'm old, I love to sing and dance. My husband asks why I didn't learn that when I was young. He says I would have been a star like my mom. I just love music now, but I'm too old to do anything with it. I've been sick, and I'm sixty-eight going on sixty-nine. I have some congestive heart failure. I must be careful with myself.

HUDSON: The health problems that come up with age are always a surprise. I certainly never imagined I'd be dealing with arthritis! I should have known from all the horses I trained. Rough work on the body.

MENDOZA: I was very active a few years ago. I was president of a club. We would go dancing and out at night. But then I got diabetes, and everything stopped. Now I'm here in my room with these four walls. That's all I do. And the music, of course. I have six kids, three boys and three girls. My oldest daughter has a thirteen-year-old daughter who likes to sing. My second oldest has a daughter who loves to sing. She sings beautifully, and she's twenty-one. Her father calls her a singing bridesmaid because she sings at so many weddings. Then my youngest daughter has two daughters who are putting a band together. All three daughters have someone who likes to sing.

HUDSON: Are they aware of the legacy of your family?

MENDOZA: Yes, they are aware. Barbara, the oldest, says she wants to sing all the time. We'll see. Now there are so many young girls that sing.

HUDSON: Did you work outside the home, even with these six children?

MENDOZA: I was always the active one. I would also work outside the home, be in clubs, and participate in the community. Until I had the sixth one, it never bothered me. I would always take my daughters wherever they wanted to go.

They [the audience] come with all their cares, their worries, their fears, their restlessness; they come. I see my job as a musician to take all that in and express it for them. Transform it and give it back, cleansed and lifted up. Kind of like a Mass.

Mandy Mercier

TELLING THE TRUTH

Gurf Morlix told me about a birthday tribute to Blaze Foley at the Chaparral Club on South Congress in Austin. There, I was reunited with Mandy Mercier, whom I had met years ago when she was playing with Ray Wylie Hubbard. We met again at Maria's Taco Xpress one Sunday. After the music ended, after we had eaten some great Mexican food, Mandy and I sat down to talk. Our connection was instant, with no obvious reason for the strong bond. We both acknowledged, at once, that we must have something important to share. Her bright eyes were shining with love as she told her own story to me.

HUDSON: There have been many times I've run into you throughout my musical odyssey. Let's talk about three moments for you when things opened up, when you had insight, when things changed for you. Three really great moments.

MERCIER: The first one, I would have to say, was getting hired to play with Ray Wylie Hubbard and his great band. I was making a living full-time as a musician with a great artist that I admired. He would fly me up to Dallas for the gigs, and he had a tour bus. We also played the folk festivals, and I would play alone with him if it were an acoustic gig. It validated me to be playing with him and Bugs Henderson and people at that level. Then I went out to L.A. and got some experience out there and won. [The award was "Female Vocalist of the Year" from the Los Angeles Chapter of the California Country Music Association in 1992; later she was inducted into the Academy of Country Music, and she was awarded an honorable mention in the "MTV Beach House Band" (1994).] You can get all that off the website [www.mandymercier.com]. The country awards were interesting because I'm not really a country artist. But I was hanging out with Lucinda [Williams] and some other friends from Texas who were in the "roots rock" scene, which found a home at the Palomino; in that particular time, the mid-1990s, country, blues, folk, and rockabilly were all part of the general "roots rock" scene in L.A.

When I came back to Austin, another defining moment was playing with Champ Hood and the Threadgill's Troubadours. That was where Janis Joplin started out, and I do a lot of blues; I had opened for Uncle Walt's Band when I first came to Austin. They were idols of mine, and so when I'd go to Threadgill's, or later, other places that the band would play, such as Gruene Hall, Champ would say, "I'm going to get Mandy Mercier up here to close it out." He had me do the finale of every single show I was at with the Troubadours. Then I hired him to do some acoustic gigs with me fairly often, but of course I wanted him to sing and play as much as I would, so in a sense we had a little duo, and I'd get to work with him one-on-one. And I'd hire the Troubadours to back me up as a band when I had a gig. That was amazing. He was the most incredible musician I've known in my life. And of course, living with Lucinda and having her success take off. We met in New York, lived together in Austin, in L.A., and again in Austin, and I've stayed with her in Nashville. We have been friends for a long time. I've learned a lot from her about a lot of things. She's kind enough to say that there's a lot of exchange between us, and we still have long talks on the phone and hang out whenever we can.

And the third moment, besides finding my way through all this, would be playing with Shake [Russell] and Dana [Cooper]. They were also heroes of mine in the early days. They were kind enough to sing on my current album, *Wild Dreams of the Shy Boys* (Wild Cantinas Records, 2001). I had opened some shows for them. I played some fiddle with Shake and sang harmony with him. I've also played with Dana—I've played with them separately and together. Their music is so complex and gorgeous. That was a real high point, not only to be accepted by, but also to be wanted by, these musicians in those contexts. Since we're talking about this in the context of women performing, I felt good getting that kind of validation from men that I admired. As a musician with equal footing. A woman player is still very much in the minority. You could be a chick singer or window dressing, as Ray Wylie used to say, but . . .

HUDSON: For me, it's how things get moved around inside me when I'm present in the music. Like this afternoon at the Taco Express Gospel Hour. What is it for you?

MERCIER: For me, music is shamanic. That's our job. The people come with all their heartache. They come with all their cares, their worries, their fears, their restlessness; they come. I see my job as a musician to take all that in and express it for them. Transform it and give it back cleansed and lifted up. Kind of like a Mass.

HUDSON: Now that's a whole lot more than just getting paid to play in a bar.

MERCIER: Right, yeah, yeah. It's become that for me. I realized that that is always what it was when it worked. Like today. I was telling you about the Sunday after September 11 when I came down here and heard Scrappy Newcomb sing "I Shall Be Released." During that line that says "Everything must fall," I just lost it. That was written over thirty years ago. There is this wonderful synchronicity in life where everything that happens feels like it was always supposed to happen and always will. When I met you, I felt that connection. I remember meeting you first with Ray Wylie when we were playing in Houston. John Vandiver was there. It was the Kerrville benefit, the Thursday before John [Vandiver] and Debbie [Davis] got killed. Fitzgerald's, I think.

HUDSON: Today was such a great reminder of where music can take us. What about the writing for you?

MERCIER: I was a student of writers for many years. Tom Pacheco was one, informally.

HUDSON: I brought him to a coffeehouse at Schreiner years ago.

MERCIER: Yeah! Really?! Well, I knew him in New York before I moved down here. I would just "sit with" [in the Buddhist sense] people I considered good songwriters. I remember Steve Forbert talking to Paul Siebel one night. He couldn't get over that song "Louise." The legend said that he wrote one line a month and it took him a year to write that song. Forbert was saying, "Louise rode home on the mail train." Like that was so important, that she be perceived as so unimportant that she had to ride the mail train. [Mandy sings a few lines of the song for me.] Listening to Forbert and Paul talking taught me a lot. I think what songwriting is about is saying it with the least amount of words. That is what was so great about Champ and Walter Hyatt in their writing. They weave these intricate harmonic chordal threads, but you could walk down the street singing the melody. It was like the Beatles. That simplicity, that ultimate simplicity.

HUDSON: I know exactly what you are talking about.

MERCIER: Right. Once I said to Larry Monroe [on KUT Radio in Austin] that Townes Van Zandt is the T. S. Eliot of our day. Songwriting is the literature of our day, just like poetry was in the 1920s, 1930s, and 1940s. Of course, we still have great novelists, but there is something very magical in Texas. And songwriting is the important literature of our day. I've been in Austin over twenty years. I went to L.A. for a while, but Texas is home. I was advertised there [in L.A.] as an "Austin artist." When I moved here, Lucinda, David [Rodriguez], Vince Bell, Stevie Ray Vaughan, and the All-Stars were all playing here in Austin. There was a blues scene, a folk scene, and more.

HUDSON: When was that?

MERCIER: Late 1970s and early 1980s. I thought I had died and gone to heaven. I had been in the scene in New York with the Roches, Steve Forbert, Tom Pacheco, and Paul Siebel. I had been a sideman — or woman? — and had a duo with a guy I met in New York, who had lived in L.A. and Texas. I moved to New Orleans with him and played a six-night-a-week gig there. That's where I really learned how to sing, singing on Bourbon Street for my rent.

HUDSON: What's ahead for you?

MERCIER: Just doing a better job at it. We haven't talked a lot about the "woman" thing in this context. I'd really like to have a guy in my life, but it's so hard when you are a woman and an artist. Men seem threatened by that. Guys who aren't musicians can't relate at all. Guys that are musicians have other issues. Especially if you are powerful! You can be a pretty little chick singer, and that's okay. Or you can get up like Yvonne did today and really deliver some oomph! Incredible. Or Janis, or someone like that. I want to be on that level. And it may mean I don't have a relationship. I was saying to a friend the other night, I don't have kids and now it's too late for that. I didn't really have a relationship with my family since I took this up. I moved down here, and there has been a rift ever since. It was okay when I studied this as a kid. At some point they wanted me to "settle down" and be a teacher or something more conventional. They always thought it was just bullshit and stupid. They didn't respect it or validate my choice. That came from other musicians, and from the audience. The audience is so essential. It's important to have all the tools to bring to the moment. Then in that moment you ask, "What does this moment need? How can I serve this moment?" By showing up and continuing to study and learn from these great musicians I get to be around.

HUDSON: I can imagine you being a mentor and helping other young songwriters. Do you have openings like that?

MERCIER: I do have some young friends who bring me their songs and who ask me about music. That feels good. I love that role.

HUDSON: Do you think there are still issues about being a woman in the business?

MERCIER: Things are different now for the younger ones coming up. And I'm glad about that. I think that ours was the last wave that paid the price. Kitty Wells and Loretta Lynn went before us, paving the way. Janis was nailed to the cross over the whole thing. For women, she was the Christ figure, I think. She was crucified because her pain was beyond endurance, literally. Ever since she did that, other women have been inspired to be powerful and strong.

HUDSON: She inspires me to be that way. I have a Janis T-shirt out in the car and wondered about wearing that Christmas Day! I saw the Janis stage show here in Austin. It was great. There are some really interesting women who paved the way.

MERCIER: In my lifetime, I truly feel like I was kept down. I had a lot of problems with discrimination in my life. It was a central problem in every way. It may sound dated, or even whiny to say now, but I really feel it's true. It's an issue both personally AND professionally. . . . Do you date a guy in the band? What happens when you lead a band of men? It was like being a woman priest in ancient times.

HUDSON: I used to run the horseback-riding program at Camp White

Pine in Canada. The year I had a staff of men was a challenging year for me. I had to ride all the broncs first to "prove" myself. Who are some other women you listen to?

MERCIER: I love the Sisters Morales and what they do. Of course, Lucinda is a friend of mine, but she's also just a great artist and an inspiration in every sense. I love Rosie Flores. She's a great player. The Hancock family is amazing. Of course, Lou Ann Barton. Other friends, too many to name, and I'll kick myself for leaving them out—my dear friend Linda Freeman, a great singer; Sarah Elizabeth Campbell, of course. Angela Strehli. Marcia Ball.

[I sent Mandy this interview in July 2004, asking her to add whatever information she wanted to.]

MERCIER: Kathleen, this interview is great. Thank you for including me. I would only add that since then I've met more amazing people, had more amazing experiences, and of course we've all had some more sadness, disappointments, and losses. It's truly an honor to be here on the planet and have the opportunity to show up. And to be even a small part of the tradition that is Texas music, and women in music.

I want to add, maybe, to what I said about feeling I was "kept down." Part of that was probably inside my own head and heart, I'm sure. I felt afraid to step out, afraid to assert myself; I would either cave in or blow up, and neither was too productive in working with, frankly, male egos. I am trying to mellow out since then. I learned a lot about that from Champ Hood. To let things roll, not to worry too much about the details, and I've seen Ray Wylie perform again several times recently and have just been amazed at the way an artist can continue to change, evolve, and grow. I hope I'm evolving! My next record is a blues album, and after that, I want to do some Cajun stuff. I found out as an adult that I'm part "France" French but also part Cajun! We did a lot of Cajun-influenced stuff in the Troubadours; that was a big part of our sound, along with blues, rock, country, and everything in between, flowing out of Champ's incredible heritage in Uncle Walt's Band.

I'd love to go to Ireland and just go around and play fiddle in pubs, since I'm half-Irish. And of course I'd love to make more records of original songs, and grow as a songwriter. I'm grateful for everything—even the struggles and the hard lessons. In Zen they talk about taking away all that is not essential, and then the punch line is—that's everything! But what you're left with is also everything—the essence. The pure truth you can't express in words, maybe, but then again—maybe with words and music!

I feel completely fulfilled doing what I do . . . because I really know that it's an unconditional love I have with Willie. . . . I know I give him strength and support. And he gives me strength and support in every facet of my life . . . always.

Bobbie Nelson

HEARTACHE AND JOY

A gray sky greeted me upon awakening on Saturday, January 25, 2004, with a commitment to drive up Highway 16 to Fredericksburg, 290 to Johnson City, then north on 281 to 71 and east to Spicewood and the Pedernales Country Club. Willie's world. Bobbie Nelson and I had been talking about this conversation since the last time we saw each other. She was cooking beans for Willie, and I was carrying my tape recorder around her kitchen. We also walked Charlie, her black and white Boston bull terrier, around the golf course, me with tape recorder in tow. That afternoon was one moment with Bobbie Nelson. I remember the first time with Bobbie. Phyllis Fletcher, her daughter-in-law, set up the meeting in Austin, and we talked for a story on women that I was doing for a March publication, for Women's History Month. Phyllis stayed in touch with me over the years, always taking care of Bobbie as Bobbie took care of others. Women supporting women in times of need. Bobbie lost two sons in one year, and Phyllis lost her husband. Bobbie said to Phyllis, "I didn't think of this as an interview. I was going to have tea with Kathleen." Her gentle, sweet, angelic spirit shined down on me even then.

As I pushed on Bobbie's black metal gate and entered the front door, I was greeted like an old friend. We looked over her plants, all inside to avoid the effects of bad weather; we looked at photos on the wall; and she started a little silver pot of coffee. By 1:00 p.m. we were talking and the tape was running. The recent passing of Charlie, her dog, started us down the road of grief and loss. I learned that the loss of her husband, Michael, about fifteen years ago coincided with her choice to raise this little dog, a dog that was once theirs. One grief seems to bring up the other griefs that we carry. We also talked of the loss of two of her three sons. And the afternoon did not match the gray sky; Bobbie radiates with love, forgiveness, compassion, and generosity.

After the interview she asked, "Do you want to see my new special place?" I looked at the glass shelves of angels and the small table on her back porch with an angel sitting on it. Yes, it was a new place. We walked out into the backyard, and she showed me the new marble tombstone for Charlie, with an angel carved in white on the top and a red heart adorning the space in front of the angel. A statue of a white cat sat nearby, and the grave of her Yorkie.

We talked of the celebration that can come with death, and not just the grief and sorrow. Upon leaving, I headed to my first visit at Poodie's Hilltop Café on Highway 71, legendary for the music jams that might include Willie or Merle or Billy Joe Shaver. This is the spot where Billy Joe kept his agreement to play on New Year's Eve, even after hearing of his son Eddy's death. I looked up above the bar, and a photo of Eddy, head bent down over the guitar, seemed to speak to me. Grief and loss. I wondered how Billy Joe handled all that inside. I heard that Willie showed up to support him in this time, playing music with him through the tears. I did love Eddy Shaver. He had played a small coffeehouse series that I produce at Schreiner University in Kerrville. He came once, to help his dad out. Billy Joe didn't want to do the gig solo, even though we had little money at the time. Eddy just drove down to join him.

Bobbie shared her house and her heart with me that gray day. I left feeling as if I had been touched by an angel. She sees the angels in her life. I see the angel in her. The sweet smile as she reminisced on life with Willie as an older sister led to another sweet smile as she told me of Mama and Daddy Nelson, the grandparents in Abbott, Texas, who raised her.

HUDSON: I see all these pictures and moments as a way to celebrate life. [We are walking through her house, looking at photos of family and friends.] Let's talk about that way of seeing life. [She insists on making a pot of coffee for us first. We look at her candle of St. Michael fighting the dragon. She keeps a candle lit at all times.]

NELSON: I'm not going to try and keep things perfect. I'm always receiving things. Last night Lana [Willie's daughter] and I had dinner, and she gave me this glass elephant. My mother collected elephants, and you'll see a lot of them around. And she gave me this little dish with the redbird on it. Did you know Jody Fisher? It was hers before she died of cancer. She used to take care of my flowers and plants and my yard. She used to walk Charlie. She and Lana used to run the Pedernales studio. It was just a year or so ago that she was diagnosed with lung cancer. Jody told her that she wanted me to have this.

HUDSON: I had a special professor, Ann Ashworth, at TCU in Fort Worth. When she died, she left me a ring and several paintings for my house. I love having these memories alive around me. It's like having her in my house. She was one of the first people to really acknowledge me in graduate school by telling me that my writing was wonderful. With that friendship I began looking at the contributions of women with new eyes.

NELSON: I've had several very interesting experiences after Charlie's death. I just feel like we're still in communication. I've always had this really deep spiritual connection . . . always. Probably you could say from the way I grew up. We were left in the custody of our grandparents, Daddy and Mama Nelson. My cousin Mildred took care of us when we were little babies.

HUDSON: As I was driving up here, I listened to a set of tapes on the family, a lecture given by James Hillman. He says family today is not what it once was. I thought about Willie Nelson and Family. This band is a family in many ways. Hillman said the word "family" originally meant the dwelling place or building site rather than a set group of people. Things inside the house are family.

NELSON: I'm sure "familiar" comes from that word. That is very interesting. I think that a woman's place in society is very important and very strong. I think women can do more than men with a lot of things. [gently smiling]

HUDSON: Did you ever take Charlie with you on the road?

NELSON: No, he was a really rowdy little guy. Someone would have had to take care of him while I played the piano. He was a handful.

HUDSON: Your touring schedule looks like you never come home.

NELSON: We do come back, but we don't get to stay very long. Usually what we do is take off in December and January. But last year we did go to Norway with Jimmy Carter for the Nobel Peace thing he did. And this year we worked the first week of December. We had a little time off, then we went back to work for New Year's Eve. We played Nashville with Toby Keith. It was one of those big affairs. Then we went to Mississippi. We went somewhere else . . . maybe Kentucky. Then we came back to Austin and did that rally, a fund-raiser. Which was unusual for us. We don't usually do political things. Then we had a little time off. Then I went with Willie to do an extra little thing. We went to Seattle to play this party for Bill Gates. It was his tenth wedding anniversary. And that was wonderful.

HUDSON: Just the two of you? I have this vision of a Sunday gospel show with just the two of you. At an auditorium in my school.

NELSON: Whenever something goes emotional, I get the desire to go to the piano or go do some gospel on the radio. We haven't really done that in a while. We did do the gospel album that is just now out. You can find it, and you can buy it now. HEB stores carried it. We took two of our gospel albums and put them together, renaming it *Further Along*. Now people can get it, and it's been doing really well. Texas Roadhouse restaurants are carrying it.

HUDSON: When you and I first talked years ago, I remember an answer you gave about your favorite thing to do. It was singing gospel music with your brother.

NELSON: This was music we grew up on. Mama had us in church from the time we were born. We were there every Sunday and every Sunday night. And we had our choir practice on Wednesday night and prayer meetings. It was just our way of life.

HUDSON: I hear the strength of a woman's voice in that experience.

NELSON: Mama Nelson, Mama Nelson.

HUDSON: In the band Willie and Family, he always honors you.

NELSON: Every night we perform!

HUDSON: You are behind the piano while everyone is focused on him and on the guitar leads. Then he says, "Take it away, Bobbie." Someone asked me about you once, not knowing who you are. I told him that there is no Willie Nelson sound without Bobbie! You do this great job of being strong and being in the spotlight. I do wonder about things you might want to say that you don't get asked.

NELSON: [after a long silence] I really don't know what has not been said. I feel completely fulfilled doing what I do. I don't need the kind of notoriety that Willie has, because I really know that it's an unconditional love I have with Willie. I know the job that we're both doing. I'm doing my part when I do what I do. It's my desire to do that. I know I give him strength and support. And he gives me strength and support in every facet of my life . . . always.

[*We continued to talk about her love for family and friends. When I heard that she lost her husband fifteen years ago, then two sons only six months apart, we shared stories of grief, loss, and faith. Bobbie will be remembered by some as the black hat bowed over eighty-eight keys on a grand piano, long dark hair flowing past the piano bench. Others will remember her lively leads on some songs during a Willie Nelson concert. Some few will know the generous woman who has an entire hat collection and is willing to share herself freely and with love.*]

I'm going to live this day like it is the last.

Lana Nelson

TAKING CARE OF DADDY

I had always known of Lana Nelson. Everyone I knew who knew her spoke highly of her, with love and respect. Kinky Friedman was the first. Then, of course, Bobbie Nelson, Willie's sister. Lana's daughter, Martha, stayed at my house in Kerrville for a week. I showcased her as a teenager at our annual writers' conference at Schreiner. I started meeting Lana for brief moments at the Willie Nelson picnics. I was standing in line to interview Willie; she was walking by quietly taking care of something. I learned later that she perceives her job as taking care of Willie and Bobbie. I sensed that in her.

I flew to Wichita, Kansas, in August 2004, to spend time with my daughter, Lisa, and her family of three girls. This trip allowed me to be with the girls and see a Willie Nelson/Bob Dylan/Hot Club of Cowtown concert at the local baseball field. This concert was one in twenty-two that were held at minor-league baseball parks. Taking the music to the people. At the end of the week, I drove the rental car back to Oklahoma City. And that Friday night the baseball tour hit town. In Wichita I was able to go back by the buses. I saw Tony Garnier, Dylan's longtime bass player, ride up on a big black bike. Their bus was hauling a trailer so Tony could have this kind of fun as well. Ray Benson was a guest. We stood out in the parking lot, and I kept my eye on both Dylan's bus and Willie's. When I saw Lana come out, I introduced myself again. She remembered me. And we made plans to talk in OK City.

In Oklahoma City, I was standing on the corner watching the buses come in. Two buses went behind a chain-link fence. How would I get a message to Lana? I noticed another young woman on that corner. I looked again. It was Carolyn Wonderland, with whom I had also been trying to set up a time to interview. Carolyn and I talked some, and Dylan's manager came out and gave her a ticket. I was left wondering. I tried to get a message back to Lana. I just stood around and waited. Finally she came out of the bus and headed to the hospitality room, inviting me to have dinner with her and talk to her there. What fun! I ate with Willie's band, listening to the banter of the road. After we ate, I turned on the tape recorder, and we had the following conversation. What an exciting moment for me.

HUDSON: I want to thank you for taking this time to talk with me. I have to believe your head is in many places right now. Bobbie spoke of you with such love and appreciation. I get the feeling that you manage a lot of what happens here on the road.

NELSON: No, it can't be managed. Everybody does his or her job here, and it goes really smoothly. I've been on the road about nine years. These guys have been out here forever. It was running smoothly when I got here, and it will be running smoothly when I'm gone.

HUDSON: What do you bring to the mix?

NELSON: Oh, I don't know. I just like to take care of Dad and Aunt Bobbie. I like to see that their immediate needs are taken care of. Dad has his office on the bus, so we do a ton of stuff coming out of that bus. I kind of help his life go more smoothly. That's my main goal; I don't know that it happens. We start our "in flight" service when the bus takes off.

HUDSON: I love the writing you do on the website. It's a great way to give people an inside look at the concerts.

NELSON: Between David Anderson, myself, my daughter Rachel, and a lady from Germany named Ruth Boggs, we manage it and get it going. It started out as just David and me. Then it kept getting bigger and more complicated.

HUDSON: I like the personal approach you take.

NELSON: Thank you very much. We just have fun. I may be a morale office! [laughter] I think this is all my dream anyway. I'll probably wake up someday.

HUDSON: Your life has been woven in with music. Do you write as well?

NELSON: I write a lot. I guess I've always enjoyed writing. *The Pedernales Poo Poo* is part of the website, a comical look at life on the road. And I write for my own personal use. I love to write. I love to read, and when you read a lot, it encourages you to want to write. I find that when I finish a book that moves me, I want to write more. Good reading ignites that spark that turns into writing for me. The same may be true in songwriting.

HUDSON: So many people are so sure they can't write.

NELSON: It's like painting. You hand them a paintbrush, and they freeze. You don't really know until you try. It might be inside of you just waiting to come out. It might just take that moment of inspiration from people, the earth, God, whatever inspires you to cause the picture or the writing to come out. It is in there. Some women might enjoy writing about their children, their mother, their father. They might just find they really are a writer.

HUDSON: I can see where that attitude inspired your daughter.

NELSON: And she inspired me! The children teach the parents after a while.

HUDSON: Have you read Sue Monk Kidd's book *The Secret Life of Bees?*

NELSON: I've heard that it was really great.

HUDSON: My mother sent it to me with her underlining. I gave it to my daughter, and she gave it to her daughter. Now that's a way to pass on influence.

NELSON: That's perfect. We can only hope to come up with an end product that inspires so many people that they want to pass it around. I just finished *The Five People You Meet in Heaven*.

HUDSON: I did too. I just read parts of it to my dad while he was having back surgery at age eighty-one.

NELSON: I'm now reading *Running with Scissors*. It makes you think.

HUDSON: You have been in the middle of what people see as "Texas music" for all your life. What are some of your perspectives on the music? What moves your heart? And we won't add Kinky to this one.

NELSON: He moves a fart! [said in true Kinkster style] I love Kinky. He's funny. So many things move me. People move me . . . all kinds of people. I'm in awe of the human race. I love to study what people think and what happens to them. The young, the old, the rich, the poor, the homeless. All people. I wonder what happens to get people on death row. There's probably nothing I can do, but my own understanding of this will help me see my own life in a deeper way. I will be better off. If you understood what made people the way they are, the world might just shift. Humans are so complex.

HUDSON: I see these stories as a way to open up understanding. I really appreciate the power of the stories we tell each other.

NELSON: Yes, yes. That's what music is, storytelling. A poem is a story.

HUDSON: What is a distinct contribution that women make to the world?

NELSON: We've made so many. Aunt Bobbie, my mothers, my daughters, my granddaughters. I loved my grandmother and my great-grandmother. If I just studied all those people, I'd learn so much. I'm like that piano player that plays for his or her own amusement.

HUDSON: Do you share your writing with anyone?

NELSON: No, I just write for me. Occasionally I'll have a project where someone wants something written, and I'll do that. I just like to write for me.

HUDSON: I feel the calm center in you. What's the source of that?

NELSON: You know Dad. He's that way; he projects that. It doesn't seem hard for me. What comes hard for me is getting upset. Once tipped over, it's not pretty. That's the same with Dad. But once he's mad, he may stay mad for an eternity. It's not easy to get him to tip over either.

HUDSON: Any words of advice for young women?

NELSON: Everyone has dreams. Just follow your heart. Learn what you can about your dream. Study what the people before you did and put your own style in it. You may never be successful financially, but you will always put out a good product. Being happy should always be the bottom line. At the end of the day, ask, "What did I do? Did people benefit from it? Was it good?" Then you can get a good night's sleep.

HUDSON: Was there a turning point for you?

NELSON: I'm sure there was. I was young, and now I'm fifty! I'm fifty. And I'm a cancer survivor. Breast cancer. Once you've been faced with a disease that could kill you, you will center yourself quickly at that point. I'm going to live this day like it is the last. I think we should all be living this way. It was really what I always knew, but this scare brought it closer to home. I know that my family, and those close to me, are the most important things in my life. My support group really is my first priority.

HUDSON: Do you have someone close you share your life with?

NELSON: Other than Dad? I have a lot of people in my life. I've changed. When I was a teenager, I had one or two best friends. I was shy. Now it seems like I have totally changed; I've opened up; I have a ton of friends. I don't keep secrets. My life is kind of an open book at this point in my life. I don't hold it all in. That can make you really sick. Dad and Aunt Bobbie are my best friends. Then my kids and my girlfriends. We call ourselves the Hormones. Back when we were in our twenties, that was funny. Now that we have none, it's even funnier! Sometimes I have cold flashes.

HUDSON: How do you describe Bobbie?

NELSON: [thoughtful pause] Like a delta flower. Fragile but strong. Steady. She's really a sweet person.

[I went ahead to the concert, loving every minute of it. Inspired by my talk with Lana, I found myself thinking about my own friends and family and their importance in my life.]

My goal is to be a better and better player. I want to be on that stage when I'm 100 years old, just playing that guitar and singing well.

Rattlesnake Annie

A FEMALE WILLIE NELSON

I first met Rattlesnake Annie at a Nashville Radio Seminar in the late 1980s. We sat and talked about Texas and about the Brazos River. In 1979, she released her self-titled album on CBS, Rattlesnakes and Rusty Water, and I loved it. We seemed to recognize a streak in each other, and I knew then that I wanted to write about her. Our paths crossed again in November 2003, this time in San Miguel de Allende, Mexico, at the International Jazz Festival. Rattlesnake and her husband, Max, had been living in Spain for many years, on the coast, and they were not thrilled with the cool weather in Mexico. Texas connections abound in all parts of the world. Audiences are mesmerized by her contralto voice, a voice that carries passion and that carries her own story. When you listen to Rattlesnake Annie, you get far more than just the song; her voice carries her heart. In 2004, Rattlesnake went into the studio in Nashville to cut a CD of Willie Nelson's songs, the continuation of a career rich with performance and production. She has played with the Harlem Blues and Jazz Band (HBJB), and she has played solo songwriter gigs. She does the blues with soul, and she lives a life "on the road," much like one of her mentors, Willie Nelson.

HUDSON: Thanks for taking the time to talk with me.

RATTLESNAKE: Thanks for including me. These kinds of books are so important. Right now, I'm going to run in here and turn my beans off so I don't have to think about them. I'm fired up and ready to go. My life right now is surrounded by gypsy flamenco professional players. I fell madly in love with flamenco; it's close to the blues. Being a solo artist, I love the guitar, and I have spent the last twenty years studying flamenco guitar and singing Spanish-language songs. Flamenco is a fantastic art form. We live in the province of Granada on the south coast of Spain. And on the seaside from my bedroom I can see only water. My life consists of getting up in the morning, having my espresso, a double, playing and singing flamenco guitar for five hours, and saying hello to all my little friends along the way, buying my groceries. I walk as much as possible. I am working on a Spanish-language album. I'm trying to stay as healthy and strong as I can. I do a lot of yoga, tai chi, and meditation. Since I spend a lot of time in Japan, I think these practices have made me stronger and more focused. I've lived in Japan recently. I record quite frequently, trying to keep all my work documented. We go between Mexico and Spain.

HUDSON: Where do you go in Mexico?

RATTLESNAKE: We go to Guadalajara, the Yucatan, and all up and down the coast, always in search of new songs.

HUDSON: I go to San Miguel de Allende each November.

RATTLESNAKE: Send me that information. There's no reason I can't go there and check it out. I was just invited to the Jazz and Blues Festival in New Zealand. I have a blues album and a jazz album with country flavor.

HUDSON: Do you miss being around Texas?

RATTLESNAKE: I come to America a lot. I come to Nashville to record. I have children and grandchildren in Dallas and D.C. I make a sweep through at least once a year. I've been married to the same guy for thirty-two years. He's my manager, and his name is Max. We're both free spirits, and we have a lot of respect for each other's creative space. We have one meal a day together. We have our own lives, even though we are together. I have a really good situation.

HUDSON: I love flamenco music, and I teach [Federica Garcia] Lorca in my world literature class. He loved it too!

RATTLESNAKE: I'm a Lorca freak too. A lot of his poems have been set to flamenco music. You can't live in Granada and not know Lorca.

HUDSON: Is there a big gypsy gathering in southern France or in Spain?

RATTLESNAKE: Not really a gathering. The Gypsy Kings are from France. There are whole communities of gypsies in Spain who are not on the road now. They were first animal traders, but now they are blacksmiths and street market merchants and musicians. There is a huge population of gypsies on the coast, and of course Andalusia is the heart of this population and the flamenco music. Now there's big money in the exportation of flamenco music. It's kind of like blues: there's nobody in the South listening to the blues.

HUDSON: I've met some flamenco players in San Miguel. The first time I heard the music, my heart felt like it was being torn out. What passionate music! Let's talk about some favorites.

RATTLESNAKE: Well, I love Mexican food. Chiles, beans, rice, and tortillas. Indian food and Mexican food are my favorites. My favorite flamenco players are the more traditional players, what I call the primitive, animal-like singers like Manolo Caracol, Camarón de Isla, and guitarist Juan Habichuela.

HUDSON: Are you a reader?

RATTLESNAKE: Oh, God, I just eat books. We don't have a television in Spain. We just don't care to be bombarded by the news. Even this summer we took a two-month period by a river in the mountains and just read. I like to read about Eastern philosophy and Buddhism. I like to read women's biographies. I love the books of Joseph Campbell.

HUDSON: I remember our first talk in Nashville, and I remember how many times I said, "Me too." Let's talk about the challenges you have faced in your life. Where are the rough spots or the dark places?

RATTLESNAKE: I think my rough places came early in my career when I learned how painful record companies can be. I guess the greatest challenge has been my individuality. It's always been a hassle because they can never put me in a slot. What bin does the record store use for my records? Record companies want you to have a label. When I signed with Sony Japan and they put me in their world music department, for the first time I felt free and understood. I'm liable to make a bluegrass album, a blues album. I've made my living my whole life from my music. I've always had a clear idea about who I am. It's always difficult for the record companies because they want to pigeonhole you. You have to make your own niche. You have to build your own audience of people who care about your music. Most people refer to my music as "Rattlesnake Music."

HUDSON: My friend Roxy Gordon, a Choctaw Indian, mixed breed, from West Texas who no longer walks this earth, gave me a couple of rattlers to wear as earrings.

RATTLESNAKE: I always wear one long rattle on my ear whenever I'm performing. It's on all my album covers. My signature.

HUDSON: Let's talk about your connection with snakes.

RATTLESNAKE: I was just born without a fear of snakes. It's the healing sign of the Cherokee. My great-great-grandmother was Cherokee. I grew up in West Tennessee in an area populated with blacks, Scotch-Irish, and Indians. Everybody had a nickname. Every cow, car, and chicken was named. My grandmother called me Rattlesnake. I was not afraid of snakes. We lived in an old house with no rug on the floor. Once I was sitting on the wooden floor by the closet door and a big chicken snake came through a mousehole, and I was touching it. So, they called me Snake. It became a part of my stage name when I moved out to Texas on the Brazos River. I let the cedar hackers cut on the land with the condition that they wouldn't kill our snakes. They started calling me the rattlesnake woman. Then I would try to get a job, and nobody knew me by any other name. We had to kill one big rattlesnake that was hanging out near the kids. We skinned it, ate it, and I kept its rattler. I wear it on my ear. That name has been a blessing and a curse. But I've realized it was the name I was supposed to have.

HUDSON: Yesterday I went to a talk on the rock art at the White Shaman Preserve outside Del Rio. The speaker talked about entering the mouth of the snake and being digested by it as a shamanic journey. And she connected the story with the images on this wall in Texas near the border with Mexico.

RATTLESNAKE: When the Indians saw their first albino rattlesnake, they thought they had encountered a god. Just like the story of the white buffalo. There used to be an albino rattlesnake at a roadside exhibit in Texas. You could pay fifty cents to see the snake. Christianity is what killed off the snake. It sits beside Buddha and represents wisdom in Asian cultures. I've sung a lot of snake songs. My friend Oscar Brown, Jr., a pop and blues songwriter, is the only one whose songs have survived using the metaphor of the snake beyond Delta blues. In fact, I have one of his songs, called "The Woman and the Snake," that was a hit single in the Czech Republic, off my Sony album. I didn't set out to create this connection; it just happened.

HUDSON: I have a black rubber snake on the dashboard of my car. It makes some people nervous as I go through a car wash. And I have this spiral image tattooed on my forearm. Something about the serpentine calls to me. I do see the image as representing movement, unfolding energy. I was going to ask you about your perception of spirituality.

RATTLESNAKE: Having lived and worked in Japan for about sixteen years, I see the real value of a practice in a culture. I grew up in the Bible belt, and I don't see any use for organized religion. A lot of things led me to seek my own spirituality, a fairly normal thing that people do. Yoga, tai chi, meditation, and Buddhism have led me to spirituality. The thing I have sought from the beginning is an international career. I have recorded in many languages: Czech, Russian, Spanish, Japanese, Maya, German, and more. That's been my passion. I've recorded with Chinese players. I've mixed flamenco with my original music. When I got my first CBS record deal, I headed right to Europe with the intention of having a global career. I can remember from the time I started singing at the age of eight and got paid that I never wanted anything else to do. That was my passion.

HUDSON: My immediate reaction upon hearing the news of an attack on September 11, 2001, was not "What are they doing to us?" Rather, "What have WE done to each other?" I was pleased and surprised that I see myself as a citizen of the world. I had a sense of an international family.

RATTLESNAKE: I was in Japan when it happened, so I saw it from another perspective, not being home. So, yeah. I have this famous Japanese friend who is the Japanese Bob Dylan. I translate songs for him and other Japanese artists. I have studied Japanese, and I can speak my stage dialogue. I get a direct translation, and I work with the artist to be sure I don't change any meaning. He said to me, "I just don't understand why they say 'God bless America.' Why don't they say 'God bless everybody'?" I have a huge sense of being part of the whole world. I have a hard time in the Bible redneck part of the world. I have a lot of Muslim friends, having spent time in Morocco. It's only twelve miles over there, and Spain was occupied by the Moors for 700 years. It was very painful for me and my friends to hear some of the language around this.

HUDSON: Let's talk about how you feel about your life now. What are you looking forward to in the future?

RATTLESNAKE: I have accomplished and done everything I've ever imagined doing . . . and a whole lot more. My goal is to be a better and better player. I want to be on that stage when I'm 100 years old, just playing that guitar and singing well. Just to keep on going, that's my goal. This is the first time I've been home in a year. I'm in Nashville recording an acoustic album, a real traditional album with some of Willie's old songs that I've been playing forever. My closest relationship with any musician is with Lonnie Mack. We've been like family for about twenty-five years. I got to record with the old Muscle Shoals rhythm section before they retired. I always eventually end up being drawn back to a certain sound. I'm a country blues musician. That's what I really am. All my stuff has a blues influence. On my new blues album, *Southern Discomfort*, I have a great duet with Bill Monroe cut at Bean Blossom on a cassette tape from the soundboard player doing blues. He's scat-singing behind me. Nobody's ever heard him do such a thing. I'm kind of a musician's musician. You know what I'm saying? It's always the blues, and real bluegrass is influenced. It appears on my CD *Southern Discomfort*.

HUDSON: I've been producing a tribute to Jimmie Rodgers, "America's Blue Yodeler," here in Kerrville for about eighteen years.

RATTLESNAKE: I was a good friend of his grandson, Jimmie Dale Court. And I recorded some songs by Virginia Shine Harvey, a cousin who grew up in the house with Jimmie Rodgers. The relationship with that music has always been really strong in my life. Jimmie Rodgers certainly listened to some blues. I wrote and recorded a tribute song to him, "Jimmie Rodgers." It appears on my CD *Country Living*.

HUDSON: My first love in music has always been the blues. In fact, I've heard flamenco music described as the blues, the music of the country people.

RATTLESNAKE: You know, I grew up close to Memphis and worked in the field all the time with blues people. I have mixed my original music with flamenco on my CDs *Indian Dream* and *Painted Bird*. I tried to make it in blues before I succumbed to country music. The connection you are hearing with blues and flamenco is the minor keys used, as well as the birthplace with the *campesinos*, a people suppressed. You can feel the connection. I can sing blues for a bunch of gypsies, and they get it.

HUDSON: Katie Webster called it the music of celebration: "Look what's happened to me, and I'm still standing."

RATTLESNAKE: Did you ever meet Lonnie Mack? He wrote "Wham" for Stevie Ray Vaughan, and Stevie worshiped him. He once said that he played music because of Lonnie Mack. Lonnie is like an unsung hero. He wrote my first three CBS singles, which were funky, country, blues, bluegrass songs. Odetta is another person very important to me. In fact, Janis Joplin calls her name as an influence as well.

[Rattlesnake Annie and Max joined me in San Miguel de Allende on November 27, 2003. We attended some of the jazz performances and walked the streets. We ended up in her apartment on Hidalgo, sharing stories.]

HUDSON: You were just telling me about an experience when Odetta came into your dressing room, sat knee to knee, and gave you suggestions about the power of meditation before performing.

RATTLESNAKE: That was my very first meeting with her. I was in Memphis singing blues and missed the folk scene. This meeting was at the Lone Star Café in New York. Bob Wade, the artist who put the Iguana over the top of the café, sold it to those guys, hoping they would think it was an armadillo. I was the opening act at the Lone Star Café. I got up on the iguana to be photographed. I was the only person to be photographed on it. It's on top of a three-story building with no protection. Then Odetta invited me to come to her house that evening. The night I met her, she had this small rag doll over her shoulder. She had a friend in another country whose child was near death. She had this doll on her for prayers for this child. She said, "I want to help you and teach you some things. I've learned a lot on the road. I'm coming to you mostly out of guilt. Guilt is my middle name. Janis Joplin reached out to me, and I did not receive her. Then I read her biography this summer where she said a lot about the 'cry' in her voice coming from Odetta."

HUDSON: I heard Odetta play live several times.

RATTLESNAKE: I was living out in Smithville once, in a cabin writing songs. I got a call that Odetta was in Nashville. I went to her hotel for a visit the next day. I called and asked her what she wanted besides vodka and orange juice. She said to bring her some soft Kleenex. She had a cold. I took some food, and we had a nice evening. She is an eternal teacher. She said, "Play something for me," then said, "I just want to remind you again about bringing more power of your guitar to make statements in the performance." You know, she plays open chords just like Dolly Parton, with those fingernails.

HUDSON: Let's talk about other influences.

RATTLESNAKE: I always loved the music of Nina Simone. When I was playing in Chicago, I wanted to find Oscar Brown, Jr., who has written some of her songs. We looked in the phone book, and there were many Oscar Browns. We picked one, dialed the number, and he answered. He came to my concert, sang with me, and took us to his home. His grandfather was the first black lawyer in Chicago. People have always fallen into my life like this.

HUDSON: Let's talk about others in your life.

RATTLESNAKE: Freddy Powers introduced me to Spud Goodall. Spud played for Tex Ritter for about twenty-seven years. He was probably the greatest country jazz guitarist ever. He started out playing in whorehouses in San Antonio. After Freddy introduced us, Spud took me under his wing. He lived in Whitehouse, Texas, and I would go stay with my friends. Spud would come to me every morning at 8:00 a.m., five days a week. He would wear a different hat and a pair of sunglasses every day. He taught me arrangements of Floyd Tillman songs, and many other songs that have really made a huge difference in my career. And Freddy introduced me to Clint Strong, another great guitar player, who worked a long time for Merle Haggard. A great jazz player. Spud always called him "Baby Guitar" because he had little short fingers. I made an album with Freddy Powers, Baby Guitar, and Dean Reynolds. I just want to say that Freddy Powers is one of the greats. I have recorded more Freddy Powers songs than anyone else's.

HUDSON: Tell me more about Baby Guitar.

RATTLESNAKE: He was a student at North Texas, and Merle lured him away with the road, all the trappings of the road. He was a child prodigy; he was playing in a jazz band when he was nine years old. Baby played me a complicated version of "Cry Me a River," and I learned it. Every time they came to town, I would go to the guitar pullings. Merle didn't like to go to sleep after a gig. Then Baby heard me play the song several months later, and he said he would teach me anytime for free. People would wait outside Merle's door to try to get guitar licks from Baby Guitar. After playing with Merle for years, he moved over to play with Ray Price. Then Baby started teaching in Reno. I went and stayed a month there, and he came to my apartment five days a week and taught me new songs and jazz guitar.

HUDSON: I want to hear that story about your gypsy friend.

RATTLESNAKE: Chato de Velez-Malaga, the singer with a great guitarist called Enrique de Melchor who plays all over the world. He is a very primitive singer, like a wounded animal. He likes the blues very much, and that is one of our common grounds. He also taught me to sing some flamenco songs and showed me things about the flamenco guitar. He was the godfather of a gypsy child, and he was required to make a party. Everyone put on their black suits, their shiny black shoes, and their tons of gold. The minute the buffet was finished, Max and I were the only "*payos.*" If you're not a gypsy, you're a *payo.* The children started dragging chairs into a circle. Everyone contributed some music. The old fat women were doing those exotic dances, and everyone was singing. It was a rich moment in music.

HUDSON: Let's hear a few more stories.

RATTLESNAKE: I was fortunate that from the beginning I knew I was going to be a musician. I've never done anything else. I earned my first money when I was eight years old with my cousins. We were a trio that sang at weddings, jails, political rallies, and anyplace else music was needed. We were about 100 miles from Memphis. It was a very black area. I worked in the fields with black workers and immigrants from Kentucky. We didn't have electricity until 1952. When I was fifteen, I saw all my friends getting married. I was being groomed to be a farmer's wife, and I hated farming. You had to shave your arms to keep the tobacco gum from sticking to the hairs on your arms. At age sixteen, I ran away to Memphis to become a blues singer. It was a great time for me. Beale Street still existed. I got to sit in with Furry Lewis, and I met Lightnin' Hopkins, one of the great Texas blues players. I realized that I couldn't make a living doing that. Before I went to Memphis, I had called a local radio station in Paris, Tennessee, and asked for a radio show doing country music. So I returned, and our trio had this radio show on Saturday. Then we won a contest. We sang at the Paris Hayride every Saturday night. One night a guy came from Nashville to choose the best artist. He had an applause meter, and we won. We went to Nashville in 1954 and were entertained by Mother Maybelle [Carter] and met Hank Snow. He welcomed us to the Grand Ole Opry, and we did live television. We were called the Gallimore Sisters. My father's twin brother had the two girls. His son, Byron Gallimore, produces Tim McGraw, Jo Dee Messina, and Faith Hill. We have a musical family. I was the only one who left home. I went to school at night and got my diploma. I sat in with Bill Black's Combo. I lived for a while in Huntsville, Alabama, where I was the featured vocalist backed by a jazz/blues trio in a nightclub where all those German rocket scientists came, from Wernher von Braun. President Kennedy came there, and astronaut James Lovell, and it was an interesting political time to be there. Then I moved to Texas and lived on the Brazos River. That's where I wrote the song "Goodbye to a River," outside Mineral Wells. They built a nuclear power plant in Glen Rose, and it just sucked the water out of that river. It became a very unsafe area in which to live.

HUDSON: Why did you come to Texas?

RATTLESNAKE: My first husband took me. We got divorced in Texas, not that Texas had anything to do with that! Then I met Max, and we married in 1970 and stayed in Texas. We bought 200 acres outside Mineral Wells and lived on the Brazos River. We thought that would be where we would live forever. The kids had animals and built cedar fences; it was our dream. Then they built the first nuclear power plant in Texas. It was the most sorrowful moment in my life, to realize that you cannot own anything. We had the great American giveaway. We gave away everything we owned and hit the road. "Goodbye to a River" became an international hit. I was invited to come to England in 1981, after BBC radio stations received over 400 requests for the song. This is what opened the gates to Europe for us. I had known as a child that I would have an international career, even though the only foreigners I had known were in the photos of the dead Japanese that people brought back from the war. I always wondered where the geese were going when I saw them flying over the tobacco patch, and I wanted to go there! The album *Rattlesnakes and Rusty Water* is not only the definitive album that got me to Europe, but it continues to be my best-selling album. It probably always will be.

HUDSON: Where does the meeting with Willie and Family fit in?

RATTLESNAKE: I went to a bar between Grand Prairie and Arlington, Texas. I met Willie and Lana [Nelson] there. He was singing. We talked, and Lana and I really hit it off. I got involved. I started going and hanging out at the guitar pullings in his room. He taught us how to be songwriters and how to share our songs. After concerts he would have everybody in his room with one guitar that we would pass around. So he really influenced me in my own individuality. I was already going to Nashville and pitching songs. It was 1974 when I ended up in the same room at RCA Records with Guy Clark and Steve Earle.

HUDSON: I've heard you described as the "female Willie Nelson." When and where did that start?

RATTLESNAKE: It started being said about me in Europe. I don't know exactly. Maybe it was the image or the songs that I sang. What a great compliment. Max used to laugh and say, "Willie Nelson is the male Rattlesnake Annie." I was always fortunate to have a good listening environment. I got a lot of good press, and I got signed by Mervin Conn, who ended up really helping my career. I toured lots of times with Johnny Cash and Jerry Lee Lewis. He would send me to many European capitals to do promotion. I would take my guitar and play on radio and television shows. One of my most incredible Conn shows included Tammy Wynette and Jerry Lee Lewis, Johnny Cash, and George Jones. Tammy had to follow Jerry Lee. We were working union houses, and you couldn't do long encores. You only got one. It was pretty hard to follow Jerry Lee Lewis and "Great Balls of Fire." "Stand By Your Man" does not follow that song. So, Mervin said, "Let's put Rattlesnake between the sets." So, as Jerry Lee was finishing up and everyone was going crazy, I had to go out there with my guitar. I started singing "Goodbye to a River." And they started lighting sparklers. That was fantastic. Patsy [Montana] wrote "I Want to Be a Cowboy's Sweetheart," the first million seller in country music.

I did a show with Tanya Tucker and Patsy Montana at a Policeman's Ball in California. There was Patsy in her cowgirl clothing and Tanya in her powder-blue limousine. I gave Patsy a copy of my album. About a year later she called my office and asked to record my song "Good Old Country Music." We became friends. She invited me out to her house, and we went over to Gene Autry's house. He presented her with a VHS tape of the movies she had been in. She was the girl singer in a lot of his movies. She came to Nashville with me and cut "I Want to Be a Cowboy's

Sweetheart" with me. She had always recorded in Chicago and L.A. This was her first time in Nashville. That was a beautiful experience for me.

In 1982 my album made it to Czechoslovakia. This Czech artist got my album, translated some of my songs, and had a hit with "Goodbye to a River." He is also my favorite duet partner. I went there, and we made an album together. It sold 100,000 copies the day they released it. We did huge concerts all over Czechoslovakia then, since my music was not threatening to the Communist philosophy.

HUDSON: You do have a connection with Texas in the imagination of our audience.

RATTLESNAKE: Well, I lived in Texas from 1964 to 1980. I lived there a really long time. I played around Northside in Fort Worth. I had small children, and we did some organic farming. This is where I was developing, meeting other songwriters. I liked the White Elephant on Northside. I also played in Mingus at a huge old wooden beer joint. It was the first city in America to have electricity. Because of the coal, there were lots of Czechs and Italians. I heard about this woman at a beer joint who had a dog that sang. [laughter] I went down there first to hear that dog sing. It sang "Sugar Blues" and "Waltz Across Texas." After I started playing, the crowd grew to about 200 families. They brought kids and picnics. A little piece of Texas musical heritage, for sure. I used that time on the river, that solitude, to hone my songwriting. I've been back to the Czech Republic every year since 1982, and also Poland and East Germany. Incredible experiences in those days, seeing the results of communism. Michal Tucny, my singing partner, died recently. Our album was called *Rattlesnake Annie and the Last Cowboy*. That's why I wrote the song "Adios, Last Cowboy." He died in 1995. I went back to do a tribute, and we had about 50,000 people come to the concert. We are folk heroes, because that was the only music allowed in the country and it brought a taste of freedom. They took us to every great theater. Oddly enough, Sony bought all those music catalogues and paid me for all those records I never got paid for. Imagine that.

HUDSON: I've talked to people who have struggled in Austin and struggled in Nashville. It seems you have the best of all possible worlds.

RATTLESNAKE: Oh, I did my street scene in Nashville. I worked hard and suffered all those rejections that everyone suffers. I finally moved to Spain and decided to hell with it. Then I got signed to CBS in Nashville, and I had to come back. As a matter of fact, my first two releases were Lonnie Mack songs. He was living in an old school bus then, outside Spicewood, Texas. I made arrangements to use Willie's studio to cut these two songs with Lonnie. His car broke down on the way, and he was late. We cut those songs that were later my singles. He picked guitar, and he was so solid that we overdubbed bass and drums. Using his guitar tracks. Can you imagine that? Not only that, he sang the harmonies without the master vocals. He's a genius. After Stevie Ray died, Lonnie made a lot of money from recordings because he wrote "Wham." It went double platinum. He bought himself a bass boat and built a cabin up in Smithville, Tennessee. In my mind, he's the greatest of pickers and a true friend. So talented. When I signed to CBS, I said that they should also sign Lonnie Mack. "Funky Country Living" was his song. It must have been about 1984 when Willie and I were on Telluride together. I sang this song, "Long Black Limousine." When I came off the stage, Lana asked me if I had seen the audience reaction. She said, "You need to cut that." Lana plays the guitar a little bit. Her daddy taught her. She could pick, and it sounded like him. We hung out that weekend, and she practiced the picking part of "Long Black Limousine." So about six months later, I went down to Texas and took Roy Huskey, my bass player from Nashville. And we got Johnny Gimble on fiddle. I cut the basic track. I asked Willie if he'd sing a duet with me. He told me a good key for him. I asked Lana to play guitar on the first half of that solo. She got into the secret vault, got out her daddy's guitar, and played the first half of that solo. Willie came riding in on his Rolls Royce golf cart, in his shorts, and he came in to cut. We played the track back, and he recognized his guitar and asked, "Who is playing my guitar?" I said, "Sister's playing it." After one song, he said, "This is fun. Let's do something else." So we cut another one from the old *Phases and Stages* album. I put together this second album, including that duet with Willie. I was living in Europe. Rick Blackburn, head of CBS in Nashville, heard my album, and they called me to come to Nashville and sign with CBS. I felt like I had already been there, but I went back. So, I signed to Columbia. And they bought those tracks, so I only cut two new tracks.

HUDSON: Did you have a group of musicians that you hung out with?

RATTLESNAKE: My mainstay was Roy Huskey in Nashville. His father was a famous bass player who had played with the Beatles, and he played on a Dylan album. Roy was a miracle who came into my life. He was the greatest upright-bass player.

HUDSON: What's the Japan connection for you?

RATTLESNAKE: Every time I made an album, I included one bluegrass song. Even on my jazz album. I recorded with this jazz trio that included Freddy Powers. I recorded "Blue Moon of Kentucky" on that album. I took it back to Bill Monroe, and he asked to play on that album. Would I! But he wouldn't sing on it because he said it would change the marketing of the record. So Bill and I became friends. On the Wimberley tour, I took my guitar down to the bar in the middle of the night. I couldn't sleep. Well, he came down and joined me. We started playing blues. We had this blues relationship. So when I played Bean Blossom in Indiana, we did "Trouble in Mind," which you will hear on this album *Southern Discomfort*, and he is scat-singing. I don't know what made me do it. I had this old blank cassette tape, and I handed it to the sound engineer to record us. I kept that in my bank vault for about twenty years. I got it out, had it mastered, and added it to the CD. We were filmed by the BBC. What an honor. He invited Max and me to his house for Christmas. We had this wonderful relationship that never had anything to do with bluegrass. It had to do with blues.

HUDSON: We've talked about how these doors keep opening for you, how players keep falling into your life. I have that same perception about my own life.

RATTLESNAKE: I think players recognize each other. I've made enough money to live like I want to live. I don't need much. I don't want to have to take care of a lot of stuff, dust stuff, pack up stuff. My songs have been translated into many languages, including Japanese, Cherokee, Spanish, French, Maya, Czech, and German. My great-grandmother was Cherokee, and that's how I got involved with the tribe and with the first woman chief of the Cherokee, Wilma Mankiller. I wrote two concept albums. One is called *Indian Dream*, and one is *Painted Bird*.

HUDSON: Tell me about Chief Wilma Mankiller.

RATTLESNAKE: I wrote this song called "Mother Mountain," and I was beginning a long Mervin Conn tour. Max was tired and had fallen asleep on the floor by the bed. I told him to go on home to Spain, and I'd go to Switzerland by myself. I saw a huge thunderstorm over Eiger Mountain. It was a first for me, then I saw an eagle flying around the mountain. This song just came to me. I thought how impossible. A Swiss friend came over to listen, and I asked about this eagle. He said there was a nest on top of the Matterhorn and reassured me that I did see an eagle. It's on the *Indian Dream* album. Then I visited a school and sang for some children. I ended up using them to sing the chorus on this song. Then Sony bought the masters for *Indian Dream* for Asia. They heavily promoted it. I was in the mountains of Japan, and one morning there was a message for me. The Expo committee wanted to meet with me. They offered me this incredible deal to use my song "Mother Mountain" as the theme song for Expo 1993. So I decided to bring some Cherokee Indian children to Japan to sing it with me. I went to Oklahoma and got in touch with Wilma Mankiller. In the meantime, I had written a song called "Cherokee Eyes" about Wilma. I had never met her at the time. I sang the song for her, and she wept. She sent me to Jay, Oklahoma, and a senator came down and brought someone to issue birth certificates for these children. They had no concept of being Cherokee. When they wore costumes, they wore pioneer clothing. Out of the clear blue, another man sent me a teacher to teach them the dances. I had a $20,000 budget to buy them clothing for the stage dances and a separate budget just for clothing to wear. Some of these children had families from the Trail of Tears. I took seven adults and thirty kids. They flew to Japan and stayed in a school there for studying forestry. I brought thirty children from Switzerland. We sang "Mother Mountain" at the Expo in English, German, Japanese, and Cherokee. I also had 100 children from Japan on the stage. I have all the film of this. It was beautiful!

HUDSON: What made you write the song "Cherokee Eyes"?

RATTLESNAKE: I wrote the entire album in Spain. I was sitting on the seaside. All was warm and beautiful. I don't know. I can't really say why. I knew that Wilma was the first woman chief of the Cherokee, and I knew that she was a political activist in Alcatraz. I had friends from the tribe in North Carolina who told me that the chiefs often squandered money. They said that Wilma was the first to be responsible. I had never even seen a picture of her.

The more you play [the guitar], the less you suck. And that's the truth.
. . . If I have a gig, some of my own needs can take a back seat. . . .
I can eat and sleep at some point in the future. I just want to keep
playing.

Carolyn Wonderland

TOUGH AND TENDER

*I had heard about Carolyn for many years. I knew of her Houston connec-
tions, and I had her CD, made with the Imperial Monkeys. I first saw her
at the Saxon Pub in Austin in 2003. Then I saw her when she appeared at
the Gospel Hour at Maria's Taco Xpress one Sunday. Later, as I waited on
the corner at the Bob Dylan/Willie Nelson/Hot Club of Cowtown tour in
Oklahoma City, I saw Carolyn again. We talked about talking one more
time. Then I read that she, Roberta Morales, and Susan Gibson were playing a songwriters circle at Casbeers. That did it. I drove in early, waited
until they finished a radio show on KSYM with Jim Beal, and caught up
with Carolyn. I am a rocker at heart, and this woman takes rock to new
limits. One night at the Saxon she pulled out a trumpet and started playing a lead. At Casbeers we saw her solo blues gig and can she pick a guitar!
We had the following conversation sitting on the curb outside Casbeers on
September 6, 2004.*

HUDSON: What excites you in your life? Let's go back to that street
corner in Oklahoma City. We were both having fun then.

WONDERLAND: I've never been so happy to not have a gig on a Friday night. I caught up with my friends and said, "Let's go." That was a beautiful thing, hearing Bob and Willie do "Heartland" together. I was bawling my eyes out. It was awesome. I had heard the stories of Hot Club of Cowtown, but I had never witnessed it in the flesh. What a band!

HUDSON: Elana is one of the subjects of this book.

WONDERLAND: Beautiful, man. And deservedly so. She rips on the fiddle.

HUDSON: Let's talk about your association with Houston.

WONDERLAND: I was born in Webster, then moved to Houston. I love Houston! I got thrown out of school there. I moved up to Austin in 1999. Right before I got thrown out of school, I started playing in a couple of little bars. There's one down the street from Fitzgerald's called Locals; I used to go in there on occasion. I went in with Miguel Trujillo once after hours when I was about fifteen. That particular night Townes Van Zandt was there. We were all passing the guitar, and they were passing the bottle. I wasn't into drinking at that time. I was driving a borrowed car. It was really cool, though. We did this songwriting swap about three in the morning. He did "Pancho and Lefty." I told him that I used to think that was my mom's song because her band always did it. That was before I heard Willie do it. Townes said, "Thanks, that is one of my most popular songs." I said, "You're such a fucking liar." The room got completely quiet. The bartender asked, "Shall we throw the kid out now?" He just gave me his guitar and asked to hear another song of mine. I ran into him a couple of times after that. I was always embarrassed that I didn't know who he was that first time.

HUDSON: Well, you were pretty young then. Who were your heroes?

WONDERLAND: My biggest hero was Little Screaming Kenny. I had seen him at a bar, and it blew my head off. I was studying piano and guitar then. When I snuck into the bar and heard this music so clean and so loud, I was blown away. I said, "That's it. That's what I want to do." He plays in the Hightailers in Houston. They still have a residency on Thursday at the Last Concert Café. He was a very respected bass player. He played a few gigs with Lightnin' Hopkins and Steppenwolf. He played with the Cold Cuts. He is such a good songwriter, and nobody played the guitar like he heard it, so he learned to play the guitar.

HUDSON: You're quite the guitar player. I just heard you on the radio.

WONDERLAND: Thank you. The more you play, the less you suck. And that's the truth. I don't do many solo gigs. It's a learning curve, to be sure.

HUDSON: How do you describe what you do?

WONDERLAND: Just chicken picking. With the head cut off. And the chicken's looking for it. I am fortunate to be in Austin. I get to play with so many different bands, and I learn so much from each one. Like the Imperial Golden Crown Harmonizers [gospel band at Maria's featuring Papa Mali, Scrappy Jud Newcomb, Sarah Brown, Nick Connolly, and Paul "Buddha" Mills]. I learned a lot playing with that group of talented musicians. I also play with Sis Deville, a group of women who are having a great time. We put on lipstick and boas and have a good time. That's Shelley King, Floramay Holliday, Lisa Pankratz, and Ann Marie Harrop. It is a hoot. Being in Jerry Lightfoot's Band of Wonder is also a great honor. It's such a treat to play with your heroes and for them to be so real, genuine, and kind. Jerry's band includes Vince Welnick, Barry "Frosty" Smith, Charlie Prichard, Larry Fulcher, John X Reed . . . what a privilege. I've been able to play regularly with folks like Guy Forsyth, get to record with lots of folks, and release *A Loose Affiliation of Saints and Sinners* CD, all thanks to letting the great city of Austin help define me. I'm a lucky dog!

HUDSON: What are some of your influences?

WONDERLAND: I've always loved bands that play all styles of music while retaining their identity, i.e., the Grateful Dead, Doug Sahm, Billy Joe Shaver. And my mama, a whole lot. She used to play in a band called Badlands when I was growing up. They played at a pizza parlor in Bellville, Texas, of all things. We all call her Kathy Mamaland. She's growing with it. [laughter] She doesn't play much now. She does special education during the day. I gave her a bunch of new strings for her birthday, in the hope that it would encourage her to play again. I used to go with her to her gigs, take quarters out of the tip jar, and go play video games. I would halfway pay attention, sing harmony, and be a goofball. I did play on all her guitars growing up. She's the reason I don't play with a pick. I got really into the guitar and into Pete Townshend. I did the windmill on my mom's Martin. I was never allowed to play with a pick again. I also got to jam with Allison Fisher while I was growing up in Houston. She's like a Charlie Christian bebop player. Growing up and playing with her was cool. We had a little duo for a while. There's this beautiful woman named

Joyce Bradsher. She passed away a few years ago. She used to always let me come up and sit in with her bands. From Houston there are so many people who showed me great kindness, like Joe "Guitar" Hughes, Teri Greene, Calvin Hall, Big Al Bettis, and Uncle John Turner. I grew up down the street from Lavelle White. Then I followed her to Austin. She kills me. And these days I really get inspired by the guys in my band. Cole El-Saleh and I duet a lot, and Scott's always studious.

HUDSON: What is your schedule like now?

WONDERLAND: When a record comes out, we're on the road most of the year. This is the year we are writing and recording more. Not so much travel.

HUDSON: Do you have a specific routine when you write?

WONDERLAND: No, I have such terrible discipline. I have no discipline. A lot of times songs hit me when I'm driving. Since I don't drink anymore, I'll drive late-night shifts. After Art Bell goes off the air, the peace and quiet can call forth some songs. I just hope I can retain the chords until I get someplace I can stop and get the guitar. I enjoy making songs up on the spot with my band; it really keeps us all on our toes and feels good to let words just fall out of one's mouth, you know? My band now, this week's lineup, includes Scott Daniels, who has been playing guitar with me forever. We've been together about five or six years. We've known each other since we were kids. Cole El-Saleh on keys. He's phenomenal. He's amazing. Bobby Perkins has been playing bass with me for a while. And drums are kind of a gig-to-gig thing.

HUDSON: I loved the time you whipped out a trumpet.

WONDERLAND: I used to play it when I was a kid. My cornet is all stopped up since I took it to the Sturgis bike rally this summer. I need to clean it up. My kind local mailman, who financed our *Bloodless Revolution* CD, gave me his trumpet. It is very nice, a cool old one, about a 1918 model from France.

HUDSON: I have noticed that when I open a magazine, the lineups at venues and festivals are mostly men.

WONDERLAND: I think it's kind of a night-to-night thing. The Harmonizers are an example of this. Last week it was me, Nick, and Buddha. The others were on tour. Then three weeks ago the whole front line was all girls. We had Cindy Cashdollar, Shelley, Sarah Brown, and myself. That was more than half the band.

HUDSON: Let's talk about a favorite song.

WONDERLAND: Most of the songs I've been writing these days are coming from a politically upset kind of place. I've been throwing away more than I've been keeping.

I've come to the decision that if you are doing a bunch of finger pointing and backbiting, it's not serving any purpose. I try to write songs that are aware and perhaps angry but have some sense of resolution. I also include material from my own life. "Feed Me to the Lions," a song on *Alcohol and Salvation*, is a song that I couldn't play live for years. It was just too close to home. There's another old song, "She Sings Amazing Grace," and I didn't play that live either. When I wrote it, I kept saying that it wasn't something I would write. Then I decided it was something my friend Melissa would say. I found out she had died that very day. So it was really bizarre. I never do that one anymore. So, I still don't have a favorite song. It's kind of like having kids. . . . you can't favor one over the others.

HUDSON: How does your choice of the road affect the rest of your life?

WONDERLAND: I have to be around folks who understand this. It makes you realize that you're going to live cheap to do what you want to do. I don't balance much of anything. I don't want to say that I'm selfish, but I know that's what it is. If I have a gig, some of my own needs can take a back seat. I don't want to do anything at someone else's expense, but if it's food or sleep, I'll just say, "Skip it." And hit the road. I can eat and sleep at some point in the future. I just want to keep playing. I try to find a rhythm with this odd schedule, because when we're on the road, that's ALL there is. Four or five of us in one van—drive, play, eat, sleep, rinse, and repeat for 15–70 days. I absolutely love it. I have no social life, but that's worth it. Sometimes the road changes everything. In February 1999 we were creamed by an eighteen-wheeler on an icy stretch of mountain highway in Elko, Nevada. Two of us were hospitalized, the van was totaled, and I met my guardian angel. Got a Ryder, missed two gigs, opened for the Paladins in L.A., drove home, and almost everybody quit the band. I figured I just had to get back on that damn horse again and again and again, so I keep rolling. I like being in a lot of different bands and playing with a lot of different folks. Shoot, I'd like to go play in Bob's band!

HUDSON: Have you met Bob Dylan?

WONDERLAND: Yeah, it was beautiful and bizarre and now that the rumor mill is done with it, I suppose I should set the record straight. About a year and a half ago, Easter 2003, I got a call from Ann Marie [Harrop], who was having lunch with him and Ray Benson. Apparently Mr. Dylan just asked out of the blue how to get a hold of Carolyn Wonderland. She called me. I was in Houston, so I hauled ass up to Austin. I thought it was going to be five minutes of hello. When Bob went to Houston the next day, he called me to come and play with him. Not at the gig, but at the sound check. It was so much fun. It was such a hoot. I've seen him play more often than most other bands. I mean, there's him, Los Lobos, and the Paladins. It's a distinct thrill to play with him. He's so giving as a guitar player and all-around musician. I know he's bad ass, but when you're up there with him, he's supportive of what you're doing. So musically, there's that. I have very much enjoyed the time we spent together. I appreciate the experience of meeting someone I admire and greatly respect. To him be additionally kind and so great to hang out with only leaves me hoping our paths cross repeatedly.

HUDSON: And you have no idea how he heard of you?

WONDERLAND: I asked him, and he said he'd heard of me for years. That doesn't tell me who I need to buy a cheesecake for. He said something like "I can't believe you're not famous." I thought, "I can't believe you've even heard of me." I do have my suspicions. I did think about this for a long time, and all roads lead to Doug Sahm. So, I lit up a big candle to him and thanked him.

HUDSON: Do you hear the Janis Joplin comparison often?

WONDERLAND: Occasionally. I can think of far worse comparisons than that one. It's a hell of a thing. I can't live up to that. I can't sing that well. I met her guitar player, Sam Andrews, when I was about eighteen. He gave me some sound advice. He said, "You know, you need to play and sing your own songs. If you go do her songs now, that will be all you do the rest of your life." I thought about that and took his advice. He steered me in the direction to respect the folks that come before but realize that it isn't you.

HUDSON: Do you have something in your life that keeps you centered?

WONDERLAND: My family and my band. And, on occasion, I'll thumb through this Rumi book and see what he has to say. He's the man. I like *I Say Me for a Parable*, about Mance Lipscomb. It only came out in hardback, and I must have bought that book about four times. I kept giving it away to people. I enjoy reading, doing yoga, painting . . . but I'm lazy. Sometimes all I need is tea, a prayer, and a nap!

HUDSON: Glen and I were doing a seminar with Landmark Education when he stood up and declared that he was going to finish that book on Mance.

WONDERLAND: Beautiful. That was a life changer for me. I'm always into reading about folks. It was written phonetically, and it really caught his story.

HUDSON: What is your biggest challenge now?

WONDERLAND: Just the perpetual letting go of control, knowing that it's all going to be cool. My friend Judy said, "Life turns out the same. Whether or not you choose to give yourself an ulcer is all you have control over." I used to be so scared about running a band and all the changes that came along. After doing it for fifteen years, it still breaks my heart when someone leaves the band. I was born November 9, 1972. I guess the challenge is still to write the perfect song. It may come, but I love the transformation and play with all of my being, every note I play.

HUDSON: Well, I was born in 1945, and we have thirty years between us. It still feels like I'm talking to the pro.

WONDERLAND: Thanks. I'm excited about playing with Susan Gibson and Roberta Morales. I'm feeling pretty damn honored to be working with Instruments for Orphans. I can't believe they asked me to be on the board of directors. They've been really cool about it. We're in the process of collecting instruments. Then I want to train some musicians to go into the houses and play for the kids.

[Carolyn added the following information in 2006, after playing the Texas Music Coffeehouse at Schreiner University.]

The case stemming from my arrest and subsequent night in jail at a war protest was thrown out after two years. Yahoo! I said I was acting within my rights! I also recorded Billy Joe Shaver's "Honky-Tonk Heroes" with Asleep at the Wheel and am working on our next CD with Mr. Benson. Double yahoo! "Judgment Day Blues" from the *Bloodless Revolution* CD is on Ruf Records' 2005 release *Blues Guitar Women*, which is a two-CD history of women blues guitarists compiled by Sue Foley. Instruments for Orphans is doing GREAT. We have instruments in homes in Austin (www. instrumentsfororphans.org). I won Guitarist of the Year in 2004 at the Houston Press Awards—weird, huh? And I was on a panel of speakers at UT's Instruments of Freedom Forum with Kinky Friedman, Jerry Jeff Walker, Marcia Ball, Roky Erickson, David Garza, and others. You know, everyday I get up, find my ass and my guitar, and GO! Thank God.

It's omnipresent with me, that balancing and integration of a professional life with a personal one.

Elana Fremerman (James)

FIDDLING WITH BOB

On Sunday, March 2, 2002 (Texas Independence Day and Don Walser Day), at Maria's Taco Xpress in Austin, I met Elana Fremerman. Gurf Morlix was performing, and he told me that I should be talking with her, so he introduced us. It's always good to have this kind of recommendation. Gurf is a musician and a producer of very interesting music. Elana and I talked over tacos on another Sunday morning. Then I heard her play at the Continental Club, and I was thrilled to see the variety in ages that were listening and responding to the lively trio Hot Club of Cowtown. I also followed her on tour for two concerts in Kansas with Bob Dylan and Willie Nelson. Bob called her out to accompany him on "Highway 61 Revisited." His look of joy as she took the lead was a moment in musical history. He stood up behind that keyboard he was playing, looked over at her, nodding his head in encouragement, and let her rip on that fiddle! Her trio plays a regular gig at the Continental Club on South Congress in Austin when the band is not on tour. And this trio tears up the place, playing rag, swing, jazz, and blues.

HUDSON: What are you doing now, what led up to this time, and where are you going?

FREMERMAN: Our band is on vacation right now. We usually set out to tour at the end of March and come back in early November. We come back for brief periods of time during the year, but it's a pretty grueling travel schedule. It's me and two guys. We fly sometimes, but we travel a lot. We are taking some time to get away from each other right now, play music with other people, and think about our next record. We want to make a live album, and I think Lloyd Maines is going to produce it. He produced our third record. We're going back out in three weeks, so I'm trying to go out socially as much as possible and get out of the total band frame of mind. I've never been married, and I'm kind of dating someone, so this is some time we can have to spend together—you know, to see if we should keep spending time together! I use this as a time to strike out on my own and be a "regular" person rather than just a band member.

HUDSON: I've talked with other women who have stories about the challenge of having a relationship/husband and continuing to be on the road. Often we don't ask men how they fit it all in, but we do ask women this question. I wonder what that implies.

FREMERMAN: I could talk about that for two or three hours! It's omnipresent with me, that balancing and integration of a professional life with a personal one. Actually, for the last year I've really started thinking about my priorities. I love playing the violin, and I love my band. But I wonder if my priority now should be finding a mate. I have lots of friends with a traditional family life—-a mate and children. I find it incredible and great that they do that. So, I've been kind of thinking that maybe they are doing the right thing, and I'm not doing the right thing. Their lives seem to reflect the deep human values that almost everybody has, but I look at my life and think, maybe mine doesn't. Or maybe it just reflects different ones. Over the last few months, though, I've been appreciating the freedom that I do have, and I'm obsessed with playing the violin. The violin kind of takes hold of me and makes me play it. In a way, I'm its instrument. [We look up and see Whit, one of her bandmates. We laugh about the meeting. He invites her to go to the mall later to shop. We laugh some more.] That's Whit—he's the guitar player in our band.

HUDSON: Let's talk about the band. You have three pieces—violin, guitar, and standup bass. You play violin, right? Is that what you call it? What about "fiddle"?

FREMERMAN: People are always asking about that. There are different styles on this instrument. Johnny Gimble will say, "If you stomp your foot, it's a fiddle." I've heard people say that if you're playing for tips, it's a fiddle, but when you're getting paid, it's a violin.

HUDSON: I particularly like "a violin sings, a fiddle dances," which I read in a book by Nadja Salerno-Sonnenberg [a hugely successful and eccentric classical violinist].

FREMERMAN: The band has consistently been the two of us, Whit and I, but we hope our bass player, Jake, stays with us. He's great. Whit and I started the band in 1997 in New York. We had a year in San Diego, then five years here. [counting] Oh—I guess that was eight years ago, not five—time flies!

HUDSON: Let's talk about the name for a minute.

FREMERMAN: The name Hot Club of Cowtown was Whit's idea, because we play a hot club jazz style of music from the 1930s—hot, danceable jazz featuring violin and guitar, like the Hot Club of France, which was Django Reinhardt and Stéphane Grappelli playing together before World War II in Paris. We write a lot of songs in that hot string jazz style. But because we also love western music and Bob Wills music and fiddle tunes, we decided to call it Hot Club of Cowtown. It also takes away some of the pretension of being a "Hot Club" band, since there was really only one. In the *New York Times* art section today, Marc O'Connor is featured talking about his new recording with his Hot Swing Trio, where he is doing basically the same thing without the western element. This article talks about how elegant and fluid his trio is. And it is. We are going for a grittier sound. Our sound is a reflection of Texas musicians playing hot string jazz music of the 1930s. We jam with a lot of old-timers right now. Recently we have been playing some shows with Johnny Gimble at festivals. We jammed at a Texas Folklife Festival event not too long ago, and most of the people there were in their seventies. That's sort of our niche!

HUDSON: Are there women who have influenced you?

FREMERMAN: I don't even think about that. But sometimes I stop and look around and notice that I'm absolutely the only female in the situation. Louise Rowe is a bass player who played with Bob Wills, and I've gotten to know her a little. There are a few that I've met who are really elegant, cool, and hip, like Cindy Cashdollar. The older you get, the fewer women are in bands, I've noticed. Many times, I'm the only female around.

HUDSON: Before you did this kind of music, did you have any women who influenced you?

FREMERMAN: My mom is a musician; she plays the violin. I've been playing violin since I was five. She's a classical violinist, and I used to hear her practicing around the house. She was a professional violinist and performed with the Kansas City Symphony, and she had a trio with my stepdad. My stepdad at the time played harpsichord and piano for traveling shows and also played in the Kansas City Symphony sometimes. So growing up I saw her making a living playing violin—and them making a living playing music. I think that can make a huge difference in being able to envision life as a musician. I never really wanted to do exactly what my mom was doing, but the vision was certainly important. She would put on her black velvet orchestra clothes and her Chanel No. 5 and come in and kiss me goodnight and call the babysitter. I would love it when she was gone on a weekend night, because we could stay up late, watch Love Boat, and eat macaroni and cheese and Oreos. Sometimes I will find myself standing over the sink having a bowl of cereal before going to a gig, and I'll think, "Oh my God, I'm turning into my mother." That was a valuable experience. She is one of our biggest fans, and she comes to hear us play when she can. She's still a professional musician.

HUDSON: I really identify with what you're saying. When something has called you, it becomes difficult to see how you can shape a relationship around that. It's not going to look traditional.

FREMERMAN: You're so right. Just in the last four to six months, I've been looking at this. I'm thirty-two now. My mom watched me play violin as I was growing up and would sometimes say, "You just might be meant to be a fiddle player," as opposed to a classical violinist. I used to find it offensive that she would say that because to me that seemed lowbrow, or like I was a failure, a failed violinist. I never understood what a fiddle player could be—I thought it was a bunch of screeching old-timers sitting around drinking moonshine, or that you played in a Top Forty country band or something, or just bluegrass music. I'd never even heard the kind of music I'm playing now. Back then I'd say to her, "Don't say that. It might come true!" She's also said to me several times, whenever we've been talking about all this, "Your life is going to look different, but that doesn't mean it's wrong. You may not want to have kids."

HUDSON: That's exactly the advice my mother gave me. "Please don't try to make your life look like something. Don't put a square peg in a round hole. Just be yourself, and it may not look like what you are expecting." Ah, this great advice from mothers.

FREMERMAN: At thirty-two I'm at a place in my life to take stock and see what patterns I've created and re-created in my life. I try to always monitor that and be aware. I don't want to be on auto-pilot. Maybe my mom's right. And my life will not be traditional. That doesn't mean I can't marry and have a family. It just might look really different from my friends.

HUDSON: Have you had some kind of training in this concept of choice leading to patterns?

FREMERMAN: No, but my mom is a psychiatric nurse. [laughter] She'll say, "The biggest predictor of the future is the past." I'll say, "No, don't say that!" In my past I've never been married. In order to move forward, I don't need to be obsessing about a personal life. Not being so hard on yourself is the first step in making a change. Sometimes I'll find myself thinking, "What's wrong with you? Why are you living this solitary life as a vagabond?" You know what, if I'm enjoying doing that, who gives a shit?

HUDSON: Let's talk about place a little.

FREMERMAN: I went to Barnard College in New York City, and there was this girl I knew named Maydelle who was really classy, elegant, and cool, and she was a dancer from Texas. I've always thought Texas was in a league of its own. If someone like that could be hewn in Texas, it compounded my respect for the state. She was urbane, elegant, and well-heeled. I also did some horse-wrangling in Colorado. By the time I left New York in 1996, I had a map of Texas behind this desk where I was sitting. I would just gaze at it. I went to Bob Wills Day in Turkey, Texas, by myself several times in the mid-1990s. I was obsessed. Whit and I moved to San Diego in January 1997, and we played for tips for that entire year in parks and farmers' markets—fiddle tunes and jazzy stuff. I thought that if people in San Diego are interested, maybe we would have even more success in Texas. We moved here exactly a year later, and in three months we had a steady happy hour at the Continental Club, found a booking agent, and got signed to HighTone Records. All the wonderful things that have happened to us started within three months of moving here.

HUDSON: I know lots of people who have spent a lot of time trying to get a regular gig and a record deal. HighTone is a nice label. How do you account for this?

FREMERMAN: Yeah. I don't know. There were other people on the label who had seen us play on tour, and they recommended us highly. We almost signed with another label, and Larry Sloven kept calling right up to the time we went to the studio. We realized we didn't have enough of a budget from the first label, and Larry called, again, saying, "I'll double their budget and overnight it to you." And so we said okay, and that was in 1998. We are about to do our fifth album with them. As long as we don't expect any royalties [laughter], we're doing fine. Yes, the label has been good for us. Many artists, apparently, get a record advance, but that becomes the money you pay back with sales of your records. The longer we've done this, the more we learn about the music business. I think HighTone saw that we are a very ambitious trio that tours all the time, which is good for sales. We tour from March to November.

HUDSON: Pretend you are someone in an audience watching the Hot Club of Cowtown. Describe what you see.

FREMERMAN: I don't mean to sound self-aggrandizing, but I'll tell you what people have told us. You'll see when you come to see us. One thing we always hear is "It's obvious you just love what you are doing." All three of us are younger than you might expect to be playing this style of music, so we often surprise people, I think. In this genre, we're the youngest. People often ask how we got into this kind of music. We are very energetic, and we have more in common with the Red Elvises or a rock band or a punk band than we do with a country or swing band. We enjoy each other. Whit and I have gone through many permutations in this relationship. At one time we were boyfriend and girlfriend.

HUDSON: I wondered about that!

FREMERMAN: It was difficult clawing our way out of that and resuming our musical friendship. When we play together, there's just enough tension and animation to make it fun for us and for the audience. I feel like we're the kind of band that can please any audience. If people could just see us, there would be no stopping us. We haven't been able to get very good distribution or a video. We're like an NPR darling band, but that audience is probably mostly forty-five-year-olds and over, who are more cerebral and oriented toward older and more intelligent things anyway.

We are preaching to the converted. But we have no doubt we could slay a much broader audience if we could just get in front of them.

HUDSON: I can see a younger audience loving what you do.

FREMERMAN: Yes, if we could get in front of them. Then I think, "Time's ticking. I can't be wearing snake pants for the next ten years. Or could I?"

HUDSON: So, you have someone you're dating now?

FREMERMAN: Yes, and he's much, much older than I am. And that's okay. He's in the same business, though. We're both going out on the road, different roads. I'm trying to stop thinking that I only have a black-and-white choice. That I have to quit it all and go buy furniture and have a baby. There's got to be a different way to do it. I haven't done things the normal way my entire life, and I tend to get things done. The things I want to have happen seem to happen, although not always on the schedule that I might want.

HUDSON: Yeah, I have that sensation in my life as well. What are some songs you like? Some people? We've already talked about Cindy Cashdollar.

FREMERMAN: Yeah, I love her. She's so cool. Our strength is a live show and the joy and energy that we have. I love tons of old western swing tunes. I love playing fiddle tunes—"Take Me Back to Tulsa," "Ida Red," "Sally Goodin," "Orange Blossom Special." I love it when Johnny Gimble plays with us, and we do twin fiddle parts together on tunes like "Little Betty Brown," "San Antonio Rose," "Maiden's Prayer," and "Silver Bells." So many good songs for the fiddle. On and on and on. We do a lot of standards, too. That's the beauty of having your own band. If you like a song, just get up and do it. No one is telling us what to do. We also love to play the songs we write. Whit and I do the writing. The last record that Gurf produced for us contained three or four songs from each of us, so the record was mostly original songs. I wrote four songs for it. That was a challenge for me. You know, you start working with your instrument, then you play in a band that's touring, and people come up and ask if you are going to sing. Then they start asking if you write your own material. Each of these questions has inspired me to explore those directions. Then you start singing as well as playing your violin. People like Billie Holiday, Elvis, or Frank Sinatra did not write their own material—they were stylists and interpreters. This emphasis on original writing is a new thing. Today the focus seems to be on the personal expression of the artist's own voice, and a belief that unless you wrote something yourself, it is somehow a cover. The truth is, though, you can play "Stardust," by Hoagy Carmichael, and it can be the most expressive, beautiful thing in the whole universe. Who cares if Willie Nelson didn't write "Georgia"—does that make it any less great when he sings it?

HUDSON: I have come around to an appreciation of the stylist, the interpreter, as artist. I was such a snob about the importance of the writing that I often overlooked other equally important talent. Just listen to Willie doing "Stardust." Now that's an original interpretation. George Strait doesn't do any of his own writing, and he has just become the performer to have the most number-one hits ever!

FREMERMAN: The only songs we play are songs we love.

HUDSON: So, the future, which you are constantly looking at, brings what?

FREMERMAN: We take this time off to plot and strategize and set goals to make sure certain things happen. We briefly had a manager last summer. We hope to get one this year so someone can advocate for us within the industry in ways we ourselves cannot. We've become so much stronger as a band, especially in the last year. We've had two write-ups in the *New York Times* in the last four months. What we do complements this movement of Americana music or back-to-the-roots approach. We're not really like the Dixie Chicks or Gillian Welch, but we do have more in common with them than with a lot of other bands. Traditional instrumentation makes a difference. We need to connect with that perfect manager who could get us in front of bigger audiences. We do have a major booking agent, Buddy Lee Attractions. They are in Nashville, and they get us in good places with big country acts, and that's very valuable to us. Lloyd Maines produced our third record and is going to produce our live album. He's such a wonderful person, just the coolest guy—he makes everything better just by being around.

HUDSON: I love the work he's doing with Terri Hendrix. Both are so humble. How did you get hooked up with Gurf? He's so talented, and I know he's been working with Ray Wylie Hubbard, both producing and playing.

FREMERMAN: Do you know Tom Russell? He is on HighTone, and we met at the Monterey cowboy poetry gathering. He kept saying, "Gurf is your man." We didn't really have any specific ideas, but Whit and I met him, and we decided to do an album with him. I guess that was on the strength of Tom's recommendation. He's artsy. He's from New York, and I think there's a part of his character I identify with. I'm a New York-ophile. One of my favorite songs on that album is our version of "Chip Away at the Stone."

[On March 17, 2005, while attending a conference for writing teachers in San Francisco, I read that Bob Dylan and Merle Haggard were performing at the Paramount in Oakland, CA. I raced over via BART and attended the show. Elana Fremerman was now front and center, playing wild and beautiful fiddle on every song with Bob Dylan. "This is a new chapter in my life," she called out to me as she left the theater. She was smiling big. Elana now performs as Elana James.]

My mom actually said, "I don't want my daughter to be somebody special." . . . They always say that I'm the queen without a crown. Everybody says my crown is the accordion.

Eva Ybarra

LA REINA DEL ACORDEÓN

I heard of Eva Ybarra first from another musician, Ray Symcheck. He was playing accordion with a group, and he said, "You must talk with Eva." He was right. I drove up to her home in San Antonio, catching her on July 9, 2004, as she prepared for an evening gig with a trio, playing at a local hall at a quinceañera. The first thing she told me was "I don't get to sing much when I play with this trio. I hope you get to hear my band as well." She was dressed in her traditional mariachi clothing, and we sat down for a few minutes on the couch. I love her spirit and her attitude. We talked about her relationship to her family, the role of her mother, and her own creative approach to life. When you talk of music and San Antonio, La Reina del Acordeón, Eva Ybarra, is in the conversation. And she performs across the country, representing this genre as "La Reina."

HUDSON: I teach in San Miguel de Allende each year with Schreiner students. I love Mexico, the culture and the language. Once at the conjunto festival, I talked briefly with Narciso Martinez, now deceased. Chris Strachwitz from Arhoolie Records was at this festival. I know he's important in documenting this music. Let's talk about your story of this music.

YBARRA: Well, I started playing accordion at the age of four, and at six I was playing professionally with my family. They give me good support. I was born here in San Antonio. All my life I've been playing. I started singing at age five. My mom wanted me to learn to play the piano. My brother played accordion. He formed a group, and he named it Pedro Ybarra y los Chamacos. And then little by little I started playing with them. My dad was my manager. We had a lot of gigs. Then my dad passed away, and I had a hard time. It wasn't the same. I was one of six children. My mom didn't want me to be a star. She wanted us to just play for the family. I didn't want that. I wanted to be somebody special. I had to mind my mom; she was rather strict. I got calls from Puerto Rico as well as Mexico. My mom didn't want me to leave the country. My mom actually said, "I don't want my daughter to be somebody special." I had to mind my mom. My dad was afraid that something might happen to me. He would talk to my mom. Then she told me my dad was afraid too.

HUDSON: I can see that your parents really cared for you.

YBARRA: When I was thirty-five, my mom still didn't want me to go out and play. They called me to Puerto Rico. I wanted to go. I said, "Mom, I'm a lady now. I'm going to take good care of myself." I went on television and performed in a lot of towns around Puerto Rico. My mom had a dream that something happened to me. I was fine. When I came back, my dad told me he was kind of tired. They encouraged me to do my thing. That's when I started living on my own. I miss my parents. I was about forty-five when I lost them.

HUDSON: I'm fifty-eight now. My parents are in their early eighties, and I feel very lucky. I talk to my parents about five times a week! Those conversations with my mother, who is the supreme listener without judgment, are such a joy. And now Dad and I are really talking about ideas. It seems I had to overcome some idea that he was the family judge.

YBARRA: I know it's not good to be a Mama's or Papa's girl. They say "mamitis," like you still take the bottle. In Spanish, I was "hija de dominio." I mind them all the time. Is that the right word?

HUDSON: When did "La Reina" get added to your name?

YBARRA: They always say that I'm the queen without a crown. Everybody says my crown is the accordion.

HUDSON: Many of the women I talk to say that issues around being a woman still exist. Club owners treat them differently.

YBARRA: When I went to Puerto Rico, I had some concerns. My mom prayed a lot for me. Something wrong happened to me. This guy wanted to abuse me. I never told her what had happened. This man paid me, then came to my room and kissed me. He wanted something else. I want to mention this because I don't want something to happen to other young ladies out there. Every lady he made a contract with, they had to sleep with him. I got out of this because of the prayers of my mom. I kept telling him that I came to sing. He even pushed me to the bed and got on top of me. I kept saying to please let me go. I was praying inside. "What's Mom going to say?" I said. "I know you're a good man and you'll let me go." I couldn't breathe. With the prayers of my mom, he let me go. An answer to a prayer. Nothing happened to me.

HUDSON: What kind of groups have you played with?

YBARRA: First my family, then mariachi groups. A man from Rosina Records heard me singing with my brothers. He wanted to record me, and he wanted only my name. My brother wanted his name there. That was a hard time. Finally Pedro insisted that they put his name as well. It's a company from San Marcos. That's where the Blue Notes used to record. He told me that we were the first conjunto group he had ever recorded. We recorded for other companies. Reloj Records was one. I took another group with me.

HUDSON: How did you meet Ray Symcheck?

YBARRA: [with a smile] Oh, that's a good one. I was playing at a festival, and someone recommended him to me. It was nice working with Ray. He's not macho like the Tejano. We get along very well. We recorded two CDs with Rounder Records in Boston. We also recorded with Dina Records, and I recorded on Magdan Records.

HUDSON: Did you start off speaking Spanish in your home?

YBARRA: Yes, my mom said, "We're Mexican first. We're not going to forget our language." My parents were also born in Texas. My grandma was born in Coahuila. Her mother was in Texas, but she went to Mexico because my great-grandfather wanted his child to be born in Mexico. I love Mexico. I have performed there.

HUDSON: I know there are many different kinds of music related to Mexico—norteño, cumbia, *la onda chicana*, and mariachi.

YBARRA: I love mariachi.

HUDSON: I just talked to Stephanie Urbina Jones at her baby shower, and she had a song called "Mariachis Always Make Me Cry." I find that to be true for me.

YBARRA: That's right! When I record my singing with mariachis, I sing sentimentally. They make me cry too, because of the feeling. I like to sing sentimental songs. And when I sing with a group more allegria, I feel happy, and I want to dance. I also sing *corridos*. Gloria Garcia is the songwriter and the vocalist of this group. We work together with a mariachi group. There's a lot of jealousy with mariachis. They won't let me sing. I feel bad, like I'm nothing there. Sometimes when I sing, people ask for more songs. They like ladies. The men don't like that.

HUDSON: I have noticed, in talking with women, that there are all kinds of ways that women get pushed aside. Some are subtle. I, too, have had this experience in academia. The men get promoted first and are not held to the same standards.

YBARRA: We play a lot of festivals. I played for a big festival in Seattle, and we play out of state quite a bit. I like having my own band. Every year we play the Conjunto Festival. Ray performed with me in Houston and Louisiana. We hope to go to Europe. We were going to go once with Flaco Jimenez, but suddenly we were just forgotten. Some political issues. Maybe the men didn't want a woman on the tour. Let me add this one thing before I have to leave. I was working with a group one time, playing keyboard and accordion. I always stand in the center. I'm used to it. I was the only lady in the group. The bandleader asked me to move to the back of the group, putting the men in front. I said, "Okay, no problem." Then a drunk guy in the audience asked, "How come that lady is in the back? How come the best musician is in the back?" [We laugh together at this.] He also said, "Remember what I say. She will be in the Hall of Fame someday. And you are nothing." I was embarrassed.

[I went to the quinceañera *with her and heard her amazing soulful voice on several of my favorite songs. The men were reluctant to have her sing. I had to request it. The hall was huge, but when Eva sang, she had all eyes and ears on her. La Reina. As with many of the women in this collection, her life is worthy of a full study, a book. This conversation is just a beginning.]*

CODA

We have completed this journey together. A reading of these interviews creates a text, as each reader brings a point of view to the story. At times during this project, I made lists and set clear goals. At other times, I talked with the women who showed up in my life. At all times I was inspired by the stories I heard. Each one made a difference in how I see my own life. This book of stories told by women informs us about the human condition. We can see what we all have in common, as well as what we do not share. I see the web of our connections in this collection of interviews.

Women are closely connected to the rhythms and cycles of life. Circles of language and meaning radiate out from each conversation. While some might prefer a linear, chronological way of seeing and thinking, this collection points to other ways of knowing and seeing. Connections. Just as women and men have distinct communication styles, so the stories in this book carry distinctions. One type of research shows that men communicate for power (vertical communication), and women communicate for relatedness (horizontal). I like the image that that creates in my mind: a crossroads, a point where the two meet before heading off in other directions. Let this book take you down a path that circles back on itself from time to time, honoring all ways of knowing. Our culture stresses the linear and rational, while a significant percentage of our culture knows the value of the circle. Yes, we know it in our bodies as well as in our minds and spirits. Like one of my teachers, Paula Underwood, author of *The Walking People,* I celebrate the three-strand braid where we weave learning into wisdom by honoring body, mind, and spirit in education and in personal transformation. I see the women in this collection as also honoring this pathway.

My last musical adventure before releasing this manuscript into the hands of the University of Texas Press and Theresa May was the night of March 16, 2005, at the Paramount Theatre in Oakland, California. Elana (Fremerman) James was on tour with Bob Dylan. Our talk at Maria's Taco Xpress a year earlier did not include the seeds for this huge opportunity. Or did it? As I watched her take her own playing to new heights, accompanying and sometimes leading both Bob, on keyboard, and his entire band, I watched a woman fully present in the middle of her own dreams. As she left the show, she smiled back at me, saying, "Something to add to my chapter!"

Driving across the roads of Texas, waiting until the appropriate time to talk, hoping for a return call: all were part of the process that created this collection. I offer this group of women as the tip of a big iceberg. I see them as shining jewels in a mine that is deep and rich. I honor them as they choose a way into the forest where there is no path. I challenge each reader to incorporate the wisdom gathered here, to look for ways to create a more balanced world where we can all weave learning into wisdom.

Due to my own enthusiasm, engendered by the women I interviewed, this project grew beyond the covers of this book. You can read more interviews and historical material on the worldwide web at www.kathleenhudson. net.

RECOMMENDED READING

Barkley, Roy R., ed. *The Handbook of Texas Music*. Austin: Texas State Historical Association, 2003.

Bolen, Jean Shinoda. *Goddesses in Everywoman: A New Psychology of Women*. New York: HarperCollins, 1984.

———. *Goddesses in Older Women: Archetypes in Women over Fifty*. New York: HarperCollins, 2001.

Carson, Mina, Tisa Lewis, and Susan M. Shaw, with foreword by Jennifer Baumgardner and Amy Richards. *Girls Rock! Fifty Years of Women Making Music*. Lexington: University Press of Kentucky, 2004.

Dawidoff, Nicholas. *In the Country of Country: People and Places in American Music*. New York: Pantheon, 1997.

Edwards, Carolyn McVickar, and Kathleen Edwards. *The Storyteller's Goddess: Tales of the Goddess and Her Wisdom from Around the World*. New York: Marlowe, 2000.

Malone, Bill C. *Country Music, U.S.A*. Austin: University of Texas Press, 2002.

Mendoza, Lydia, and Yolanda Broyles-González. *Lydia Mendoza's Life in Music* (American Musicspheres). London: Oxford University Press, 2001.

Oermann, Robert, and Mary Bufwack. *Finding Her Voice: Women in Country Music, 1800–2000*. Austin: University of Texas Press, 2003.

Pearlman, Mickey, and Katherine Usher Henderson. *A Voice of One's Own: Conversations with America's Writing Women*. New York: Houghton Mifflin, 1992.

Reid, Jan, and Scott Newton. *The Improbable Rise of Redneck Rock* (Jack and Doris Smothers Series in Texas History, Life, and Culture, No. 12). Austin: University of Texas Press, 2004.

Sternberg, Janet. *The Writer on Her Work*, Vols. 1 & 2. New York: Norton, 1991.

———. *The Writer on Her Work: New Essays in New Territory*. New York: Norton, 1992.

Willoughby, Larry. *Texas Rhythm and Texas Rhyme: A Pictorial History of Texas Music*. Dallas: Texas Monthly Press, 1984.

Wood, Roger. *Down in Houston: Bayou City Blues* (Jack and Doris Smothers Series in Texas History, Life, and Culture, No. 8). Austin: University of Texas Press, 2003.